STUDIES AND TEXTS 112

Manor, Vill, and Hundred
The Development of Rural Institutions in Early Medieval Hampshire

ERIC KLINGELHÖFER

T he foundation of the medieval world was its rural institutions. This book challenges the accepted views on the origin and development of the English shire and parish, as well as manor, vill, and hundred. Archaeology and toponymics supplement pre-Conquest charters and Domesday Book in detailing the early medieval history of eighty-seven manors in central Hampshire, the heartland of Anglo-Saxon Wessex.

The author identifies early Saxon territorial units as geographically discrete regions defined by watersheds. Such tribal areas were comprised of local geographic districts, here called 'archaic hundreds,' the central places of which became the later royal manors and 'kingstons.' Open fields, nucleated villages, and the chartering of 'bookland' from tribal land made the archaic hundred obsolete, and throughout the late Saxon period its functions devolved into the local institutions of manor, vill, and hundred.

The ninth-century Danish invasion of Wessex caused the ancient territories to be replaced by the more efficient shire system; the Church more slowly abandoned the missionary *parochiae* of archaic hundreds for the medieval arrangement of village parishes under cathedral superiority. Since all these institutions developed principally in the centuries between 800 and 1000, medieval England was effectively an Anglo-Saxon creation.

STUDIES AND TEXTS 112

Manor, Vill, and Hundred

The Development of Rural Institutions in Early Medieval Hampshire

Eric Klingelhöfer

PONTIFICAL INSTITUTE OF MEDIAEVAL STUDIES

ACKNOWLEDGEMENT

This publication has been supported by a grant from the
College of Liberal Arts, Mercer University.

CANADIAN CATALOGUING IN PUBLICATION DATA

Klingelhöfer, Eric C.
  Manor, vill, and hundred

(Studies and texts; ISSN 0082-5328 ; 112)
Includes bibliographical references and index.
ISBN 0-88844-112-6

1. Land tenure – England – Hampshire – History. 2. Local
government – England – Hampshire – History. 3. Feudalism –
England – Hampshire – History. 4. Hampshire (England) –
History. 5. Land tenure – England – History. 6. Local government
– England – History. 7. Feudalism – England – History. 8. Great
Britain – History – Anglo Saxon period, 449–1066. I. Pontifical
Institute of Mediaeval Studies. II. Title. III. Series: Studies and
texts (Pontifical Institute of Mediaeval Studies) ; 112.

DA670.H2K55 1992   942.2'701   C92-093823-X

This book is dedicated to the memory of F.W. Maitland, whose personal copy of Farley's *Domesday Book* once was in daily use on my desk. It now resides more safely in the Eisenhower Library rare book room at Johns Hopkins.

Contents

List of Figures

Abbreviations

AJ	*Archaeological Journal*
AHEW	*The Agrarian History of England and Wales*, ed. H.P.R. Finberg, vol. 1 (Cambridge, 1972, 1978)
ASC	Anglo-Saxon Chronicle: C. Plummer, *Two of the Saxon Chronicles Parallel* (Oxford, 1892-1899); D. Whitelock, *The Anglo-Saxon Chronicle, A Revised Translation* (New Brunswick, N.J., 1961)
ASE	F. Stenton, *Anglo-Saxon England*, 3rd. ed. (Oxford, 1971)
B	Charter in *Cartuliarum Saxonicum*, ed. W. de Gray Birch (London, 1885-1893)
DB	*Domesday Book*, ed. A. Farley (London, 1783)
DB Hants	*Domesday Book. Hampshire*, ed. J. Munby (Chichester, 1982)
DBB	*Domesday Book and Beyond*, ed. F. W. Maitland (Cambridge, 1897)
ECW	*Early Charters of Wessex*, ed. H.P.R. Finberg (Leicester, 1964)
EHD	*English Historical Documents c. 500-1042*, ed. D. Whitelock (London, 1955)
F	Charter in *ECW*

Gesetze	*Die Gesetze der Angelsachsen*, ed. F. Liebermann (Halle, 1898-1916)
HRO	Hampshire Record Office
HE	Bede, *Historia Ecclesia*, ed. C. Plummer (1896; repr. Oxford, 1966)
K	Charter in *KDC*
KDC	*Codex Diplomaticus Aevi Saxonici*, ed. J.M. Kemble (London, 1839-1848)
Liber de Hyda	*Liber Monasterii de Hyda*, ed. E. Edwards (London, 1866)
MSCC	*Medieval Settlement: Continuity and Change*, ed. P. Sawyer (London, 1976)
"Micheldever"	E. Klingelhöfer, "Manor, Vill, and Hundred: Rural Development in the Region of Micheldever, Hampshire, 700-1100," Ph.D. dissertation, The Johns Hopkins University (1985)
Mon. Angl.	*Monasticon Anglicanum*, ed. W. Dugdale (London, 1718)
ODEPN	*The Concise Oxford Dictionary of English Place-Names*, ed. E. Ekwall, 4th ed. (Oxford, 1960)
S	Charter in P. Sawyer, *Anglo-Saxon Charters, An Annotated List* (London, 1968)
VCH	*The Victoria History of the Counties of England: A History of Hampshire and the Isle of Wight*: vols. 1, 2, by A. Doubleday (London, 1900-1903); vols. 3, 4, by W. Page (London, 1908, 1911)

Preface

> For my part, I have never been able to understand the anxiety to
> identify the district known, in later days, as a "Hundred" with an
> original hundred warriors, or hides.

J.H. Round, *Feudal England* (1909), p. 98.

With typical acidity, Horace Round dismissed the Anglo-Saxon origins of
English local government. For Round, such traditions were primitive in
contrast to the administrative achievements of the Norman clerks. Anglo-
Saxon institutions were inefficient and insufficient, object lessons of what
a medieval state ought not to be. More admirable were the Normans and
their grim Duke William, conquering and ruling a people who had claimed
neither strength in the bonds of fealty nor pride in the name of vassal.

This book holds the opposite premise: that there is real value in the
search for early political and social institutions, including the hundred. From
Maitland and Jolliffe to Stenton and Sawyer, proponents of an Anglo-Saxon
dominant gene in English medieval government have looked to the hundred
as a key element in institutional development. I chose the Hampshire chalk
downland, the heartland of Wessex, to search for evidence of early
territorial units. This area not only has one of the greatest concentrations of
surviving Anglo-Saxon charters, but also an archaeological record difficult
to surpass. Both conditions are not unrelated to the proximity of the Anglo-
Saxon capital, Winchester, which was in fact the reason for my familiarity
with and interest in the region. In the early 1970s, I learned first-hand of its
historical and archaeological riches, through my participation in the
Winchester Excavations, investigating the city proper, and in the MARC3
excavation team, exploring the adjacent countryside in advance of the M3
motorway construction.

The evolution of the rural landscape and institutions in the region of
Micheldever, Hampshire, was the subject of my 1985 doctoral thesis for
The Johns Hopkins University. That study used documentary,
archaeological, toponymic, and geographic sources to recreate the shifting
patterns of settlement and land-use and determine their relationship to land
holding and local territorial units. Subsequent research and thought on the
first of the subjects has led to the publication of the monograph, *Settlement
and Land Use in Micheldever Hundred, Hampshire, 700-1100.*[1] Its conclusions for middle Hampshire, that no case can be made for continuity of the

---

[1]   Transactions of the American Philosophical Society, vol. 81 part 3 (Philadelphia,
1991).

Romano-British countryside beyond the sub-Roman period, and that the medieval villages and field systems were established well before the end of the Anglo-Saxon period, have since been paralleled in Della Hooke's study of localities in Berkshire.[2]

Further study has also revised and expanded the other theme of the dissertation research: how the dynamics of settlement and land use in middle Hampshire related to landholding practices and local territorial units. This book explores the origins of English local institutions in Anglo-Saxon Hampshire, and sets their development in the context of the growth of a regional, then national, monarchy.

Of primary importance is the discovery of discrete geographically-integral blocks of land which in the eighth century comprised one hundred hides, or households. These 'archaic hundreds,' originally natural groupings of population, were soon adopted as administrative districts by the Church and the Christianized kingdom. At the same time, however, agricultural change led to the formation of the vill, a nucleated village with its surrounding lands. The steady spread of this new entity caused the division of the earlier, larger district into three categories of smaller units: the manors, parishes, and hundreds that assumed the economic, spiritual, and political functions of the 'archaic hundred.'

An unexpected finding was that these elements were often reassembled into new groupings during the late Saxon period, resulting in territorial units and arrangements that have the appearance of greater antiquity. Indeed, many territorial links among such groupings in the Domesday Book date only from the preceding century. The sequence of manorial, parochial, and juridical development is one of alternating fission and fusion, a pattern most likely further repeated in the fluctuating economic climates of the later Middle Ages.

A case study of one of the archaic hundreds proposed in this work has already appeared in print.[3] In it, I examined details of the pre-Conquest charters of the upper Itchen valley and reinterpreted the boundaries of the Anglo-Saxon manors. Originally, the land within the valley-defined territory may have known as 'Itchen,' an early type of toponym. The 'central place' of the archaic hundred was Worthy, with a major pagan cemetery, an early

---

[2]   Hooke's findings, "Regional Variation in Southern and Central England in the Anglo-Saxon Period and its Relationship to Land Units and Settlement," in *Anglo-Saxon Settlement*, ed. Hooke (Oxford, 1988), pp. 123-151, unfortunately came to my attention too late to be included in this study.

[3]   Eric Klingelhöfer, "Anglo-Saxon Manors of the Upper Itchen Valley: Their Origin and Evolution," *Proceedings of the Hampshire Field Club and Archaeological Society* 46 (1990), 31-39.

church, and a royal manor. Further, the names of villages along the upper Itchen suggest the late fission of large, multi-settlement tracts; two villages have 'Itchen' as part of their name and four others have 'Worthy.'

This present study of Anglo-Saxon territorial units in Hampshire suggests an origin for medieval local institutions in a primitive district that was rendered obsolete by the appearance of the village and manor. The resulting administrative districts of parish, manor, and hundred were to form new, shifting associations in the following centuries. This complicated process—the functional division of an original unity, followed by a kaleidoscope of changing patterns—is essential to understanding the rural development of Wessex, if not southern England. Perhaps even Horace Round would now value the search for the origin of the hundred and accept the role of the 'archaic hundred' in the institutional history of early England.

This work owes more debts than did Mr Micawber. The subject of territorial divisions in early medieval Hampshire first came to my attention when I took part in Martin Biddle's excavations in Winchester; interest was renewed when I worked for Peter Fasham's MARC3 group.

The formal study of the Micheldever region of Hampshire was encouraged by my doctoral advisors, Professors John Baldwin and Michael McCormick, of The Johns Hopkins University. Mercer University faculty development grants to support supplemental research in 1985 and writing in 1986 were authorized by Deans Robert Hargrove and Sammye Greer. The archival and field research undertaken in 1982 and 1986, however, would not have been successful without the kind professional assistance and even kinder personal hospitality of Kenneth Qualman, Katherine Barclay, and Caroline Raison Schadla-Hall. Over the years, I received much cooperation from the staffs of the Hampshire County Archives, the British Library, the Eisenhower Library of The Johns Hopkins University, and the Stetson Library of Mercer University. David Hinton and Derek Keene, who perhaps more than anyone know the early medieval history of middle Hampshire and Winchester, were most helpful in suggesting improvements in the manuscript, and Margaret Gelling graciously spared the time to comment on my presentation and interpretation of place-names. Colleagues in the History Department of Mercer University, Professor Carlos Flick and Professor Emeritus Willis Glover, were kind enough to review the manuscript in final draft. The conclusions presented here are mine alone, however, as are all errors and omissions.

Above all, none of this would have been possible without the enduring patience and understanding of my wife, Alexandra.

1

The Historical Problems

When historians were formulating standards of critical scholarship and consequently defining problems of permanent significance, a century ago, the origin and development of the Anglo-Saxon manor was already the subject of intense debate. In 1892 appeared *The Old English Manor*, an attempt by Charles Andrews to synthesize the widely divergent scholarly theories.[1] Although much information has been brought forward since Andrews's time, little has been settled concerning the nature and process of early medieval rural development. In simple terms, the debate was over the question of which institution, the manor or the village, was earlier, and thus influenced the development of the other. The debate continues, but in recent years, coloured by the terminology of models and systems, it has drifted away from the as-yet unanswered questions.

The controversy is of major importance to understanding medieval history, because the manor and village are the physical embodiments of two distinct and conflicting social forces. For this study, the early manor is defined territorially as the land of one or more family's farming units, control over which was in the hands of one man or institution, the lord, and upon which the exploitation of resources was organized. The village, spatially, was the form taken by the concentration of a rural population, usually associated with a cooperative agricultural system. In the manor, society was directed from above; in the village, it was organized from below. Thus the primacy historians attribute to one or the other reveals, either intentionally or otherwise, their views on the foundation of medieval society.

The manor/village question was an important aspect of the nineteenth-century concern for tracing medieval institutions back to an ethnic or national origin. In one view, the village was thought a creation of the original German immigrants, with a manorial system developing second-

---

[1]   Charles M. Andrews, *The Old English Manor: A Study in English Economic History* (Baltimore, 1892).

arily. Alternatively, the manor was claimed to be the normal agricultural organization among the Romano-British, and was developed by the Anglo-Saxons directly from existing structures, or indirectly via later Celtic traditions, whereupon the English lord of the manor then drew together the peasantry into a manageable unit, the village.[2]

Andrews tempered those extreme positions by amending the 'voluntary association of freemen' to a patriarchal tribal organization and by claiming that the Roman Church, not the Roman Empire, was the major influence in the creation of the English manor.[3] His efforts were unthanked and ignored.

Fin-de-siècle nationalistic concerns are anachronistic and of faint interest today, but the little-read Andrews makes a good starting point for a review of the ensuing scholarship. The historical debate on the origin of rural institutions has been broad, deep, and acrimonious, reasons enough to note with care the various contributions. But in such a crowded and well-argued field, a new model of historical development necessarily challenges previous authorities. The problem that it attempts to solve must be placed in its historiographic context by reviewing previous scholarship in some detail—before the argument for the new model is offered. Readers unfamiliar with the field require an overview of the scholarship independent of my findings and judgments. Those acquainted with the material will want to note the interpretation given here of various points of discussion and underlying assumptions about the early medieval world. For clarity, the development of rural institutions is best organized in four topics: land tenure, administration, settlement, and synthesis.

LAND TENURE

Land tenure is a defining characteristic of rural society, e.g., 'feudal tenure,' referring to land tenure by possession of a military fief. The *feodum* was a conditional reward for service, while an *allodium* was permanent, in

---

[2]   Andrews reviewed the positions of the scholars of the time: there was a group following Palgrave and Lewis in favour of a Welsh or Celtic origin for early medieval legal and agricultural customs; a 'Romanist' group led by Seebohm; and a third and larger contingent based on Stubbs and Freeman that sought an origin among the traditions of the continental Germans.

[3]   The idea of entities competing for survival strikes a note similar to the 'process of natural selection,' which Bishop Stubbs saw as the system by which the Anglo-Saxon tribal states sorted themselves out into the Heptarchy. See William Stubbs, *The Constitutional History of England* (1874-1878), abridged and with an introduction by James Cornfield (Chicago, 1979), pp. 18, 19.

freehold. These were of course administrative terms, and did not necessarily express the complexity of actual tenurial conditions, stated and unstated.

Evidence for land tenure is present in the most common surviving record of the pre-Conquest period, the charters. Because the details of these documents can be readily compared to better-known later medieval land-holding arrangements, tenurial conditions have been used extensively as a basis for speculation on the structure of Anglo-Saxon society and on the more concrete institutions of the manor and village. Five years after Andrews' *The Old English Manor* appeared, Frederick Maitland published the magisterial *Domesday Book and Beyond* (1897), which contained a flood of information on land tenure, generally substantiating the claims of the Germanists.[4] This effort, moreover, was supplemented by a work which even more closely addressed the question of primary institutions, Sir Paul Vinogradoff's *Growth of the Manor* (1905).[5]

Maitland considered Anglo-Saxon landholding to have originally been by clans or tribes, under the authority of national kings. He proposed that the Anglo-Saxon charters, following a standard Roman formula, conferred a 'superiority' over the land. What was granted by the King first to church and lay nobles, and later conveyed by them to others, were the alienable fiscal and judicial rights over the land. For Maitland, this devolution of central control led to the formation of the manor as an economic and juridical entity. Lordship was closely tied to manorialism, and was not an earlier institution. Drawing comparison from Continental lordship, Maitland contended that the ancient Frankish *senior* had not necessarily possessed legal rights over his *vassi*, men who entered a lord's protection and swore to support him. It was only in the tenth century that English kings legislated against the lordless man by insisting that everyone should have a superior, a lord who would be responsible for his behaviour, thus fostering vassalism, if not feudalism. To Maitland, land was not held privately in the villages, nor was it communal, but rather a co-ownership of individuals. The catalyst for change was the Danish invasions, which he thought might well have given a certain amount of liberty to peasants in Danish-occupied areas, but the much higher dues to the state for the greatly increased expenses for defence elsewhere caused the subjugation of the free peasant.[6]

---

[4]   F.W. Maitland, *Domesday Book and Beyond: Three Essays in the Early History of England* (Cambridge, 1897).

[5]   Sir Paul Vinogradoff, *The Growth of the Manor* (London, 1905), 2nd ed., (New York, 1951).

[6]   *DBB* 232, 283, 340-341.

Sir Paul Vinogradoff added to Maitland's explanation of the rise of the manor by enumerating certain steps in that process. He believed that it was misleading to search for tribal organizations in Anglo-Saxon England, because the family farm, or 'hide,' was from very early on reckoned a constituent part of the 'hundred,' an administrative area which he thought originated in a military group of one hundred warriors, and not a tribal organization. Moreover, Vinogradoff considered the hide to have been not an absolute measure of land (as had Maitland), but an equal share of a *tun*, or rural settlement. He found the communal aspect of the village to be the key element to early medieval development, and sought corroboration in Anglo-Saxon social terminology. As the term 'foldworthy,' defining a free man, was equated with right of pasture (the importance of which gave the village 'a decidedly communalistic bent'), so the associated term 'mootworthy' revealed the position of the *tun*'s court meeting, or 'moot,' as the nucleus of rural administration.[7]

For Vinogradoff, the evolution of the manor was expressed in the growth of rents and services, but especially of the 'demesne,' land which the lord did not parcel out among the villagers but reserved for himself. Territorial lordship does not necessarily imply a demesne, Vinogradoff argued, and what may have been originally little more than a storehouse for tribute in kind developed into a demesnial farm with its dependent holdings. He followed Maitland's theory that along with the political reorganization during the Danish Wars, came heavy burdens upon the peasantry, which reduced their status from free tribesmen to dependent serfs.[8]

But contradictory conclusions were drawn from the same sources. In *Anglo-Saxon Institutions* (1905) H.M. Chadwick examined the evidence for early land tenure and concluded that landholding was originally not by family or clan, but was given out by the king to support an individual loyal follower (*gesith*) either directly, as an official (*comes regis*), or indirectly, as a member of the *gesith* class (a *gesithcund man*), presumably via a royal office. He stressed that in the Danish invasions, as after the Norman Conquest, the land was divided up from above, in pyramidal descent according to rank and allegiance, and he proposed that this had also been the case in Anglo-Saxon tenure, which was the result of a similar conquest.[9]

H.R. Hodgkin's *History of the Anglo-Saxons* (1935) extended Chadwick's hierarchical view of early English society, with the claim that

---

[7]   Vinogradoff, *Manor*, pp. 145, 151, 181, 199. But for Maitland's rejection of the village as a political institution, see *DBB* 350, 353.

[8]   Ibid., pp. 224, 265.

[9]   H. Munro Chadwick, *Studies on Anglo-Saxon Institutions* (Cambridge, 1905; repr. New York, 1963), p. 375.

the army was not drawn from a national body of freemen, but a small select group of warriors, the king's companions. Hodgkin sided with Chadwick in his assertion that "with the exception of the king himself, every individual in the nation owed obedience to a lord," but he differed in his view of the Anglo-Saxon conquest and settlement, seeing a slow replacement of Celts by Germans, and thus leaving open the possibility of some continuity of traditions.[10]

The views of Maitland and Vinogradoff, however, were forcefully repeated and expanded by Sir Frank Stenton's *Anglo-Saxon England* (1943). Stenton believed that the independent free peasant landowner was depressed into villeinage by the spread of the manorial lordship, a control over land and production. Manorial lordship was joined in the late Saxon period by territorial lordship. The medieval manor was formed when two actions occurred: the money or food rent that villagers paid the lord (formerly the king) was converted to labour services on a demesne; and individual peasants surrendered their lands to the lord, receiving them back as his men, under his protection and control. When normal governmental jurisdiction was replaced by territorial lordship, the transformation was complete.[11]

In 1958, the Stenton thesis, while not criticized in L.C. Latham's essay on "The Manor and Village,"[12] was challenged by another paper, "The Origins of the Manor," by T.H. Aston. Questioning the view that manorialism slowly developed in the late Saxon period to come to fruition under the Normans, Aston argued that in fact the reverse had occurred - that a noticeably reduced demesne land in twelfth-century estates proved that the classic demesne manor was then in decline. Examples in Domesday Book of the leasing out of the demesne suggested to Aston that manorial institutions were already in decay soon after the Norman Conquest. He also firmly disagreed with Maitland's concept of "superiority over the land," and asserted that only later did charters distinguish between the land and the rights over it, and that grantees of the early charters had full landlord rights. Lordship was the dominant social institution, and the ties of lordship were always "more vital and effective" than those of kinship. There was no such thing as an unattached landowning peasantry. Land upon which the lord had settled dependents, the *gesettland* of the late seventh-century laws, Aston

---

[10] R.H. Hodgkin, *A History of the Anglo-Saxons* (Oxford, 1935), pp. 135, 203, 208-210, 590-593.

[11] *ASE* 470-472.

[12] L.C. Latham, "The Manor and the Village," in *Social Life in Early England*, ed. G. Barraclough (London, 1960), pp. 29-50. The introduction by Barraclough reveals that Latham's article had been considerably revised. The introduction was dated 1958, so Latham must have already completed the paper by that date.

equated with the taxable *utland* of Domesday as distinguished from tax-exempt *inland*, or demesne. He concluded that the classic demesne manor had been the normal economic unit of the Anglo-Saxon period.[13]

In that same year, Eric John joined in the attack on the 'Germanists' with the publication of *Land Tenure in Early England*. In it, he examined the conditions under which land was granted by charter as 'bookland,' and those that applied to unchartered 'folkland.' He argued that in the earliest charters the monarchy did not grant total immunity, but retained the "three common burdens" attached to the land, i.e., military service, and fort and bridge construction. It was only later, he asserted, in the second half of the tenth century, that full immunities appeared, and there it was a case of powerful churchmen, with close ties to a feudalized France, who received extraordinary authority from a weakened monarchy. Much of John's argument rests upon his interpretation of the tenurial arrangements in the bishop of Worcester's Liberty of Oswaldslow, and the identification of it as a unit designed to supply a ship and men for the national defense.[14]

These arguments were supplemented by those of H.P.R. Finberg, who concluded in *The Early Charters of Wessex* (1964) that the late tenth-century church reform was also the occasion for much production of 'post-dated' land grants, usually defining manorial rights that had been either undocumented or unspecified in the original charters. Consequently, much material that had been discarded by Stubbs, Stevenson, and Stenton as spurious, Finberg accepted as late tenth-century compilations of earlier records and conditions, and associated with the contemporary cathedral reforms.[15] Elsewhere, Finberg argued for a servile Anglo-Saxon peasantry, even asserting that a 'carlton' or 'charlton' was not a settlement of independent peasant *ceorls*, owing allegiance to the king alone (as Stenton

---

[13]   T.H. Aston, "The Origins of the Manor in England," *Transactions of the Royal Historical Society* 5th ser. 8 (1958), 59-83. For the following topics, see: demesne manor in decay p. 61; ties of lordship p. 62; landlord rights p. 64; Ine's 'gesette land' as non-demesnial pp. 67-68; dependent peasantry p. 73. For Stenton's claim that the ties of kinship were only slowly replaced by those of lordship, see *ASE* 314-318. John F. McGovern showed an alternative explanation to Aston's 'gesette land' in "The Meaning of 'Gesette Land' in Anglo-Saxon Land Tenure," *Speculum* 46 (1971), 589-596.

[14]   Eric John, *Land Tenure in Early England* (Leicester, 1958), pp. 113-139. See also W.H. Stevenson, "Trinoda Necessitas," *English Historical Review* 29 (1914), 689-703. Oswaldslow 'triple' Hundred has been the object of intense scholarship. See Maitland, *DBB* 304-318, for a pre-Norman military tenure; Stenton, *ASE* 485-486, 681-682, only a service tenure; Marjory Hollings, "The Survival of the Five-Hide Unit in the Western Midlands," *English Historical Review* 63 (1948), 453-487; C. Warren Hollister, *Anglo-Saxon Military Institutions* (Oxford, 1962), pp. 54-55, 96-99, 112-113.

[15]   *ECW* 214-248.

maintained), and surrounded by lands that had individual lords. Rather, the 'charlton' was a manorial unit upon which serfs were settled, and its name as recorded was due solely to the fact that, as it was a royal estate, the royal servants who drew up the documents referred to the holding by its functional term.[16]

The combined arguments of Aston, John, and Finberg present a picture of pre-Conquest England strikingly different from Stenton's. For them, an incipient lordship was not far removed from the Continental seigniory. In this England, there was little room for democratic or egalitarian traditions.

More recent scholarship has continued to examine the relationship between social organization and early medieval landholding, again with conflicting results. The connection between family and hide was analyzed by John McGovern, who saw an evolutionary change from a society based upon the family to one based upon property. As the term 'hide' adopted the definition of the Roman law *fundus* and provided the Anglo-Saxons with the concept of an estate that could consist of non-contiguous property, a society based upon the family evolved into one based upon property.[17] On the other hand, the hide may have been a generic holding of freemen and not associated with a particular sense of 'family.' If social positions were relative, then they cannot be taken as attributes of a single social class. As a noble *gesith* may be *hlaford* (lord) to a peasant *ceorl*, so a *ceorl* may be *hlaford* to a bondsman *laet*, or any other person of low status. Lordship was thus not restricted to the nobly-born, but was rather a legal term expressing rights over others.[18] Scholars like Donald Bullough have cautioned that early medieval society was based far more strongly upon kinship than the

---

[16] H.P.R. Finberg, *Lucerna, Studies of Some Problems in the Early History of England* (London, 1964), pp. 144-160.

[17] John F. McGovern, "The Hide and Related Land-Tenure Concepts in Anglo-Saxon England, AD 700-1100," *Traditio* 28 (1972), 101-118.

[18] T.M. Charles-Edwards argued that the concept of the workforce of a hide needed revision; it was farmed not only by a *ceorl*'s family, but also by his dependents. This identification would still keep to Bede's definition of the hide, or *mansus*, as the holding of one family, but the potential variations in the size of such units could be great indeed. See "Kinship, Status, and the Origin of the Hide," *Past and Present* 56 (1972), 3-33.

Much of the information of Anglo-Saxon social status is drawn from the *Rectitudines Singularum Personarum* (presented and translated by Whitelock, *EHD* 1: 364-372), which is considered an Anglo-Norman treatise, but generally reflects late Anglo-Saxon society. It lists the rights and duties of the *thegn, geneat, gebur, cotset,* and serf. See *DBB* 227-237; *ASE* 473-479.

institutionally derived sources admit, but at same time this kinship was more circumscribed by other social forms than some historians have assumed.[19]

ADMINISTRATION

The major problems in early English administrative history are two-fold: the origins of the late Saxon administrative institutions, and the relationship between the late Saxon government and that of the Anglo-Normans of the next century. The organization of the tenth- and eleventh-century kingdom was, above the local level, by hundred and shire. The origin of these institutions is not known. They were not present in the initial conquest and settlement, having no origin in the Germanic past. Neither did they appear in recognizable form in the earliest records of the seventh and eighth century. Their creation therefore must have occurred between the seventh and the tenth centuries, but the details can only be surmised.

H.M. Chadwick investigated the early medieval rural district called the hundred, which he contended was native to Wessex alone, and was a part of the administration established by Alfred's descendants over a unified England. He identified the predecessor of the hundred as a pre-Alfredian division, the *scir*, comprising several hundred hides and dependent upon a royal vill where the customary dues were paid and justice was given out.[20] This interpretation is in keeping with Chadwick's hierarchical view of Anglo-Saxon society.

Maitland saw the original local administration transformed in two ways. First, tribute for the king's *feorm* (living expenses for a certain

---

[19]   Other opinions, however, continue to flourish. The original free status of the Anglo-Saxon peasant, particularly in the Danelaw, is a theory that retains adherents: *ASE* 502-525. See also Henry Loyn, *The Free Anglo-Saxon* (Cardiff, 1975), and Barbara Dodwell "The Free Peasantry of East Anglia in Domesday," *Norfolk Archaeology* 27 (1971), 145-157.

Thus far, social and economic historians of the early English period do not seem to have used the Marxist explanation of class identity which Hilton, Kosminsky, and to some extent Hallam, have given for the rural development of the later Middle Ages: R.H. Hilton, *The English Peasantry in the Later Middle Ages* (Oxford, 1975); E.A. Kosminsky, *Studies in the Agrarian History of England in the Thirteenth Century* (Oxford, 1956); H.E. Hallam, *Settlement and Society: A Study of the Early Agrarian History of South Lincolnshire* (Cambridge, 1965).

Donald Bullough makes the point, however, that the documents reveal kinship to have a much more limited definition than sociological historians have assumed ("Early Medieval Social Groupings: The Terminology of Kinship," *Past and Present* 45 [1969], 3-18).

[20]   Chadwick, *Institutions*, pp. 239-248, 260-262.

number of nights) was once a uniform royal system. Rights to this tribute were granted by the king and in fact became the source of manorial dues. Secondly, jurisdictional areas were grouped by hundreds, with justice given out in each hundred court or 'moot.' These also were granted by the king, often as entire hundreds, then as smaller areas still measured as a fraction of a hundred, and later as 'sokes' no longer considered derivative parts of an hundredal jurisdiction. The alienation of royal control over the legal rights of the populace in certain areas was the source of manorial authority.[21]

J.E.A. Jolliffe took a different approach, claiming that the basis for the older administrative units, represented by at least some groups of hundreds should be equated with a 'folk,' the *regio* of Bede.[22] Following Chadwick, he based the earlier unit upon a royal residence, a *curtis*, which developed into the later *villa regalis* or 'kingstun.' But this framework was broken down by the spread of the demesne-based manor and a subsequent immunity from fiscal and judicial administration. Jolliffe did not think that those changes were part of a linear progression of maturing social forms, the "natural and even necessary stage" of feudalism, as seen by Maitland.[23] Rather, Jolliffe saw the reverse: "folk and folk law is the basis of a stable government," and "feudalism was but an interlude intruding for a time upon [the folk's] millennial endurance."[24] Each unit of Jolliffe's 'folk' was levied a fixed round sum to support the king, rendered annually as *feorm* or *gafol*, and it governed itself under 'folklaw.' In this model of a society of near primitive purity, there is no room for the lord; any modification of the direct links between king and folk is intrusive. To him, "the *feudum* was enemy to the folks," and it seems that what was not 'folk' was *feudum*.[25]

Helen Cam made notable contributions to the study of local institutions, especially the hundred. She drew attention to the private hundred, or 'hundredal manor,' which she believed displayed "features

---

[21]   *DBB* 92-93, 286, 351.

[22]   J.E.A. Jolliffe, "The Era of the Folk in English History," in *Oxford Essays in Medieval History Presented to Herbert Edward Salter*, ed. F.M. Powicke (Oxford, 1935), pp. 1-32. He considers the 'federative' manor to have had Celtic origins, p. 15. For his comments on the Yorkshire hundreds, see pp. 22-23, and for those in Cornwall, p. 15.

[23]   Ibid., pp. 166-167; *DBB* 223.

[24]   Jolliffe, "Era of Folk," pp. 7, 8.

[25]   Ibid. Jolliffe argued that the debates on feudalism and the origin of the manor had overshadowed the role of the folk. He seems to suggest that the folk-groups were somehow self-governing, with royal reeves perhaps restricted to collecting the *feorm*.

suggesting a remote antiquity," perhaps preceding Alfred's reign.[26] She traced the histories of these estates back to manors of ancient royal demesne, finding that they could generally be proven to have been 'farmed' by the king's officers. While accepting Chadwick's identification of the royal *tun* as the focal point for an early administrative system, Cam seriously questioned Jolliffe's suggestion of a popular, even non-Saxon origin for these territorial units.[27] Such an earlier entity, she believed, may well have been set at 100 hides in Wessex, and while not the same thing as the hundred of the tenth century, it was nevertheless an administrative district "with a royal rather than a popular basis."[28] Furthermore, Cam suggested that the earliest endowments to the bishoprics "carried with them rights which crystallized into titles of hundreds," and thus the poorly documented hundredal manors of the ancient dioceses may well preserve original territorial units and the administrative powers within them.[29]

Sir Frank Stenton considered the round figures of the assessment of public burdens relating to the king's *feorm* and other service duties, compared to more precise contemporary Anglo-Saxon administrative figures (e.g., fines). He explained that this did not mean that such round figures represented a portion of a hundred's dues, because they appear "two centuries before there is any evidence that hundred courts existed for the adjustment of unequal assessments." The round figures, he argued, must then have been determined by an alternative political entity, which he identified as a primitive township moot. He also proposed that the early *regiones* had self-governing moots, and they supplied the king with his *feorm* and his *fyrd* (national army) in units of round hundred hides. The origin of the hundred may thus be sought in the growth of monarchical institutions, whereby royal administrative districts replaced a system of tribal *regiones*.[30]

---

[26]   Helen Cam, "*Manerium cum Hundredo*: The Hundred and the Hundredal Manor," *English Historical Review* 47 (1932), 353-376, repr. in Cam, *Liberties and Communities in Medieval England: Collected Studies on Local Administration and Topography* (Cambridge, 1964), pp. 64-90. See also her "Early Groups of Hundreds," in *Historical Essays in Honour of James Tait*, ed. J.G. Edwards, et al. (Manchester, 1933), pp. 91-106.

[27]   Cam, "*Manerium*," pp. 69, 87.

[28]   Ibid., p. 90. She found fault with Jolliffe's concept of the 'folk' because the pre-hundredal system of tribute-paying areas based on royal 'tuns' has every aspect of a royally constructed income-producing apparatus, and not that of a natural, organically evolved, and loosely democratic, governmental system.

[29]   Helen Cam, "The Private Hundred Before the Norman Conquest," in *Studies Presented to Sir Hilary Jenkinson*, ed. J. Conway Davis (Oxford, 1957), pp. 50-60.

[30]   *ASE* 287, 298-301.

SETTLEMENT

Settlement studies, and their contributory disciplines of historical geography, archaeology, and toponymics, give data on the physical location and character of the rural population.

Noteworthy settlement studies of specific locales have been those undertaken by Barry Cunliffe in Eastern Hampshire, C.J. Arnold in Sussex and the Isle of Wight, Peter Wade-Martens in East Anglia, Margaret Faull in Yorkshire, and W.J. Ford in Warwickshire.[31] Detailed studies concern not only early medieval village locations but also early estates, as revealed in the boundaries attached to many Anglo-Saxon land charters.[32] Increasing evidence for continuity of land use and territorial division within the countryside suggests that some of the parish boundaries of medieval England may have existed from the earliest days of Anglo-Saxon occupation, or before, but there is also evidence for a complex transition in the late Saxon period from dispersed settlements to recognizable medieval villages.[33]

---

[31] Barry Cunliffe, "Saxon and Medieval Settlement-Pattern in the Region of Chalton, Hampshire," *Medieval Archaeology* 16 (1972), 1-12; C.J. Arnold, "Early Anglo-Saxon Settlement Patterns in Southern England," *Journal of Historical Geography* 3 (1977), 309-315; Peter Wade-Martens, "The Origins of Rural Settlement in East Anglia," in *Recent Work on Rural Archaeology*, ed. P.J. Fowler (Bradford-on-Avon, 1975), pp. 137-157; Margaret Faull, "Roman and Anglian Settlement Patterns in Yorkshire," *Northern History* 9 (1974), 1-25; W.J. Ford, "Some Settlement Patterns in the Central Region of the Warwickshire Avon," in *MSCC* 274-294.

   But see also W.L.D. Ravenhill, "The Form and Pattern of Post-Roman Settlement in Devon," *Proceedings of the Devonshire Archaeology and Exploration Society* 28 (1970), 83-94; P.J. Fowler, "Small Settlements and Their Contexts in Western Britain, First to Fifth Centuries AD," *Proceedings of the Royal Irish Academy* 76c (1976), 191-206, for the West; and C. Phythian-Adams, *Continuity, Fields and Fission: The Making of a Midland Parish* (Leicester, 1978), for a close examination of a small area. A settlement study of middle Hampshire is presented in Eric Klingelhöfer, *Settlement and Land Use in Micheldever Hundred, 700-1100*, Transactions of the American Philosophical Society, vol. 81 part 3 (Philadelphia, 1991).

[32] A recent review of the methodology is *Recording Historic Landscapes: Principles and Practice*, ed. Peter Brandon and Roger Millman (London,1980). For a good example of the process, see Geoffrey Hewlett, "Reconstructing a Historical Landscape from Field and Documentary Evidence: Otford in Kent," *Agricultural History Review* 21 (1973), 94-110.

[33] The material is extensively reviewed in P.J. Fowler, "Agriculture and Rural Settlement," in *ASE*, 23-48. Christopher Taylor has argued forcefully for the late change in settlement type, in *Village and Farmstead: A History of Rural Settlement in England* (London, 1983). See also Ann Goodier, "The Formation of Boundaries in Anglo-Saxon England: A Statistical Study," *Medieval Archaeology* 28 (1984), 1-21.

A regional and national level offers more scope for the limited historical and archaeological data.[34] Wendy Davies and Hayo Vierck combined settlement studies with the list of peoples in the eighth-century Mercian tribute record, the Tribal Hidage, to try to identify and explain the arrangement of unequal-sized political units in the middle Saxon period.[35] Even Maitland noted that whilst the Anglo-Saxons may have settled in peasant villages similar to those they had left on the continent, there was also evidence that "German kings and earls took to themselves integral estates, the boundaries and agrarian arrangements whereof had been drawn by Romans, or rather by Celts."[36]

Jolliffe referred to the "federate manor," an estate composed of several village units, not necessarily contiguous. He saw the ultimate origin of this manorial form to have been the federative unit of the 'folk,' which at times was fossilized in a 'soke,' i.e., folkright over folkland under private or royal lordship.[37] T.H. Aston proposed that even though most settlements had been created by the dependents and followers of one man, evidence for this primary stage had been obscured by the "discrete estate," a landholding "covering more than one significant settlement" (and identical to the federate manor). Declaring that "the structural variations in the cells of discrete estates, even in the cells of one estate, are of the utmost importance in manorial history," Aston theorized that the discrete estate was part of an original land pattern, but the subsequent process of creating and dissolving those units helped destroy the "unity of lordship and settlement" that was the basis of the primitive estate.[38]

Glanville Jones, a historical geographer, contended that the early English "multiple estate," with a central settlement and a number of

---

[34] E.T. Leeds, *The Archaeology of the Anglo-Saxon Settlements* (Oxford, 1913); R.G. Collingwood and J.N.L. Myers, *Roman Britain and the English Settlements*, Oxford History of England, Vol. 1 (Oxford, 1936). Unchanged in the 1968 reprint, it was substantially revised in J.N.L. Myers, *The English Settlements*, Oxford History of England, Vol. 1B (Oxford, 1986), based upon findings presented earlier in his *Anglo-Saxon Pottery and the Settlement of England* (Oxford, 1969).

[35] W. Davies and H. Vierck, "The Contexts of Tribal Hidage: Social Aggregates and Settlement Patterns," *Frühmittelalterliche Studien* 8 (1974), 223-293.

[36] *DBB* 351.

[37] Jolliffe, "Era of Folk," pp. 15, 18.

[38] Aston also suggested that outlying land such as *berewicks*, (barley farms) had little or no demesne and were similar to the *coloni* settlements dependent upon late Roman villa estates, "Origins of the Manor," pp. 76, 77. A recent refinement of his theory concludes that "the variated social and agrarian landscape" resulted from the multiple effects of the late Saxon expansion of settlement ("The Origin of the Manor in England *with* a Postscript," in *Social Relations and Ideas: Essays in Honour of R.H. Hilton*, ed. T.H. Aston [Cambridge, 1983], pp. 1-43, esp. 42).

dependent ones, had the same organization as the Welsh *maenor*.[39] Jones, and Jolliffe before him, believed that the pre-Danish *scir* of Northumbria, a considerably smaller territorial division than the late Saxon shire, represented an already existing settlement grouping of Celtic origin, which the Anglians took over with no apparent change. Jones found in Sussex and Wiltshire pre-Saxon multiple estates which he located documentarily or inferred from late medieval hundredal centres. Jones did agree with Aston's view of the original servile condition of the Anglo-Saxon manor worker, but he asserted that the setting was not that of an integral unit where a lord's *-ingas* group of dependents worked a single estate from a single village. He proposed that the Celtic, pre-Saxon multiple estate with its scattered bond hamlets gave explanation enough for the servile conditions Aston found in the early manor.[40] These landholdings, he further claimed, had developed the range of local resources to the point where the lands each controlled would have included a mixture of all available topographic and vegetative types.[41]

SYNTHESIS

Having reviewed the relevant contributions to the study of early medieval rural landholding, administration, and settlement, we may turn to syntheses of this material. For the past generation and longer, one view has predominated: a free peasantry's descent into villeinage, as refined and advanced by Sir Frank Stenton. He accepted the free peasant landowner of Maitland and Vinogradoff, "owning the land which supported him, though farming it in association with his fellows, and responsible to no authority below the king for his breaking of local customs." The customs themselves were strictly Germanic, and in spite of occasional surviving British and

---

[39] G.R.J. Jones, "Settlement Patterns in Anglo-Saxon England," *Antiquity* 35 (1961), 221-232. Jones's multiple estate seems identical to Aston"s 'discrete estate,' Jolliffe's 'federal manor,' Maitland's 'integral estate,' and Gelling's 'conglomerate estate.' But also see B.H. Slicher van Bath, *The Agrarian History of Western Europe, AD 500-1850* (New York, 1963), pp. 46-47, for remarks on manor type.

[40] G.R.J. Jones, "Basic Patterns of Settlement Distribution in Northern England," *Advancement of Science* 72 (1961), 192-200.

[41] For localities in Wales, Sussex, and Northumbria, Jones equated the extent of early estates with the later medieval boundaries of the administrative units of the Welsh *cantraf*, the English hundred, and the Danelaw *wapentake*. By grouping all settlements with labour services or tribute due to an ancient manorial center, and by adding any jurisdictions pertaining to that centre, he claimed the early existence of complex forms of estates. See G.R.J. Jones, "Multiple Estates and Early Settlement," in *MSCC* 14-40.

Roman place-names, the British strain left no significant impression in English society. The basic holding was the hide, the amount of land that could support one family, and the unit used for tribute assessment to the king, as 'folkland,' or to an immunity-holding lord as 'bookland.' The fact that whole-number assessments of 'family lands' in each village paying toward the royal *feorm* remained unchanged for centuries convinced Stenton that social organization was based upon the village, not the farm. The community was organized at one level by the village, and at another by the tribe. The early territorial division, *regio* or *ge*, was similar to the German *gau*, and originated "in tribal settlements, not any deliberate division of the land for administrative purposes."[42]

There is clearly a wide difference between Stenton's view of early medieval rural history and the results of Finberg's work on charters, Jones's study of the multiple estate, and Aston's search for manorial origins. Yet, according to Peter Sawyer, the historical debate has been ill-founded; insufficient evidence has led historians to believe that there had been only minimal development of the Anglo-Saxon countryside. He documented the amount and nature of the tribute coming from the land to suggest that in many places the Saxon estates "were already being fully exploited in the seventh century." He questioned the extent of the shift to an arable economy, noting the presence in the early documents of substantial cereal as well as pastoral products. Rejecting the presumption of largely unsettled areas that appear in historical geographies for the early medieval period, Sawyer labelled Domesday Book unreliable as a guide to eleventh-century settlement. It did not list minor settlements separately, but treated them as integral to the manor to which they were attached. This was particularly common with villages in wooded areas, and nearly all these settlements, Sawyer claimed, were actually of Saxon date but only appeared in the documents later, when they were detached from their parent manor. The main development in early medieval rural history was, in fact, the fragmentation of the large Anglo-Saxon manor.[43]

---

[42]   *ASE* 277 (the peasants landholder); 286 (the village); 279 (the hide); 293 (the *gau*); 314-315 (irrelevance of Britons); 318 (no actual landownership).

[43]   Sawyer's views are best summed up in "Introduction: Early Medieval Settlement," in *MSCC* 1-10, and in "Anglo-Saxon Settlement: The Documentary Evidence," in *Anglo-Saxon Settlement and Landscape*, British Archaeological Reports 4, ed. T. Rowley (Oxford, 1974), pp. 108-19. His earlier work reflected much of the same thinking, e.g., "The Wealth of England in the Eleventh Century," *Transactions of the Royal Historical Society* 5th ser. 15 (1965), 145-164.

    Moreover, recent archaeological findings, particularly botanical and zoological data, is strong evidence for a more developed economy than earlier assumed, and a rural hinterland which apparently served well the needs of the urban communities of the early

Peter Sawyer also challenged the view of the static medieval village. The permanence of rural habitation has become a less viable view, following the archaeological evidence that villages would change not only their names, but also their locations. Some new settlements may have been founded before and after the Conquest, but for Sawyer, it was a time of "shifting, not expanding settlement."[44]

The developing revisionary synthesis has important ramifications for social and institutional history. If the lord and manor were early, even primary, elements in pre-Conquest England, then the village community of free landowning peasants would have been very rare, if indeed such a community ever existed. In this regard, Anglo-Saxon England would have been similar to the Continental kingdoms. Furthermore, the origins of the later English democratic institutions can no longer be ascribed with easy assurance to a primitive village community of 'yeoman' peasantry, but will have to be sought, however tenuous the descent, in some expression of a society organized and directed from above.

---

medieval period. See P.J. Fowler, "Agricultural and Rural Settlement," in *ASE* 23-48; and "Farming in the Anglo-Saxon Landscape," pp. 271-280. For a broader—if controversial—viewpoint, see Richard Hodges, *Dark Age Economics: The Origins of Towns and Trade A.D. 600-1000* (London, 1982).

[44]   Sawyer, "Introduction," in *MSCC* 6.

2

The Emergence of the Vill

We have seen that the great question of early English rural history has been whether the manor or the village was the formative unit of rural life. Yet a solution to the manor/village question does not necessarily address other social and political problems.

If the manor was the primary institution, then it still must be determined at which point it entailed lordship, as recognized in the later Middle Ages, rather than a basis of wealthy, independent farmer/warriors. Furthermore, at what level of social grouping was allegiance institutionalized? It may have been a simple collection of neighbouring farms and nearby relatives, which later, because of the agricultural changes, coalesced into a village. Or perhaps there was no viable political grouping below the tribe. Hereditary kingship might be a likely form of tribal leadership, but the earliest English records generally show only a tribal confederation or 'national' king, under whom a *subregulus* or *dux* may have enjoyed a status superior to an 'ealdorman.' If neither of these institutions, the village or the tribal sub-group, was the principal vehicle of political association before the Danish wars, was it then the hundred? Even if the Wessex hundred had been a distinct territorial entity before the late tenth century, it may have been formed in quite different ways. It could have originated in a group of neighbouring freeholders, perhaps lords, or equally well have been created as a block of land over which a leader granted authority to one of his lieutenants.

The unresolved questions are valid enough, but it is also necessary to place them within the context of scholarly opinion. The 'orthodox' view, as promulgated by Maitland, Vinogradoff, and Stenton, holds that institutions brought by the original German immigrants developed into English ones, largely independent of any other society. Revisionists claim that English society could not help but be affected by the other cultures on the island - there had to be important elements of continuity between the Roman and Celtic worlds and that of the Anglo-Saxons who replaced them. In agricultural history and settlement studies, the revisionist argument has developed wide-reaching theories based on the pattern of landholding by 'multiple estates.' But just as there is no uniform explanation of its origin, there is as yet no fully accepted interpretation of how this territorial unit was replaced by the pattern of landholdings observed in the late eleventh century. That a great conglomerate estate existed until its dissolution in late Saxon times, never to be reassembled, is an assumption that must be tested. It can be adequately examined only in a well-documented locality where such a territorial unit is known to have existed at least by the eleventh century. Middle Hampshire is a promising regional setting for a comparative study, because its pre-Conquest history is comparatively well-documented and it contains the large ancient hundredal manor of Micheldever. This writer used multidisciplinary research techniques at Micheldever to trace the evolution of settlement and land use from the post-Roman period to the beginning of the twelfth century.[1]

MICHELDEVER HUNDRED AND MIDDLE HAMPSHIRE

The Micheldever region of Hampshire (see Figure 1.1) offers valuable historical and archaeological resources for early medieval studies. The Hundred with its centre (*caput*) of the same name is situated at the headwaters of the Test and Itchen rivers in central Hampshire, straddling the road between Winchester and Silchester, and covering an area about ten miles square. It was a *villa regalis* (the king's 'tun' of a royal manor) in 862 AD when the West Saxon council purportedly met there, and its charter of 900 (S360) refers to a *gemot hus* (meeting house) on the estate.[2] Soon after the death of Alfred the Great in 899, Micheldever was granted by his son to the then-founded New Minster of Winchester, later called Hyde Abbey. The extent of these lands, generally corresponding to the later Hundred, are estimated at 12,200 acres.[3] For over six centuries it remained in the hands of the monastery, except immediately after the Conquest, when William I briefly confiscated most of the New Minster's property. Henry VIII sold off the lands, with the hundredal rights and several manors going to one of his favourites, Thomas Wriothesley, later first Earl of Southampton, and one manor going to Winchester College, which still possesses it. The privately owned lands have passed through only two families since the Dissolution, thereby assuring a degree of continuity in land ownership and use.

---

[1]   See Eric Klingelhöfer, *Settlement and Land Use at Micheldever Hundred, Hampshire, 700 to 1100*, Transactions of the American Philosophical Society, vol. 81 part 3 (Philadelphia, 1991).

[2]   See H.M. Chadwick, *Studies on Anglo-Saxon Institutions* (Cambridge, 1905; repr. New York, 1963), pp. 256-257, for a brief discussion of these early references.

[3]   Francis Henry Baring, *Domesday Tables* (1909), pp. 192-193.

The wealth of historical resources is composed primarily of the exceptionally large number of pre-Conquest charters surviving for Hyde Abbey, including those for the Micheldever estates. No less than five charters with bounds survive for Micheldever properties, and another ten describe the boundaries of adjacent manors, most of which were owned by Winchester Cathedral and their records kept in its archives. The Micheldever charters were copied into a cartulary which survives in appended sections to regnal chapters in the fourteenth-century Hyde Abbey chronicle, the *Liber de Hyda*, published in the Rolls Series in 1866.[4] This particular cartulary is unusual because each charter's attached lists of bounds is triplicated in Latin, Anglo-Saxon, and Middle English. This detail is not present in the other two extant, but unpublished, Hyde Abbey cartularies, nor in the remaining two related items: an abbey 'miscellany' and the famous illustrated New Minster charter of refoundation by King Edgar.[5] Other valuable information appears in the relevant Domesday Book entries, in the Hyde Abbey cartulary and manorial records, and in early post-medieval state records and maps.

The value of this documentary material is increased by the continued rural nature of the Dever valley (as it has been called locally), which has changed little in the past century, with only slight suburban growth from Winchester. This has left the field boundaries, road systems, and village plans largely intact, excepting alterations made by Georgian estate management and earlier enclosures of the common fields. Consequently, place-names gleaned from the documents may be checked against surviving physical locations. Careful examination of the specifics of soil types and conditions, water availability and flow, and topographic features, should

---

[4]   *Liber Monasterii de Hyda*, Rolls Series 45 (London, 1866) ed. Edward Edwards. Edwards proved that this manuscript was the lost original upon which an abridgement by Stowe survives as British Museum, Lansdowne MS 717.

[5]   The other two cartularies are in Brit. Mus. Cotton MS Dom. A xiv and Harleian MS 1761. The miscellany is Stowe Park MS Ecclesiastica ii. 32, and the Edgar charter is Cotton MS Vespasian A viii. Descriptions of all four are given in Edwards, ed., *Liber de Hyda*, pp. lxxxvii-xciii.

Dugdale's *Monasticon* itemized the contents of Stowe MSS Press III No. 32 (Harleian MS Domitian xiv) in Sir William Dugdale, *Monasticon Anglicanum*, ed. John Caley, Henry Ellis, and Bulkeley Bandinel, vol. 2 (London, 1819), pp. 432-434. *A Catalogue of the Manuscripts in the Cottonian Library Deposited in the British Museum* (London, 1802), very briefly describes Cotton MS Vespasian A viii (435) and Domitian xiv (574). *A Catalogue of the Harleian Manuscripts in the British Museum* vol. 2 (London, 1808), pp. 205-207, provides a listing of each of 88 entries for the Harleian MS 1761 cartulary. These documents are presented in G.R.C. Davis, *Medieval Cartularies of Great Britain: A Short Catalogue* (London, 1958), p. 121.

produce patterns against which settlement locations, communication routes, and agricultural resources can be compared.

Micheldever Hundred and its setting in middle Hampshire proved to be a rewarding subject for early medieval rural studies. The research there established field systems and other physical features of the medieval landscape, and identified manorial boundaries and other territorial divisions. It correlated this spatial evidence with that for settlement date, size, and form, and determined the change or continuity in the patterns of settlement and land use.[6]

The findings of the Micheldever study bear upon several historical problems: not only the level and direction of the early medieval economy, but also the complex relationship between village, manor, and hundred. The reconstruction of the rural development of this locality, and by extension, its region, presents the opportunity to evaluate the concepts of the multiple estate, the village community, and the territory of the 'folk.'

SETTLEMENT AND LAND-USE PATTERNS: A SUMMARY

The emergence of the village habitation as the dominant form of medieval peasant settlement marks a fundamental change in the basis of rural life, but the date and reasons for its appearance are a matter of debate.[7] Reviewing the archaeological debate on the dating of village formation and its relationship to the strip-field system, Martin Welsh doubted a direct cause-and-effect relationship of changes in farming practice leading to nucleated settlements, questioning "whether the strip field system emerged early enough to explain the abandonment of settlements and cemeteries in the seventh and eighth centuries."[8]

---

[6]   The Micheldever study also examined the Roman settlement pattern, in order to see what continuity there may have been between the Roman and Saxon periods. The survey found no grounds for assuming a direct continuity, but the sub-Roman period may have witnessed such little competition for land and ability to control it, that the subsequent 'dispersed' settlement may have actually been an agrarian anarchy. The farmers of the sixth and seventh centuries may also have been both Celtic and Germanic, each in too few numbers to establish an archaeologically noticeable pattern. See Klingelhöfer, *Settlement and Land Use*, pp. 61-75.

[7]   See Frederick Cheyette, "The Origins of European Villages and the First European Expansion," *Journal of Economic History* 37 (1977), 182-206.

[8]   Martin G. Welsh, "Rural Settlement Patterns in the Early and Middle Anglo-Saxon Periods," *Landscape History* 7 (1985), 13-25, citation from p. 20.

The change from early Saxon to late Saxon patterns of settlement at Micheldever, presented in detail elsewhere, can be summarized here.[9] The strongly linear, valley-based early Saxon settlement of the Micheldever region is drawn from the combined evidence of archaeology and place-name studies. One must note that like all settlement distributions, it does carry with it the bias derived from the fact that cemeteries are more readily discovered than habitation sites, and that toponyms are restricted to those sites that continued to be occupied or that happened to be mentioned in a surviving early medieval document. In Hampshire, early medieval settlement is thought to have often been dispersed.[10] The conditions of the fifth to eighth centuries would certainly be appropriate for such a pattern. A low population was then thinly spread over a landscape that contained light soils exhausted by over-use and heavy soils too difficult to be exploited successfully by a limited technology and work force. The result was a settlement pattern of individual farmsteads occasionally clustered into hamlets.

The pattern changed to a centralization or nucleation of settlement, with larger populations increasing the competition for resources and agricultural practices simultaneously moving from independent to cooperative farming. By the tenth and eleventh centuries, this process had spawned the fully-developed 'classic' manor and village. But the large estates of middle Hampshire left little room for the establishment of unitary manors (one manor for one vill), which elsewhere may have been a further factor encouraging the nucleating of villages. Because of the incomplete development of what was a standard pattern in the Midlands, for instance, the Micheldever region has several instances of settlements that were too close together to evolve into fully-formed villages, with adequate population, church, independent manorial court and customs, etc. They are therefore similar to the 'polyfocal' villages that Christopher Taylor believes coalesced in the mid- to late Saxon period.[11]

An example of the changing settlement pattern in the Micheldever region can be found in the Candover valley, a tributary of the Itchen east of

9   Klingelhöfer, *Settlement and Land Use*, pp. 75-84.

10   See David A. Hinton, "Hampshire's Anglo-Saxon origins," in *The Archaeology of Hampshire, from the Palaeolithic to the Industrial Revolution*, Monograph No. 1, Hampshire Field Club and Archaeological Society (Winchester, 1981), pp. 56-65, esp. 59-60.

11   See C.C. Taylor, "Polyfocal Settlement and the English Village," *Medieval Archaeology* 21 (1977), 189-193; and "The Anglo-Saxon Countryside," in *Anglo-Saxon Settlement and Landscape*, ed. T. Rowley (Oxford, 1974), pp. 5-15. Taylor's views have been further developed in *Village and Farmstead: A History of Rural Settlement in England* (London, 1983).

Micheldever. Data on pre-Conquest settlements come from three sources: archaeology, documents (mainly charters), and place-name studies. Even though the valley contains much evidence from the Roman period (three villas and at least five other Romano-British settlements), traces of the Anglo-Saxons are few. One pagan burial lies in the upper reaches of the Candover valley, but present occupation and day-to-day activities taking place on the valley floor have brought to light no evidence of an early Saxon presence. Nevertheless, the stream name 'Candover' (Celtic, *Cein-dwfr*) is applied to three villages (Brown, Chilton, and Preston Candover), which are first recorded separately in the thirteenth century. Such a stream-name indicates early settlement, though not necessarily at the village sites. Four other medieval villages in the lower Candover valley are recorded before 1100: Abbotstone, Swarraton, and Bradley in tenth-century charters and Weald in the eleventh-century Domesday Book. The *tun* names of four villages suggest a fairly late date of settlement, in the eighth century or afterwards. The two villages with wood-names are probably even later, formed only at the end of the Anglo-Saxon period. The picture is obscure. There is no archaeological evidence to suggest that nucleated settlements occupying the Candover valley bottom were early; their name-elements also argue against this. Yet the valley was indeed inhabited earlier; a pagan burial and the survival of the name 'Candover' from Romano-British usage suggest continuing, if widely dispersed, settlement.[12]

Another example is the Somborne valley, a tributary of the Test river downstream from the Dever. Here again, direct archaeological evidence is absent, but an Anglo-Saxon charter refers to 'pagan burials' on the valley slope. Like the Candover, the Somborne gave its name to three medieval villages (King's, Little, and Upper Somborne). Somborne (*Swinburna* of Domesday Book) is Anglo-Saxon, not Celtic in origin, but its use as the name of habitation suggests that this valley was also settled early. Yet the three other medieval village names (Ashley, Crawley, Sparsholt) were all wood-names first and appear. as such (probably uninhabited) in Anglo-Saxon charters.[13]

The Dever valley itself underwent a parallel development, but here archaeology provides more positive evidence. Pagan burials discovered in the Dever valley seem to have no relationship to later medieval settlements and cemeteries. Habitation sites there appear to have been abandoned around

---

[12]   Margaret Gelling, *Signposts to the Past: Place-Names and the History of England* (London, 1978), pp. 191-214; Gillian Fellows-Jensen, "Place-Names and Settlement History: A Review," *Northern History* 13 (1979), 1-26; Klingelhöfer, *Settlement and Land Use*, pp. 70, 77-81.

[13]   Klingelhöfer, *Settlement and Land Use*, pp. 78-79.

the eighth century, with no continuity of settlement going into the late Saxon period. At Micheldever, Southbrook Tithing lies on the south side of the stream. It was one of three adjacent, stream-side settlements with separate field-systems within Micheldever Manor. Yet uphill in Southbrook Tithing is a small, early-mid Saxon habitation site that must have been abandoned when the Micheldever manor's village lands were established. Ninth and tenth-century charters of the Micheldever area also point to lost settlements or their habitants, suggesting a pattern of dispersed settlements that was replaced by the medieval pattern of nucleated villages along valley bottoms.[14]

The Micheldever findings complement the results of excavation and fieldwork elsewhere in Hampshire, especially the research at Chalton, situated on the chalk downland near the Sussex border.[15] More distant settlement studies relevant to this summary are discussed in Chapter 7, where the broad range of conclusions presented here are placed in the context of the current debate on early medieval rural development.

Farmsteads, hamlets, and possibly cemeteries were commonly abandoned on the Hampshire chalk ridges in the mid-Saxon period. The seventh to ninth centuries witnessed a shift in population to fairly equal-sized settlements in the valleys. If the valley locations were already inhabited (as is likely for good sites), then this increase in population alone would have converted hamlets into villages. It must have been a general movement, for the vills, or townships, as fossilized in parish boundaries, show little variation in size. The common size of vills and the relatively standard placement of villages in the valleys testify to an even distribution of resources in an homogeneous geography. But there is no evidence for an Anglo-Saxon institution powerful—or interested—enough to so radically remake the landscape.

The particulars of settlement at Micheldever and comparative details of other archaeological work are not in themselves essential to our consideration of the broad changes in early medieval rural development. Villages in middle Hampshire formed along streams, while elsewhere they may have been sited upon ridges lines or roadways, or were evenly

---

[14]   For example, the *fritheling dic* of Wonston's charter (S374), the *Ticcesham* and *Herpesham* of the Micheldever charter (S360), and even the lost *Sudberie* recorded in Domesday Book for Bermondspitt Hundred and probably lying in the upper reaches of the Candover valley ("Micheldever," p. 539).

[15]   See Michael Hughes, "Rural Settlement and Landscape in Late Saxon Hampshire," in *Studies in Late Anglo-Saxon Settlement*, ed. Margaret Faull (1984), pp. 65-79. Hughes has been involved in the Chalton research, and reports on fieldwork and interpretations beyond those of Barry Cunliffe in "Saxon and Medieval Settlement Pattern in the Region of Chalton, Hampshire," *Medieval Archaeology* 16 (1972), 1-12.

distributed about a region. The important factor is not in fact the settlements themselves, but that they signify a regrouping of both population and resources—in particular the land claimed by each population centre. Settlement and land use are of course two important, characteristic activities of a population, but a population's spatial self-definition is its territory.

Evidence of the early medieval landscape suggests that the entire Dever valley comprised an early Saxon territory.[16] Much of the eastern half of the valley was wooded, while wide tracts of the western valley seem to have been pasture land. Reflecting to some degree the geographic conditions of soil type, drainage, and elevation, this duality of land use also suggests that zones of land use were much larger in the early Saxon period than in the late Saxon period. The Dever valley was treated as a single economic unit, measuring roughly, with woodland common to all inhabitants in a great arc centred on the upper periphery, and common pasture land available at the lower end. This 'community-wide' division of land use is exactly what one would expect in a territory made up of farmsteads and small hamlets, with group responsibility for permanent pasture and woodland. It could only flourish in a period before the appearance of a discrete cooperative agricultural unit, the vill.

The division of the valley into separate vills and manors might have occurred as late as the land dispersements recorded in the ninth- and tenth-century charters that first document the existence of the narrow blocks of land later to become medieval parishes. In this case, it could be argued that the legal partition of the valley unit into individual manors forcibly splintered the common rights to pasture and woodland into separate resources for each vill. Rarely, however, do late Saxon charter boundaries appear as arbitrary, new land divisions that cut through existing field systems and even settlements. In most cases, the boundaries seem to be long-established divisions between land units, which suggests that the vill began to emerge at Micheldever some time before the charters were drawn up.[17] This occurred most likely in the eighth century, when a general mid-Saxon settlement shift can be archaeologically demonstrated for

---

[16]   Klingelhöfer, *Settlement and Land Use*, pp. 127-129, fig. 5.3.

[17]   Ibid., pp. 125-127, fig. 5.2. The major field system units in Micheldever manor had hedges dating back to the late tenth century. In some instances, moreover, portions of these hedgerows appear to be even older, dating from the eighth century.

Although hedgerow analysis has its proponents, it is not a widely used research procedure. See David A. Hinton, *Alfred's Kingdom: Wessex and the South 800-1500* (London, 1977), p. 110; and Geoffrey Hewlett, "Reconstructing a Historical Landscape from Field and Documentary Evidence: Otford in Kent," *Agricultural History Review* 21 (1973), 94-110; but also note Cyril J. Johnson, "The Statistical Limitations of Hedge Dating," *Local Historian* 14 (1980), 28-33.

Hampshire.[18] The charter process that 'booked' holdings as private or seigneurial and left the 'unbooked' land as public or royal, can have no bearing upon a vill that preceded it by a century or two.

There is reason to believe, therefore, that the Micheldever valley had a 'community-wide' rural economy in the early Saxon period, with resources for sheep rearing and swine herding allocated on the basis of the entire valley unit. At some time between the eighth century and the tenth century, this primitive unity dissolved into a pattern of separate village holdings, strip parishes that ran from the river up to the crest of the watershed ridges to include all necessary land types. The village lands were typically separated by banks, ditches, and hedges; all evidence suggests that they were economically independent entities.

The division of the Dever valley into lands belonging to each vill put an end to the sharing of resources beyond the level of village members. This same period saw the rights and responsibilities of the wider community devolve upon new institutions, the manor and the hundred. As lord of Micheldever, the New Minster controlled directly the extraneous parcels and lands that did not fit the pattern of equal portioning among the strip-parish vills. Thus the Domesday record shows not only the impressive regularity of the streamside farming communities, but also the small detached holdings that were scattered along the watershed between the Micheldever and Candover valleys. Yet in the pre-Conquest period the strip pattern to land units was just as evident on the eastern half of the Dever valley (where most of the land remains to this day in the single, large manor of Micheldever), as it was in the western half of the valley (where separate manor/vills can be traced back to at least the ninth century). An important conclusion of the Micheldever study is that the formation of the vill and its lands was an economically directed change, and could not have been brought about by the dismemberment of a royal estate into small, 'private' holdings. The implications of this change and its relationship to developments in land ownership and royal service are topics to be explored in the following chapter.

---

[18]   Field survey, excavation, and reinterpretation of documentary material led Hughes to propose at least one general population movement (see "Rural Settlement and Landscape," pp. 74-76). At Chalton, one site (Church Down) was abandoned during the eighth century at the latest and one site (Manor Farm) began in the late eighth century; occupation of the Cowdery Down site is thought to have ended in the eighth century. Hughes went on, however, to evoke "a continuously changing pattern" to explain the vagaries of other dating evidence (p. 77). Perhaps it could be better described as a slowly evolving pattern, in which the downward movement of population eventually deserted the ridges to coalesce in nucleated settlements in the valleys.

3

The Development of the Manor

As changes in land use brought about an evolution of the landscape, so the rural economy was similarly affected by changes in Anglo-Saxon landholding. At first, all lands appear to have been ultimately claimed by the *gens*, tribe, or folk. The king dispensed these lands as royal favours, but only with the consent (or at the behest) of the *witan*, the council of nobles. It seems that before the introduction of Christianity in the seventh century, the standard practice had been a verbal assignment of lands for the upkeep of a mature warrior, done in council with the senior nobles. The junior warriors were attached to households of the king, the royal family, and great nobles. As seen in the heroic epic, *Beowulf*, these younger men waited for opportunities for advancement and permanent landholding, opportunities which usually came from prowess in battle.[1] Pagan priests and their temples had probably been supported by a combination of allotted lands and offerings, though some may have been more directly linked to the king, as part of his role of religious leader of the folk.[2] The Christian church in England, however, intended from the start to continue its standard practice of holding land in perpetual ownership. The creation of chartered land or 'bookland,' as opposed to royal and *witan* distributed 'folkland,' can be directly attributed to the establishment of the Church in the Anglo-Saxon kingdoms. Precisely how the original differences in form and recipient evolved into the division between permanent, inheritable property, on one hand, and life grants, on the other, is a much debated point, but the overall trend is well recognized.[3]

---

[1]   The poetic term *heal-thegn* (*Beowulf*, line 42) concerns the young warrior retainer in a lord's hall. See *Beowulf, with the Finnsburg Fragment*, ed. C.L. Wrenn, 3rd ed., rev. by W.F. Bolton (London, 1973), p. 102.   On lordship and the *gesith* class, see Dorothy Whitelock, *The Beginnings of English Society* (Baltimore, 1952), pp. 35-57, 64-65, 85-88.

[2]   For the role of the king in pagan and Christian worship, see William A. Chaney, *The Cult of Kingship in Anglo-Saxon England* (Manchester, 1970); and J.M. Wallace-Hadrill, *Early Germanic Kingship in England and on the Continent* (Oxford, 1971), pp. 47-71.

[3]   *ASE* 306-314.   A lengthier examination of the nature of 'folkland' and the development of 'bookland' is by Eric John, "Folkland Reconsidered," in *Orbis Britanniae and Other Studies* (Leicester, 1966), pp. 64-127.

The early medieval Church held the monarchies of David and Constantine as models of worldly authority. With this Christian catalyst, the institution of kingship underwent a rapid development. A strong Christian monarchy affected landholding in two principal ways. First, the traditional requirement for status and material reward had been the fulfilment of common duties to society (folk, tribe or kingdom), but was now superseded by loyalty to the person of the monarch. Secondly, a limited proprietary right over common, clan or 'kinship' property was replaced by personal tenure and possession. Both developments created in southern England a type of early medieval landholding little different from that found elsewhere in northern Christendom. It marked the political and economic integration of Wessex and its fellow kingdoms into that region of the world, western Europe, where there was a similar welding of Roman institutions onto Germanic societies.

Examination of the early medieval manors of the Micheldever region of middle Hampshire provides details of these developments. This chapter will demonstrate how significant patterns of manorial hidage assessments form the basis for grouping manors into small territorial units, perceived as the earliest stage in the evolution of manorial land divisions. To explain this phenomenon, several observations on estate formation and ownership are drawn from particulars of the region. Hidage arrangements and changes in estate territories point to overall patterns of landholding. With supplementary material from Anglo-Saxon law codes, the context of the early medieval manor is considered, and compared to current theories of rural development. Finally, the proposed patterns of landholding and the overall manorial development serve as the basis for reconstructing a regional evolution.

THE HIDAGE OF THE MIDDLE HAMPSHIRE REGION

To find an overall pattern to the territorial development of the manor, on the local level, one must first reconstruct the physical extents of all manors within an area of study, taking care to eliminate the effects of later tenurial and jurisdictional changes.

Information on the manors comes from several sources: 1) boundary clauses of the Anglo-Saxon land grants; 2) hidage assessments recorded in the grants, in lists of ecclesiastical properties, and in Domesday Book; 3) boundaries of the later medieval parishes and manors, which commonly appear in maps accompanying the tithe awards and common enclosures of the early nineteenth century. Of the three sources, the most important are the boundary clauses, which even when part of a spurious

document of pre-Conquest date, nevertheless remain as credible evidence for
early medieval divisions between lands that may or may not have been transferred at the time or among the parties claimed by a charter. Sir Frank
Stenton described the charters of the first three quarters of the tenth century
as a 'monotonous series,' but noted their particular value for topographic
studies, because such charters typically have detailed boundary clauses.[4]

The estates in question were granted in typical charter or diploma
form, with various divisions within the *protocol, corpus,* and *eschatochol.*[5]
The boundary clauses were not part of the *corpus* included among the *clau-
sulae,* but were appended to the end of the document. They were invariably
in Old English, and were occasionally translated into Latin in post-Conquest
confirmations, though such clauses no longer appeared in new charters. The
earliest boundary descriptions were short, with only a few major landmarks,
but the later ones contained detailed references to specific points: field
boundaries, ditches, trees, etc.

It is impossible to accurately reconstruct from these lists of landmarks the physical extent of Anglo-Saxon manors 'from the armchair.' Even
with a knowledge of local topography, place-names, and archaeology, it
remains a difficult and tedious effort. H.P.R. Finberg noted a generation
ago: "There is much work still to be done on Anglo-Saxon charter boundaries ... it will be slow, laborious, and costly work, involving much tramp-
ing over difficult miles, as well as long searches in libraries and muniment
rooms."[6] Despite their negative aspects, these primary sources offer clear
opportunities for original and important contributions to early medieval rural
history. As Nicholas Brooks has written (coincidentally concerning the
Micheldever bounds):

> Tracing the boundaries of an Anglo-Saxon charter on the modern map and
> on the ground is one of the most rewarding forms of research. The excite-
> ment of discovering how a particular landscape has changed or remained
> the same, over a thousand years cannot easily be equalled. But it is diffi-
> cult to present the results of such work without suppressing the uncertain-
> ties and difficulties that must remain.[7]

---

[4]   Stenton, *Latin Charters of the Anglo-Saxon Period* (Oxford, 1962), pp. 287-291.
[5]   The standard form referred to is presented on pp. 84-85; see Leonard E. Boyle,
"Diplomatics," in *Medieval Studies: An Introduction,* ed. James M. Powell (Syracuse, N.Y.,
1976), pp. 89-102.
[6]   H.P.R. Finberg, *The Early Charters of Wessex* (Leicester, 1964), p. 11.
[7]   N.P. Brooks, "The Oldest Document in the College Archives? The Micheldever
Forgery," in *Winchester College: Sixth-Centenary Studies,* ed. Roger Custance (Oxford,
1982), pp. 189-228 at 196. Brooks covered ground similar to that at "Micheldever," pp. 385-
395. His interpretation of the boundary clause of S360 differs at some points from my own,
but further consideration on my part has reduced the differences between them.

The manorial extents and hidages of the estates around Micheldever are surveyed in Appendix A. Using the results of the survey, one may compare pre-Conquest manors, the changes their hidage underwent, and the particular groupings from which they were removed by grant, lease, or bequest.

Examination of manor boundaries and hidages yields two general results. The first is that in many areas, hidage assessments of the earliest recorded grants can be compared to figures for the same manors in the Domesday Book. By establishing applicable ratios of change between these figures (a one-half reduction is common), and by using the corporate assessments for the Old and New Minsters' holdings, one can attempt to restore the alterations and reductions evident in the Domesday figures. The result is an 'original' hidage figure for each land unit. Its reliability will depend upon its sources: some are taken from firm documentary evidence; others are estimated by the equivalency of manors of similar size, geography, and land-use.

The manorial survey also revealed a geographic determinant to early land holdings. The earliest boundary clauses in the Anglo-Saxon charters indicate that the divide between water catchment areas was the dominant factor in determining the extent of early medieval estates in the area under study. In fact, all the early medieval manors of middle Hampshire appear to have been formed from discrete topographic units based upon stream catchment areas.

The coincidence of early medieval territorial units with certain topographic elements has been obliquely noted in several instances. In Hampshire, while identifying Kings Somborne as an early royal manor, Rosalind Hill found that in the northern part of Kings Somborne Hundred, the territory "on the eastern bank of the Test from Stockbridge Down to Farley Mount ... had a sort of convenient geographical unity."[8] The actual Somborne catchment unit does follow the general lines of the later hundred, but extends beyond it to include other manors, especially those on the west bank of the Test. Professor Hill's appraisal of the topography was of course limited by her dependence on later medieval hundredal boundaries as a guide to early royal estates. Similarly, Katherine Barker has reconstructed for the Malmesbury-Sherborne region ancient territorial units that have a tendency to represent a catchment area, but also include manors that are not topographically associated.[9]

---

[8]   Rosalind Hill, "Some Parish Boundaries in Hampshire," in *MSCC* 61-65.

[9]   Katherine Barker, "Institution and Landscape in Early Medieval Wessex: Aldhelm of Malmsebury, Sherborne and Selwoodshire,' *Proceedings of the Dorset Natural History and Archaeological Society* 106 (1984), 33-42.

Investigators of manorial origins use the same method to collect their evidence for the existence of the great 'multiple estates' of the early medieval period. G.R.J. Jones has used the surviving records for hundredal, parochial, and seigneurial jurisdictions of Sussex and Yorkshire as the basis for his recreation of large land units, which he claimed dated back to the earliest medieval period, or further back into the Roman or British Iron Age.[10] This procedure has been valuable for Professor Jones and for others trying to push the origins of some medieval hundreds back to earlier epochs. Manorial boundaries in Wessex have been suggested by Desmond Bonney to have among their components the landmarks, field edges, and even estate borders from previous periods.[11] His analysis of the coincidence between early boundaries and pagan Saxon burials does suggest that some later medieval land units were already present in the early Saxon settlement. Unless there was widespread abandonment of the region, the Germanic occupants would have found it difficult to ignore the long-established presence of estate and field boundaries of the lands they had taken over. Of course, it is likely that much depends upon the degree to which those boundaries had a physical presence.

Even as Anglo-Saxon charter boundary clauses are used to trace the lines of early manors, and their hidage figures can be used to check the relationships among estates in an area, these scanty sources have been applied to the modelling of an ill-defined, but static early manor, the complete fragmentation of which is characteristic of the early medieval period. At Chalton, Hampshire, Barry Cunliffe used archaeological survey and charter boundaries to conclude that the break-up of an original multiple estate was associated with the replacement of its centre, excavated upon Chalton Down, by low-land settlements that became the nuclei of medieval villages.[12] In the east Midlands, Charles Phythian-Adams has used charter boundary clauses to recreate a 'great estate' that extended on both sides of Watling Street. This estate, he believed, was either the result of a fusion of smaller Saxon estates, or the survival of a rural unit that preceded the construction of the Roman road.[13] For Northamptonshire estates along Watling Street, Brown, Key, and Orr found a strong correspondence

---

[10]   G.R.J. Jones, "Settlement Patterns in Anglo-Saxon England," *Antiquity* 35 (1961), 221-232; and "Early Territorial Organization in England and Wales," *Geografiske Annaler* 43 (1961), 174-181. More recently he has apparently modified some of his positions.

[11]   Desmond Bonney, "Early Boundaries and Estates in Southern England," in *MSCC* 72-82.

[12]   Barry Cunliffe, "Saxon and Medieval Settlement-Pattern in the Region of Chalton, Hampshire," *Medieval Archaeology* 16 (1972), 1-12.

[13]   Charles Phythian-Adams, *Continuity, Field and Fission: The Making of a Midland Parish* (Leicester, 1978).

between the boundaries of Saxon charters and those of the medieval parishes. Here Domesday ploughland figures from the separate vills add up to an assessment of an original thirty hide unit. These researchers concluded that the large multiple estate had split up before the late Saxon imposition of the hundred system in the Midlands created artificial units of 100 hides with "little regard of earlier or indeed existing tenurial arrangements."[14] Excavations at Rounds, Northamptonshire, have led its archaeologists, Cadman and Foard, to search for the context in which an area of traditionally dispersed settlement would begin to create nucleated villages. They proposed that a 'Greater Raunds' territory had broken apart into several townlands (vills), with the new open-field systems administered from townland centres that had previously been hamlets.[15]

This study of middle Hampshire differs from the preceding examples because it concerns a larger area. Perhaps due to this scale, the hidage totals for the topographically-determined groupings of estates here present a new and revealing pattern. One might assume that a combined hidage assessment of these manor groupings is likely to be a multiple of ten hides, reflecting a condition whereby manors were assessed in round figures of five or ten hides.[16] If their extents were determined in part by major topographic factors such as watershed divides, these 'natural' groupings of estates might be thought to represent some of the larger 'multiple estates' or combinations of them, which as ancient and 'natural' economic units would have received large but varying assessments. Varying hidage totals for each grouping would thus reflect the natural diversity of economic values based upon soil productivity, land use, and size of individual estates. The attitude of the Domesday assessors supports this last assumption, because their assessments appear to have been specific where possible, and standard where necessary.

The survey's hidage totals for the topographic groups of middle Hampshire, however, do not yield figures confirming these assumptions of assessment variability. On the contrary, where one might expect variation, there is a uniform pattern (see Figure 3.1). The totals of documented and estimated hidage figures detailed in Appendix A show an unmistakable

---

[14]   A.E. Brown, T.R. Key and C. Orr, "Some Anglo-Saxon Estates and Their Boundaries in South-west Northamptonshire," *Northamptonshire Archaeology* 12 (1977), 155-176.

[15]   Cadman and Foard are more successful in suggesting the primary manor site than in defining its territory, "Raunds: Manorial and Village Origins," in *Studies in Late Anglo-Saxon Settlement*, ed. Margaret L. Faull (Oxford, 1984), pp. 81-100. Figures 6 and 7 do not explain the significance between 'natural' boundaries (undefined) and 'arbitrary' boundaries. The resulting unit of 'Greater Raunds' seems to be totally artificial, while obscuring certain natural boundaries.

[16]   *ASE* 646.

repetition: Upper Itchen ca. 100; Alre 100; Tichbourne 50; Candover 92; Micheldever 158; Somborne 93; Middle Test 99.5; Upper Test ca. 199. The eight topographic units into which all the early manors of middle Hampshire have been grouped have totals within 10% of multiples of 50 hides: to be exact, one 50 hide group, seven 100 hide groups, one 150 hide, and one 200 hide group.[17] They are readily identifiable as the 'pre-Alfredian' equivalents of the half-hundred, the full hundred, and the double-hundred.[18]

This early hidage pattern is obtainable only because the archives of the Old and New Minsters, later Winchester Cathedral Priory and Hyde Abbey, respectively, preserved a number of early references to hidage assessments. No doubt most documents survived because they were supporting material for the efforts by these wealthy and powerful institutions to transform their holdings into the great hundreds of Micheldever and Chilcomb/Fawley. Elsewhere in southern England, the earliest hidage assessment is usually that of Domesday Book, but similar surveys could be undertaken for other areas that have large numbers of surviving early charters, especially around the ecclesiastical centres of London, Canterbury, and Worcester.

The significance of the middle Hampshire manor groupings is that they point to a coherent territorial unit that existed before the establishment of the late Saxon hundred system. Such a territorial unit represents a type of pre-Viking 'multiple estate' perhaps typical of this part of Wessex. According to this Micheldever 'model,' the basis of rural assessment was a valley or catchment basin. The entire valley usually received an 100 hide assessment, which was probably divided proportionally among its landholders. Although most of these valley units were assessed at an even 100 hides, exceptionally small ones had 50 hides, and larger ones had 150. The assessments were only roughly representative of the size or productivity of a valley unit; there is no evidence for early units of, say, 20, 40, or 80 hides, or for figures that would even more accurately reflect the natural disparity between valleys. The relation of this unit to the tribal territories of the pagan period and to the administrative jurisdictions of the late Saxon period is discussed in the following chapter, but the particular figure of assessment, at 100 hides, is surely the precursor of the later hundred.

---

[17]   The manorial division between the Micheldever and Candover estates does not necessarily respect the watershed divide. If 8 hides were shifted from the former to the latter (as might well better fit a land-use division following the chalk lands on either side of the heavy clays and woods between Micheldever Wood and Thorny Down Wood), the result would be a more precise 100 and 150 hides.

[18]   *ASE* 298.

Yet, it is hard to find in Wessex a medieval hundred that actually had 100 hides in it. Whatever the function of the 'valley unit' or 'archaic' hundred, the later hundred seems to have retained the assessment-name of the earlier unit. The topographic factors upon which the archaic hundred was based no doubt coincided to some degree with the pattern of original Saxo-British landholding, by blood-related groups or by settlers placed there by a local authority.[19] One may even conclude from the survey results that an early grouping of landholding and settlement in valleys or catchment areas was recognized and used by a central authority that made standardized assessments of tribute due from such areas, and who went by the name of *Gewissae, West Seaxna,* or *reges Anglo-Saxorum.*

Subsidiary territorial units often did not have habitation names, but geographic ones. The *Meonwara* and the *Wilsaetna* were the inhabitants of the Meon and Wyly valleys. But it may be that these terms referred not only to the dwellers along these streams, as is generally assumed, but also to the entire valley units, their full catchment areas. Thus a reference to the *Meonwara,* or simply to the Meon, concerned the whole of its catchment area, just as *Wihtawaru* and *Wihta* referred to the whole of the Isle of Wight, and *Kantawaru* referred to Kent. Similarly, the early meaning of Micheldever (*Micendefer*) and Candover (*Kendefer*) was presumably not villages by those names along the banks of the streams, but to all the lands and settlements within their respective valley units. This interpretation is supported by the charter evidence of Appendix A, where 'x' amount of land 'at Micheldever,' 'at Candover,' or 'at Tichbourne' was not necessarily part of the later medieval vill or parish. It may or may not have been on the course of the stream; it could have been anywhere in the catchment area. Thus the 10 *mansae* of land at Micheldever given to the Old Minster in 904 (S374) did not lie in Micheldever manor or even in Micheldever Hundred. Rather, the charter concerns Wonston manor, which lies downstream on the Dever and was never tenurially associated with the Micheldever holdings of the New Minster. Adjoining Wonston was Stoke Charity, which must have been the land 'at Micheldever' in the Old Minster's eleventh-century list of estates (S1821). Similarly, the lands granted 'at Tichbourne' (S385) were Cheriton and Beauworth villages, and in the Domesday Book, one of the Somborne manors appears to have been the vill of Stockbridge.[20] In each

---

[19]   See Martin Biddle, "Hampshire and the Origins of Wessex," in *Problems in Economic and Social Archaeology*, ed. G. de G. Sieveking, I.H. Longworth, and K.E. Wilson (London, 1976), pp. 323-341.

[20]   Stockbridge was identified as the 14–hide Domesday holding of William of Eu at Somborne in *DB Hants* at 32,1 n., referring to Rosalind Hill, "The Manor of Stock-bridge," *Proceedings of the Hampshire Field Club and Archaeological Society* 32 (1975), 93-101.

case, the charter locational terminology, 'at ...,' cannot be reconciled with the extents of the later medieval vill or parish. The lands of the examples can be identified as specific estates within a catchment area, but distinct from the vills bearing valley toponyms (i.e., Micheldever, Tichbourne, Somborne).

Another clue to the extent of early great estates is the repetition of a name among neighbouring villages, examples of which are well known in Hampshire. To consider only north Hampshire groups with stream names, the Sombornes and Candovers of this study can be joined by the Wallop, Andover (Ann), Hurstbourne, and Clere groups.[21] This situation occurs in Wiltshire and Berkshire as well, citing only the better known cases of the Collingbournes and the Lambournes.[22] The recurring feature of name repetition has long been known to result from the division of large estates, but the physical dispersal of settlements and their lands no doubt often took place before the recorded or tenurial division. The apparently greater number of examples in Hampshire than elsewhere suggests that the legal division of large manors occurred later here, or perhaps a strong tradition of the great estate was preserved in the local nomenclature. In either case, the presence of related manors throughout middle Hampshire shows that it was a wider, regional phenomenon, one perhaps dependent to some extent upon the topography of the Wessex Chalk downland, or upon the nature of early medieval settlement here, which itself was strongly influenced by landforms and geology. Peter Sawyer proposed that:

> the settlement of Anglo-Saxon England did not develop through colonization of peripheral sites from centres which were established in the first phase of conquest, but ... as the fragmentation of large multiple estates ... . A few of these great estates, particularly those held by kings or churchmen, survived well into the Middle Ages, but their origin must be sought in a past which was already ancient when our documents begin in the seventh century, and that is a matter for the archaeologists and students of place-names.[23]

[21]   The villages are Nether, Middle, and Upper Wallop; Andover, Abbot's Ann, and Little Ann; Hurstbourne Tarrant, Stoke-by-Bourne, St. Mary Bourne, and Hurstbourne Priors; Highclere, Burghclere, and Kingsclere.

[22]   These are Collingbourne Ducis and Kingston; Winterbourne Dauntsey, Gunner, and Earls. Of course there are many instances of repeated names in England, but they do seem to have a high frequency in the Hampshire, Wiltshire, Berkshire region.

[23]   Peter Sawyer, "Anglo-Saxon Settlement: The Documentary Evidence," in *Anglo-Saxon Settlement and Landscape*, ed. T. Rowley (Oxford, 1974), pp. 108-119 at 116.

In middle Hampshire, Micheldever was one of those great estates that survived into and beyond the Middle Ages. For that reason it is valuable in its own right, but the hidage figures suggest that it was once surrounded by great estates of similar size, and that this was a regional norm. We may now examine the nature and descent of the recorded manors to test the validity of both the 'Micheldever' model of the multiple estate and Sawyer's theory of development by fragmentation.

TENURIAL ASPECTS OF THE MANOR

Considering the early medieval manor in the abstract, we will examine three tenurial aspects. First, the process by which large estates were formed may reveal how their constituent parts, the manors, were treated. Secondly, there is the possible influence royal possession may have played in the development of a manor. Thirdly, the identity of charter donors indicates the segment of society from which properties were transferred, and may permit a temporal or spatial pattern to be observed. Consideration of all three factors helps place the early medieval manor in the context of the forces that dictated its tenure and descent.

Characteristics of Estate Formation

Early medieval estates were created in several ways. Aside from the single moment of disposition by the king, estates were also formed by the gradual accretion of lands around one or more original holdings. The lands may have been acquired by royal grant, or by the conversion of leasehold into ownership, an ill-defined concept at a time when custom and local memory may have had more authority than titular legalities. Leasehold was impermanent tenure (usually for a fixed term) with either single or annual payments usually in money, but occasionally in exchange for something of commensurate value. For the Anglo-Saxons, freehold was permanent possession, equivalent to allodial holding. It was eliminated by the Norman establishment of universal military tenure from the king.[24]

Micheldever manor itself is an example of a large estate created by a single grant. Before 900, all the Micheldever valley seems to have been

---

[24]   But see Peter Sawyer's thoughts on the subject: "1066-1086: A Tenurial Revolution?" in *Domesday Book: A Reassessment*, ed. P. Sawyer (London, 1985), pp. 71-85.

traditional royal/tribal 'folkland.'[25] In the grant of 900 (S360), Edward the Elder gave a large part of the valley to the New Minster in Winchester, a foundation established by his father's will. Within the next century, most of the Micheldever valley was bestowed upon religious houses, principally the Old and New Minsters. This seems to have been typical of middle Hampshire; by the tenth century, the Old Minster may have owned large 'core' estates at Chilcomb and Alresford for at least two centuries. Easton and the other manors south of the Itchen, as well as nearly the entire Tichborne valley, were eventually brought into the Cathedral's huge Chilcomb estate. Portions of Ropley and Medstead were originally attached to the Alreford manor, while neighbouring Wield and Abbotstone joined them in the tenth century. One part of the Dever valley belonged to an outside manor: the small vill of Hunton was a detached part of the Bishop's manor of Crawley, west of Winchester.

Of the non-ecclesiastical landholders, the most important for which records survive were the earls of Wessex, Godwin and his son Harold, and their family members. In the Micheldever area, the lands of Earl Godwin and his heirs were not extensive enough to have been the basis of a coherent estate. After the Godwin family was granted the adjacent Po[o]lhampton and Quidhampton manors in the eleventh century, the remaining royal lands available for grants in north-central Hampshire comprised only unpromising upland tracts and a few scattered manors in the more fertile valleys.

In most cases, title documents concern a royal grant or a private bequest, but there is occasionally the record of a donation with a 'life annuity' clause, whereby the institution payed an annual lease for the property to the donor and his spouse until their deaths. In other cases, there is no record of how a property was acquired. Doubtless many were simply unrecorded donations, but other cases may well have been usurpations of titles to lands that the churches had been given only in leasehold. Indeed, the late tenth-century rapid succession of West Saxon predecessors of Alfred may have left the royal donations and leases in some confusion, which the Danish wars and Ethelwulf's 'Decimation' (a reputed bestowal of one tenth of royal property upon churches) no doubt multiplied. Similarly, the short reigns and sudden deaths of Edmund, Eadwy, and Edward the Martyr, as well as the rapid demise of Ethelred, Swein, and Edmund Ironside during the second Danish wars, provided opportunities for converting questionable titles into long-held possessions.

---

[25]   In the Micheldever valley, there is no evidence for the alienation of land, as 'bookland,' before the charters of the tenth and eleventh century. Norton remained a royal manor in the early medieval period, so it was never 'booked.'

Several instances of pre-Conquest attempts to convert leases to freeholds are recorded for middle Hampshire alone. These documents have survived in the archives of ecclesiastic institutions, and naturally enough they include only those cases in which a layman tried to convert church land into freehold. Evidence to the contrary, of a church usurping title to royal or private land, went unrecorded or was not preserved.

Bishop Ealfrith leased ca. 875 part of Easton to a thegn and his wife, for three lives. This tract may have become separated from the episcopal lands, because it was included in the regranting of all of Easton to Bishop Brythelm in 961 (S695).[26] Edward the Elder returned the ancient manor of Alresford to the bishop in 909, after the thegn Alfred, having renewed his parents' lease, forfeited his lands through misconduct (S138). Edward stipulated that it should no longer be granted out to laymen, a custom which even if excluded in this instance, nevertheless continued into the next century on other ecclesiastical manors. Another example is the case of Drayton. The New Minster had leased it (ca. 1000) for one life (S1420), and Canute returned it to the New Minster after he had mistakenly granted it to the son of the former tenant (S956). In addition, the Domesday Book noted that land at Headbourne Worthy had been leased by the Cathedral for three lives, and that Ralph de Mortimer was the third and final landholder. Unfortunately for the Old Minster, the Mortimers were too powerful to be dislodged, and they usurped title to the manor—or perhaps received it as a 'gift' from an institution wanting friends in high places.

Bookland, Folkland, and Royal Demesne

The evidence for the Micheldever region suggests that little estate formation took place in the eleventh century, though the Godwin family may have tried to create new blocks of holdings here, as they did elsewhere. Middle Hampshire was clearly dominated by Church holdings. The bishop, the Old and New Minsters, and the smaller houses had taken most of the good-quality land. Royal demesne land at Kings Worthy, Barton Stacey, and Kings Somborne could not readily be detached from the Crown. This left a much reduced amount of land to be held of the king/state in life tenure, as was the ancient custom with 'folkland.'

In the eleventh century and probably earlier, there was a *de facto* division between three kinds of royal manors. The first (recognized *de jure*) comprised the royal family's personal lands, which were inherited, dispensed, and bequeathed, as seen in the wills of Alfred and Eadred (S1507

---

26   This charter may in fact be a confirmation, but it is not so stated.

and S1515). Secondly, unchartered land remained as 'folkland,' owing dues to the king, and was held in life tenure by those members of the Anglo-Saxon warrior aristocracy who had not the power or influence to obtain a charter.[27] Because such charters are less frequent in the last century before the Conquest, the remaining common-held lands may have been safeguarded by the *witan* council of nobles from further depletion that would only disrupt the social solidarity of the thegn class and undermine its military effectiveness.

There was also the royal demesne, a *de facto* third type, where the land was neither 'book' nor 'folk.' Some small tracts at Barton Stacey were held by royal officers in 1066, and the lease of pasture land there rendered a good cash return. Yet the royal demesne manors do not appear among the properties that the royal families bequeathed, bestowed, and exchanged. The king drew most of his revenues from demesne land, using it to support his officers and agents. It was not granted out to institutions or bequeathed to family members, as 'bookland,' nor was it held by a succession of warrior dependents, as 'folkland.' But it would be an oversimplification to say that demesne land became such only when all the other land had been alienated. In Kent and elsewhere, Jolliffe saw the ancient royal vills as demesne centres to which tribute was brought from the surrounding 'folkland.' As the following chapter discusses, many such vills became centres of hundreds and were later the *capita* of royal estates.[28]

Figure 3.2 illustrates the Domesday division between royal demesne land and 'folkland.' In 1086, this distinction was translated into the terminology of the Norman state as manors where William was his own tenant-in-chief. The map shows that royal demesne holdings were valuable valley holdings, while royal lands that had tenants were all in the less productive uplands. Yet even in the eleventh century, more alienation took place in the Micheldever area; Little Somborne was split off from the large royal manor of Kings Somborne as a separate holding. One is again confronted with the dismal truth of early medieval monarchy—to keep its political power, it had to surrender its economic base.

The Venerable Bede had earlier worried about a similar problem. In a 734 letter to Egbert, Archbishop of York, he wrote that because the king was granting royal lands to men falsely claiming to build monasteries upon them, religion was weakened and there was "a lack of men to defend our territories from barbarian invasions."[29] The long-term problems of

---

[27] See Eric John, *Land Tenure in Early England* (Leicester, 1960), *passim*.

[28] J.E.A. Jolliffe, "The Era of the Folk in English History," in *Oxford Essays in Medieval History Presented to Herbert Edward Salter* (Oxford, 1935), pp. 1-32.

[29] *EHD* 1: 740-741.

Anglo-Saxon landholding may therefore put later medieval arrangements in perspective. The eventual adoption of feudalism by most of western Europe suggests that it was viewed as an acceptable, functional way of organizing the material rewards of power in a society for which the Roman rights of landownership and corporate entity had proved incompatible to the German traditions of folk right and kingship.

Manorial Donors

One must also consider the persons and institutions, other than the king in concert with the *witan*, by whom manors were given or bequeathed. First, the king could act as a private donor. When Edgar booked Middleton to himself in 968 (S727), he presumably intended to give it to his wife, Aelfthryth, who used it to found Wherwell Abbey. Kings often bequeathed their private 'booked' lands to ecclesiastical institutions, as well as to members of the royal family. The widely scattered geography of the holdings in such gifts is illustrated in King Alfred's will (S1507), in which he gave Edward the Elder estates in six different counties, the Old Minster lands in three, his younger son lands in seven, etc.

In the Micheldever region, there are three instances of thegns giving their lands to ecclesiastic institutions—the manors of Kilmeston, Martyr Worthy, and Yavington. An independent church, St. Peter of Stoneham, held Hinton, and the Bishop of Crediton held Abbots Worthy, both manors coming into the hands of the Old Minster by 1066. Priests were donors of Leckford and Wooton St. Laurence, in the Test upland. Before it came into the Church, Quidhampton had been held by a nun, and then by a thegn.

Late Anglo-Saxon 'bookland' in central Hampshire was still a rarity outside of church property. The other holdings may have been still considered 'folkland,' available to all warriors of the kingdom, but were in fact claimed by adult family members of the last occupant. It was this sense of responsibility to his family or clan, that led King Alfred to note in his final testament: "It is my will that the men to whom I have bequeathed my booklands shall not give it away from my kindred after their death ... ."[30] He recognized that the rules under which 'bookland' was transferred were different from those that applied to the ancient 'folkland.' Alfred made this special enjoiner, which served as a simple entail, because he wanted the family to retain ultimate title to the property, while at the same time enjoying the privileges (revenues, immunity, etc.) that accompanied 'bookland.'

[30]   *EHD* 1: 492-495 (S1507).

LANDHOLDING PATTERNS IN MIDDLE HAMPSHIRE

We have concluded above that the topographical divisions of middle Hampshire, into which early hidage assessment fall, represent the matrix from which early medieval manors were formed. Specific patterns of early medieval landholding can be detailed by comparing the particulars of these territorial divisions, the descent of the manors therein (see Appendix A), and their tenurial characteristics. These patterns are addressed in four topics: reduction of royal lands, creation of new estates, detached holdings, and late Saxon estates.

The Reduction of Royal Lands

The disbursement of royal lands into private hands and the assemblage of these holdings into estates are illustrated in the accompanying maps (Figures 3.3-3.6). Grouped by centuries for easier comparison, the patterns show a steadily decreasing royal demesne. There was an expansion of royal land here under William, but the region does not show similar countertrends that may have occurred under Egbert, Alfred, and Canute. Because of the important Micheldever grant of 900, royal largesse appears to have been as great in the early tenth century as at the end of the century. This is in fact misleading. Alfred's will and the reigns of Edward and Athelstan were not particularly generous to the Church, whilst Edgar's reign certainly was, and Ethelred's too, to a lesser degree.[31] Another trend is the growth of estates held by the eleventh-century dynasty established by Godwin, Earl of Wessex. After the Conquest, however, these vast lands (few of which lay in middle Hampshire) returned to royal control.

The measure of early medieval monarchy was the amount of land it held as royal manors. Its power was ultimately derived from dynastic estates that faced pressures of erosion, increasing generation by generation. Unless reversed, the process of alienation continued until there was no more land to dispense. Royal power was then dissipated, and a new dynasty seized the throne. The newcomers were typically those very followers who had received the lion's share of royal demesne. This pattern is no less true in Wessex under Ethelwulf or England under Ethelred the Unready than it was for the last Merovingians or Carolingians. The picture of a nearly complete alienation of royal lands in Hampshire appears more dramatic than it

---

[31] Eric John argued that the House of Wessex had protected their resources in this way for several generations, and this was an important factor in the survival of Wessex. *Orbis Britanniae*, pp. 36-47.

actually was, however, because some of the royal manors had probably been granted out at a date earlier than the surviving documentary record would indicate. This is especially true in those cases where land was 'booked' to a thegn who then bequeathed his estate to a church. Furthermore, in the eleventh century, many royal lands were held for a term or for life by nobles of the court and royal officials.[32] Most non-demesne manors of the Micheldever region would have been held in this way, as the king had few other methods to reward and support his followers.

The Creation of New Estates

One aspect of the landholding changes in the centuries 700 to 1100, then, was the drastic reduction in the amount of land over which the king exercised direct control, and the concomitant multiplication of manors that were owned by, or had as their lord, a person or institution distinct from the king and Crown.[33] Another development was the creation of estates by the newly landed families and institutions, which here comprised the New Minster, the Old Minster/Bishop of Winchester (the lands of which were only decisively separated in the late tenth century), and the Godwinson family. We have noted the several ways by which the new manors were formed: by grant, by accretion, and by default or usurpation. Further, we observed that the less productive uplands largely remained as royal tenanted manors, the remnant of 'folkland,' while the valuable valley lands were occupied by royal demesne lands—and the newly created ecclesiastical estates. Some of the manors in middle Hampshire had detached holdings situated in higher terrain elsewhere, but these holdings formed no specific pattern. The detached manors, and 'combined' royal manors (e.g., Barton Stacey and Kings Worthy) were evidently the results of late Saxon property distribution and rearrangement.

The relatively good documentation for the Micheldever region, as interpreted and interpolated in the estimates for manorial hidage figures compiled in Appendix A, permits these observations. But a further basis for the landholding pattern is the agricultural and administrative conservatism of the landholders in question. Little manorial reorganization appears to have taken place during the period for which documentation is available. Estates continued to use the same land divisions they had when acquired, and their lands were only rarely reapportioned among their vills or leaseholders. Manorial units granted in the eighth, ninth, and tenth centuries

---

[32]   The Domesday Book lists only Barton Stacey, Kings Worthy, and Kings Somborne as demesne manors.

[33]   *DBB* 152-154, 241-244; John, *Orbis Britanniae*, pp. 64-127.

remained the functioning components of the estates dominating middle Hampshire in the eleventh century and usually throughout the Middle Ages. Their unchanging boundaries very often went on to serve as the basis for the ecclesiastical parish and the later civil parish.

Examples of even minor alterations to manors are few. In the tenth century, the New Minster owned a strip between Brown Candover and Chilton Candover. It was then attached to its Northington manor, as part of the Micheldever estate, but by 1066, it had been transferred to the New Minster's manor of Brown Candover. Domesday Book further notes that Woodmancott had been combined with Brown Candover, but was separated from it after 1066. The early history of Tichbourne is obscure, but it does seem that an early large manor was divided when the Bishop of Winchester leased part of it ca. 900. The leased tract did not include Tichbourne; it comprised the lands of Cheriton and Beauworth, and followed their later manorial boundaries.

Detached Holdings

A not uncommon element of Anglo-Saxon estates was the detached holding. In many middle Hampshire valley groups of manors, at least one property was separated from its manorial seat sometimes by miles. The Domesday Survey was particularly interested in such manorial associations, and these instances were usually carefully noted. In many cases, charters show that the tenurial associations had been created at the time of the grants.

The Micheldever manor is a prominent example. Drayton and Cranbourne were physically detached dependencies. Popham and Stratton manors adjoined it, and had been part of the original grant of 900, as shown by the details of the boundary clause (S360). In 1066 they were held by tenants, and were not part of Micheldever's demesne; in 1086 Hugh de Port held all four dependent manors in fief.

Earlier, the Northington dependency of Micheldever had itself a detached holding—the above-mentioned narrow strip running across the Candover valley between Brown and Chilton Candover. The bounds of this holding were appended to the late tenth-century copy of Edward's grant of Micheldever (S360) in 900. The New Minster acquired Brown Candover by 1066, presumably absorbing the strip, which does not reappear in the documents until the Tithe Award maps show it to have remained a detached part of Northington parish until the early 1800s.

In 1066, Hunton (just west of Micheldever) was part of Crawley manor in the Somborne valley. This association dated back at least some time, for it appears in the confirmation of 909 by King Edward to Bishop Frithestan of the Chilcomb estate (S376). The document itself is spurious,

but it accurately represents pre-Conquest conditions. The attachment of a
Dever valley tract to a Somborne valley manor had been made before the
end of the tenth century, when the forgery was composed, but there is no
foundation for assigning this association any greater age; it cannot claim a
remote Anglo-Saxon antiquity.

A similar document (S377) confirmed the Old Minster's title to
lands in the upper Test valley, including Overton and its attached manor of
North Waltham. Overton also held Bradley, the bounds of which prove it
to have been the nearby upland portion of Whitchurch parish (now Bradley
Farm) rather than the vill of that name east of Preston Candover.

New estates

Other estates in middle Hampshire were composite manors, formed of
several vills. Aside from Micheldever, noteworthy examples in the area
were Kings Somborne, which had several vills, Alresford and Easton, each
of which comprised at least three later manors, and Tichbourne, to which
three subsidiary vills were attached. The largest estate was that of the
Cathedral's Chilcomb manor, which held several hundred hides, but was
beneficially assessed at one hide, making it the outstanding example of this
type of early medieval 'liberty.'[34]

The Old Minster had in fact been fabricating documentary records
to support its claim to vast holdings in north-central Hampshire. Five
confirmation charters purportedly date to 909. According to H.P.R.
Finberg, these five are nearly identical to three of thirteen charters of a
syntagma collection of confirmations issued ca. 975 by the Cathedral and
Edgar.[35] They were probably created in the late tenth century in an
attempt to insert charterless holdings among those for which there were
good titles. Finberg further argues that the charters are interpolations and
compilations of earlier diplomas, amended to fit the needs of the Old
Minster.[36] Both the forgeries and confirmations may have been a response
to administrative changes, perhaps related to Ethelred's exactions from every
hide in the kingdom to pay the Danegeld. The forgeries were backdated to
Edward's reign, yet they referred to the division of property between the
bishop and the cathedral clergy. This reference reveals that they were
created no earlier than the 960s, when this division was made, as is detailed

---

[34] For Maitland's classic discussion of Chilcomb, see *DBB* 496-498.

[35] Finberg suggests that they were never actually released because "the whole
Benedictine movement was abruptly halted by his premature death" (H.P.R. Finberg, *The
Early Charters of Wessex* [Leicester, 1964], pp. 240-241).

[36] Ibid., pp. 36-38, 230-244.

in Edgar's confirmations of all lands held by the bishop and the cathedral (S818 and S827, respectively). Internal evidence suggests that the forgeries were composed under the direction of Bishop Ethelwold himself.[37]

The confirmation of 909 (ca. 975) probably had several immediate results. The titles to many holdings were more secure; the hidage for which they were accountable was enumerated; and the division between the bishop and the cathedral monastery was clearly defined. The particular form, rather than content, of Ethelwold's forgeries was probably shaped by the specific groupings of lands into which the charters are divided. These documents concern the components of five estates: the bishop's estates of Chilcomb, Alresford, Overton, and Crawley, and the cathedral's estate of Whitchurch.[38] The manors that formed these estates had been acquired by the bishop and cathedral clergy (usually as dual recipients) over a long period of time and from a variety of sources. One manor, Wonston, had been given specifically for the purpose of supporting the cathedral refectory as long ago as 904 (S374), suggesting that the division between the bishop and the chapter's *mensa* was a slowly developing concept. The groupings of manors in the forgeries and confirmations indicate how these landholdings were organized for purposes of production and administration.

Late Saxon Estate Formation
By the end of the tenth century, the piecemeal assembling of properties was nearly complete in middle Hampshire. The great ecclesiastical estates, which were to last throughout the Middle Ages, had largely reached the proportions they would keep for the next six centuries. The New Minster, the Old Minster, and the Bishop of Winchester did hold some other lands in the region, but they were either not directly associated with the great estates, or were added to them later, and consequently do not appear on Figures 3.3-3.6. Two features of the newly-assembled estates are immediately apparent: their detached holdings, and the lack of topographical unity.

---

[37]   Finberg (ibid., nos. 43/44 and 47) and Sawyer (S377 and S381) give contradictory statements concerning the recipient of the confirmation charters of Overton and Crawley. Inspection of the texts in Kembles's *Diplomata Chartarum* (nos. 1092/3 and 1096) reveals that in both cases, Edward was reputedly responding to a request by Bishop Frithestan, not the Old Minster cathedral, as Sawyer has it. In fact, the language of these two and the others attributed to 909 is identical. The clergy's confirmation of Whitchurch (K1011, F42, S378) is however differently constructed, with *familia* clearly stated and with no reference to Bishop Frithestan.

[38]   Crawley S381, Overton S377, Whitchurch S378, Alresford S375, Chilcomb S376.

To generalize, the detached holdings of these late Saxon conglomerate estates were usually the more distant, woodland tracts that were tenurially associated with larger valley manors closer to Winchester. This ought not to be unexpected; the three ecclesiastical institutions were based within Winchester, and the most desirable properties were naturally the large, valley manors near the city. Secondary gifts by the king and others would have included the more distant holdings. Many may have been unsolicited donations, inspired by personal piety. No doubt the institutions were mindful of the benefits that a central estate would gain from such holdings (e.g., extra woodland for fuel, building material, game, and pasture), but they may also have taken the opportunity to lease distant lands for a cash income.

The 'pairing' of two manors with supplementary resources was rare in middle Hampshire, the only example being the attachment of Hunton, which had good riverside meadowland, to Crawley, which was far from any major stream. Even so, Crawley held other lands at wooded Ampfield that could not have contributed much to its own wide forests. There is no evidence that any of the detached holdings represents an ancient connection between lowland and upland, or between *feld* and *weald*. In middle Hampshire of the late tenth century, rather, the recorded detached holdings were of no great age; others continued to be created in the next century.

The second feature of the newly-created estates was the lack of topographical unity. Geographic contiguity of the manors within the estates was common, and probably aimed for. But even if geographic or spatial unity was a factor, it was not an overriding principle of late Saxon estate formation. Moreover, specific topographic unity was largely ignored, as is especially evident in the peculiar division of the 'Chilcomb' holdings between the bishop and the Cathedral clergy. In each case, the component manors formed a contiguous estate, but the over-all layout was oblivious to topography. The Old Minster's Chilcomb manor included portions of three different valleys, and the bishop's 'Chilcomb' may have extended into four. At its inception, the New Minster's Micheldever manor extended far into the neighbouring Candover valley. Topography was thus not a factor for the late Saxon estate; the basis of its tenurial assemblage was the individual manor, an economic unit no longer dependent upon geographic constraints.

THE CONTEXT OF EARLY MEDIEVAL MANORIAL DEVELOPMENT

The preceding chapter described how the Micheldever valley underwent an economic transformation during the Anglo-Saxon period. It was suggested that at the beginning of the period, land use here was on a valley-wide basis, in which the valuable lower slopes were under arable farming, while most of the north and east uplands were forested, and the southwest part of the valley was under permanent pasture. Between the eighth and tenth centuries this unity was replaced by a pattern of separate village holdings. It was at this time that the manor developed as the standard unit of landholding. In this chapter, we have assessed the characteristics of manors in middle Hampshire, and we may now draw upon those findings to discuss the general development of the early medieval manor.

The manors that first appear in the records are large blocks of land, usually of forty or more hides and encompassing several later parishes. These manors were granted by the king as chartered 'bookland,' brought out of the 'folkland' over which the Crown had rights of tribute. At the same time, certain settlements were necessary focal points for the collection of tribute in the form of rents or taxes (*gabel*), and fines or profits of justice. These locations later became royal demesne manors or vills (e.g., *kinges tun, villa regalis*), and many of them were also the seats of the local court, which in the tenth century appears as a national system of hundreds.[39]

By the Norman period middle Hampshire had few royal vills. Most of the land had been granted away to ecclesiastical foundations, which held their property according to no fixed formula. They rarely split up the manorial association of vills that often happened to be listed in a charter, but at the same time, they did not impose a geographic order to the estates that they built up by donations and purchases. The vills and tracts making up a single manor were therefore often scattered. But this lack of spatial order or unity need not indicate poor management, nor is there evidence that it caused an over-all inefficiency. The perceived benefit of a reduced risk to crop loss in scattered holdings, plus the value of a traditional allegiance given to the landholder by the inhabitants of the vills, or by their lord, are possible reasons why the simple exchange of manors, leading to the unification of scattered estates, did not take place.

The Manor as a Land Unit

The early medieval manor was a legal entity, a collection of possessions and privileges that had as an economic base the land unit of the vill. The vill was also a settlement, either nucleated or dispersed, that could measure only a few families as a hamlet, or several hundred souls in an important village. Some scholars have suggested that manors were originally compound units

[39]   H.M. Chadwick, *Studies on Anglo-Saxon Institutions* (Oxford, 1905, repr. New York, 1963), pp. 249-256. For a recent treatment, see H.R. Loyn, *The Governance of Anglo-Saxon England 500-1087* (Loyn, 1984), pp. 140-147.

made up of several separately organized tracts of land, the divisions of which had a very early origin.

Desmond Bonney investigated the relationship between early boundaries and estates in Wessex. He found that not only were parochial and manorial territories often based upon ancient boundaries, but that "some small units or estates, of considerably less than parish dimensions, were recognizable entities in pagan Saxon times."[40] His argument for the origin of permanent local land units in the fifth or sixth century rests upon the conclusion that pagan burials found in charters and manorial boundaries were placed on pre-existing divisions between settlement territories. It is true that many surviving barrows are to be found on such boundaries, but this relatively limited number of earthen mounds is just as likely to represent only the surviving portion of many more barrows, most of which were destroyed by medieval and modern ploughing. Earthworks on the manor boundary (which nearly always follows field edges) had a reduced risk of destruction. It is even more likely that medieval manor boundaries commonly used pre-existing burial mounds as landmarks in the same way that they used other features of the landscape, e.g., ponds, pits, graves, trees, etc. Thus Bonney's case, though important to early medieval rural history, is difficult to prove. The only documents to describe the particulars of the early medieval landscape are charters, and their boundary clauses refer only to certain of the features that lay on or near their courses, and do not describe the landscape as a whole.[41]

Ann Goodier has analyzed the coincidence of burials on boundaries, and came to the conclusion that after the sixth century, burials may have been sited on boundaries as those boundaries were formed, a long-term process that ended with the arrival of Christianity.[42] Martin Welsh has noted that the 'significant pattern' of burials on or near boundaries needs to be explained, but he questions the view that the boundaries necessarily preceded the burials, because Bonney's assumption that burials would lie on marginal soils between settlement lands has been strongly challenged by Arnold and Wardle.[43]

---

[40]   Desmond Bonney, "Early Boundaries and Estates in Southern England," in *MSCC* 72-82.

[41]   Others have found similar weaknesses in Bonney's argument. See Martin Biddle, "Hampshire and the Origin of Wessex," in *Problems in Economic and Social Archaeology*, ed. G. de G. Sieveking, et al., (London, 1976), pp. 324-341, esp. 328.

[42]   Ann Goodier, "The Formation of Boundaries in Anglo-Saxon England: A Statistical Study," *Medieval Archaeology* 28 (1984), 1-21.

[43]   Martin G. Welsh, "Rural Settlement Patterns in the Early and Middle Anglo-Saxon Periods," *Landscape History* 7 (1985), 13-25; and C.J. Arnold and P. Wardle, "Early Medieval Settlement Patterns in England," *Medieval Archaeology* 25 (1981), 154-159.

Della Hooke considered early boundaries in the West Midlands where she found that "the internal divisions of minor townships are found within a majority of parishes," and that "these small communities had a recognized separate identity in the Anglo-Saxon period."[44] She concluded that "the present-day parish was not necessarily the basic land unit of Anglo-Saxon England, for in the tenth century and perhaps earlier, the land unit of the township was often a smaller and more compact area."[45]

There may have been many cases of burials along the borders of pagan Saxon land units that continued to function and were incorporated into the manorial framework of the tenth and eleventh centuries. But such cases are hard to prove, and Hampshire gives some examples to the contrary. At Micheldever, there was a shift of settlements around the eighth or ninth century, and the boundaries of the new land units were more for the purpose of enclosing an area of mixed land types than following a series of prehistoric barrows and pagan burials. In fact, although Saxon burials in barrows and pagan burial grounds do appear in the boundary clauses of charters of the Micheldever region, none has yet been identified firmly in the field.

The shift of population centres in the Middle Saxon period and later has led to confusion and imprecision concerning the locations of early medieval settlements. Within the century that may have passed between the issuing of a charter for one property and that for a neighbouring tract, there could have been a sizeable movement in habitation sites that continued to bear the same, or similar, names. Around Micheldever, there is the one instance of a ninth-century settlement that did not survive the next century (*Ticcesham*, S360). It was a period of population movement elsewhere in Hampshire. Nucleated settlements were abandoned at both Cowdery's Down near Basingstoke in the north and Chalton in the south; the latter was replaced by several medieval village sites that also supplanted Celtic settlements surviving into the Saxon period.[46]

The Micheldever valley, however, has not yet revealed a similar early nucleated Anglo-Saxon settlement. The pagan Saxon cemetery near Micheldever village represents a religious and social centre, but the population at the time was probably located in dispersed settlements along

[44] Della Hooke, "Pre-Conquest Estates in the West Midlands: Preliminary Thoughts," *Journal of Historical Geography* 8 (1982), 227-244, at p. 234.

[45] Ibid., p. 235.

[46] P.V. Addyman and D. Leigh, "The Anglo-Saxon Village at Chalton, Hampshire: Second Interim Report," *Medieval Archaeology* 17 (1973), 1-25; Martin Millett, "Excavations at Cowdery's Down, Basingstoke, Hampshire," *Archaeological Journal* 140 (1983), 151-279.

both sides of the Dever stream. The eighth and ninth centuries saw here the farmstead replaced by a concentrated settlement, the village.

The Manor in the Early Law Codes

The change in rural organization is echoed in the law codes of the kings of Wessex.[47] The basis of early Saxon society may have been the tribe, and the clan or kin-group within it, but the ultimate unit of social and economic activity was the household farm, the hide or *hiwisc*. It was so recognized by the state, which used it as the quantitative measure for social status and tax assessment. The hide as household was the unit for manorial dues, as shown in the Hurstbourne custumal, ca. 900.[48] The render of cloth from each household/hide at Hurstbourne was a traditional tribute, because this payment also appears in the law code of King Ine of Wessex, ca. 700.[49] Ine's laws used the hide in other ways as an economic measure: a landholder with twenty hides was to show twelve hides of sown land if he wanted to leave; with ten hides, six hides sown; etc. Ine's laws also listed the specifics of food-rent due from ten hides. In addition, the hide was used as the social and economic determinant for assessing the status of the individual. The level of hidage for English wergild compensation payments was left unstated, but it was expressly declared for Britons: five hides meant a wergild of 600 shillings; one hide meant a wergild of 120 shillings, etc.[50]

Hidage appears in a more complicated fashion as an instrument of justice, varying according to the severity of the crime. The requirement that acceptable court testimony be supported by a certain number of hides enabled the defendant or litigant to back up his own testimony, valued in the hidage of his property, with the oaths of men willing to testify to the man's credibility in the community—either oaths of many small landholders or those of fewer but greater landowners. These rules were changed over time. Some were made more lenient: a king's *geneat* (companion) with a wergild of 1200 shillings could swear for 60 hides. Others were made more

[47]   This study does not attempt to analyze the complexities of the Anglo-Saxon law codes, but simply to cite the references to the hide. Therefore, all references are to the accepted translation of the laws in Dorothy Whitelock, *English Historical Documents c. 500-1042*, vol. 1 (London, 1955).

[48]   For a discussion of the particulars of this document, see H.P.R. Finberg, *Lucerna: Studies of Some Problems in the early History of England* (Leicester, 1964), pp. 131-143.

[49]   A 'blanket' paid by each household was valued at sixpence. *EHD* 1, No. 32, law 44.1.

[50]   Ibid., No. 32: leaving, laws 64, 64, 66; food rent, law 70.1; wergeld, laws 24.2, 32.

rigorous: homicide defended by oaths required of each 100 hides the inclusion of a man entitled to swear a king's oath of 30 hides, therefore making unacceptable a defence based solely upon large numbers of smallholding kinsmen. This was further altered in the Laws of Athelstan (ca. 925), where oaths were to be supported by no more than twelve men on each side, and there was no longer a required number of hides for acceptable testimony.[51]

Place-name studies confirm what the laws imply: that the individual farmstead was the dominant early form of settlement. The actual names of settlements, however, did not include the word 'hide' or 'hiwisc.' Farmsteads were probably the original *ham* places, and were certainly so in the later terms *tun, worth, thorp, cot,* and *stoc.* The individual holding sometimes appears in the law-codes in forms other than 'hide.' Ine's laws ordered church scot to be paid from *healme* and *heorthe* (stubble and hearth = farmstead). The *frumstal* (paternal homestead) of a fatherless child was to be cared for by his kinsmen. A ceorl's *worth* (farmstead) had to be enclosed all year long, or he had no right of compensation for crop damage. This concern with the individual household did not continue in the later laws of Wessex. Those of Alfred and Athelstan were more concerned with communities, especially boroughs and districts under a reeve's authority, and with the responsibility of neighbours. For example, the attachment of cattle required the nomination of five neighbours, and an oath by one of the five, while all the men in a locality were required to ride out to take in hand the property of a malefactor.[52]

Thus the evidence of the early English laws suggests that the individual farmstead, and not the village, was the basic element in society. The village must have grown to dominance after the law code of Wessex was set down by Ine in the late seventh century. This is supported by the toponymic evidence. The presence in surviving early place-names of terms referring to single-family habitations, rather than large groups, suggests that the village was not a common form of primary settlement.[53] The change from the hide to the village may be reflected in the late Saxon laws, which in the ninth century stressed the responsibility of neighbours over

---

[51]   Ibid., No. 32: *geneat*, law 19; homicide, law 54; No. 35, twelve jurors, law 23.2.

[52]   Ibid., No. 32: church scot, law 61; *frumstahl*, law 38; worth, law 40; No. 35: neighbours, laws 9, 20.4.

[53]   Village sites that were abandoned early would of course rarely survive as place-names. It is more certain that the Middle Saxon period, from the seventh to mid-eighth century, saw many farmsteads abandoned in favour of villages. This does not mean that earlier settlement did not include villages, for archaeology shows that it in fact did. But such villages have no proven relationship to the late Saxon vills.

hide-holders, and in the tenth century finally did without the hide as a measurement of supportive testimony. By the Viking period, it seems that the hide was already an obsolete administrative term, and by Domesday, it survived only as an abstract unit of financial assessment.

Theories of Rural Development

The changes in landholding that led to the development of the manor over the period 700-1100 were to Peter Sawyer the results of the fragmentation of primitive great estates.[54] Glanville Jones sought prehistoric origins for the ancient 'multiple estate,' while Desmond Bonney thought certain manorial boundaries to have pagan Saxon, or earlier, origins, but also suggested that the late Saxon period may have witnessed the creation of new estates as well as the disintegration of ancient landholdings. [55]

Similarly, the tracing of Anglo-Saxon land units by Della Hooke and others has followed the pattern established by Sawyer and Jones. They saw early medieval rural development as the creation of independent manors out of older, royally-controlled blocks of lands, within the background of an increasingly developed countryside. Charles Phythian-Adams concluded that the tenth century in particular was "a period, not of estate or parochial creation, but one of territorial subdivision and settlement."[56] Della Hooke briefly considered the variety of forms of estate formation: "land units may be grouped together in different ways, for further subdivision can take place or amalgamation may occur."[57]

Yet this later amalgamation has not been recorded. Neither Ford nor Hooke noted any amalgamation of land units in the late Saxon period in Warwickshire or Worcestershire, respectively.[58] In a nine-parish area on the Leicestershire-Warwickshire border, Phythian-Adams traced a process of fragmentation that had started before the Danish invasions. He suggested that the original land unit may have had a Roman or sub-Roman origin,

---

[54]   Peter Sawyer, "Anglo-Saxon Settlement: The Documentary Evidence," in *Anglo-Saxon Settlement and Landscape*, ed. T. Rowley (Oxford, 1974), pp. 108-119, at 116.

[55]   G.R.J. Jones, "Early Territorial Organization"; Desmond Bonney, "Early Boundaries," p. 81.

[56]   Charles Phythian-Adams, *Continuity, Fields, and Fission: The Making of a Midland Parish* (Leicester, 1978), pp. 78-82.

[57]   Hooke, "Pre-Conquest Estates," p. 228.

[58]   William Ford, "Some Settlement Patterns in the Central Region of the Warwickshire Avon," in *MSCC* 274-294; Della Hooke, *Anglo-Saxon Landscapes of the West Midlands: The Charter Evidence*, British Archaeological Reports, British Series 95 (Oxford, 1981). See also Hooke, *The Anglo-Saxon Landscape: The Kingdom of the Hwicce* (Manchester, 1985).

while the fragmentation continued until the core was fully split up in the tenth and eleventh centuries, and by Domesday came to comprise twelve manors.[59] We have seen that Cadman and Foard proposed the fragmentation of 'Greater Raunds' into four townships, containing eleven medieval settlements.[60] Brown, Key, and Orr studied groups of manors in southwest Northamptonshire. Applying Bonney's theories of boundary origin, they concluded that the sixth- and seventh-century burials followed the general lines of estate boundaries, which had been established after the Roman Watling Street. The great estates there, they argued, must have been formed between the late first century and the early centuries of Saxon occupation. They also found that in the tenth century there were multiple estates of three to four parishes, but by the eleventh century there were only single parish manors. They concluded that the charters they used recorded the dissolution of an earlier unit by the process of royal grants.[61]

The above research activities took place in the Midlands; further north, Glanville Jones made a case for the fission of multiple estates in Yorkshire, where Margaret Faull and Gillian Fellows Jensen have found further examples.[62]

In southern England, the concept of a single movement from large estates to small manors lies at the bottom of Alan Everett's research on Kent.[63] But here, and in the west Midland and Yorkshire studies, early land units have been defined largely by associating groups of manors that had dependent holdings in peripheral areas of woodland or upland 'fells.' This pattern is thought to represent the division of a large territory reserved for the transhumance pasturing of cattle, sheep, or swine belonging to an early great multiple estate. The same detached woodland holdings are found in Sussex as well, but there and in Hampshire, studies have also found areas with early composite estates but no evidence of early medieval transhumance.[64]

[59]   Phythian-Adams, *Continuity, Fields, and Fission*, pp. 25, 30, 39.
[60]   Cadman and Foard saw a pattern of large manors with dependent townships repeated in Northamptonshire ("Raunds: Manorial and Village Origins," pp. 92-94).
[61]   Brown, Key, and Orr, "Some Anglo-Saxon Estates," pp. 155-176.
[62]   G.R.J. Jones, "Multiple Estates and Early Settlement," in *MSCC* 15-40. Margaret L. Faull, "Place-Names and Past Landscapes," *English Place-Name Society Journal* 11 (1978-1979), 24-46. Gillian Fellows Jensen, "Place-Names and Settlement in the North Riding," *Northern History* 14 (1978), 1-46.
[63]   Alan Everitt, "River and Wold: Reflections on the Historical Origin of Regions and Pays," *Journal of Historical Geography*, 3 (1977), 1-19.
[64]   Jones, "Multiple," pp. 26-35; Martin Bell, "Saxon Settlements and Buildings in Sussex," in *The South Saxons*, ed. P. Brandon (Chichester, 1978), pp. 36-53. Barry Cunliffe, "Chalton, Hants.: The Evolution of a Landscape," *Antiquary's Journal* 55 (1973), 173-190.

The 'fragmentation' model of early medieval rural development can be inappropriate when composite estates are identified on the basis of detached holdings with a presumed transhumance use, or when the model of the steady disintegration of such land units is too strictly adopted. These approaches may not distinguish between detached holdings of an ancient composite estate and those properties newly joined to a late Saxon conglomeration of manors. We have noted above several instances of the latter in middle Hampshire: the Micheldever estate; the episcopal estates of Crawley, Whitchurch, etc. The detached holdings here do not represent ancient ties of transhumance. Some are only a mile away, others twenty to thirty miles across the full width of Hampshire, and some holdings lay beyond the county borders. Most were acquired by the religious institutions only in the late Saxon period.

Other models of rural development come from place-name specialists (see Appendix B). Topographic names are now considered among the oldest, as are those names with the element *ham*, while the place-names with *-ing* are no longer thought to represent primary settlements. Names with *tun* also appeared later, and Gillian Fellows Jensen has made a study of them in the North of England.

Fellows Jensen applied the toponymic chronology to rural development, proposing that a *tun* originally meant a component of a large estate.[65] Many bear directional or positional adjectives (e.g., Middleton, Easton) that describe a position on the estate. She noted that many also have specialty names—particularly those of animals and agricultural products.[66] Furthermore, many *tun* names have prefixes denoting a group of people with a special status or occupation (examples being *wealas* and *ceorlas*), which again signify dependent units of a large estate (giving Walton, Chalton, Charlton, and Carlton). A *tun* with a wild animal or plant name referred, she believed, to an unfavourable site. However, twice as many *-ingatun* names came to be born by parishes as did *tun* names, even though *-ingatun* is considered a later formation. The origin of the latter place-name element is obscure, and Jensen suggested that *-ing* names were originally applied to districts and *tun* names to the settlements within them.

Margaret Faull addressed the problem of dispersed settlement in early medieval Yorkshire. She thought that in western Yorkshire, "the division of the countryside into townships [vills] had occurred by the tenth century at the latest and probably much earlier," but it was impossible to

---

[65]   Jensen, "Place-names and Settlement," pp. 33.
[66]   William Ford had earlier advanced the idea that this could indicate the degree of localized specialization on a great estate. See "Some Settlement Patterns," pp. 287.

determine the places within the vills before the thirteenth to fourteenth centuries, and some never did have a population centre.[67] She believed that the habitative names with *ham* or *tun* could have referred to both the estate and the township, and from this, she suggested that it was common for such names to antedate settlement names:

> the interpretation of settlement patterns by a close study of specific settlement sites to which names now belong, rather than the general areas of land making up the vills, may have to be rethought.[68]

The accumulating place-name evidence, then, reveals a new paradigm, whereby original settlement was by an area known as a *ham* or by a district with a topographical place-name. In each case, settlement may have been concentrated in one or more spots, or may have been dispersed. Archaeological work has shown that during the seventh century, a discrete habitation site, which had the place-name element, *tun*, began to appear, and the names it bore reveal that it likely represented a functional component of a larger, integrated estate. The subsequent appearance of personal name elements suggests the association of specific land-units with individuals and their descendants, first as a derivation of the possessive *-ing* suffix, then later as a more recognizable personal name, e.g., 'Osmundsham.' The manor had become the personal ownership of a vill, a major conceptual change in landholding, and it is no doubt the reason why in some areas more parishes have *ingatun* names than *tun* names. At the same time, the creation of such units out of the ancient great estates was accompanied by the appearance of habitation toponym referring to small farmsteads, often as part of woodland clearance, which once again suggests that an expansion of population and agricultural activity lay behind the estate, settlement, and place-name changes.

Appendix B demonstrates how place-names of the Micheldever region can be grouped according to the new theories of toponymic development. The frequent retention of Celtic stream names, and their incorporation into settlement names, is evidence that the Celtic population survived here to some degree, even though other Celtic words and toponym are generally rare in this region. Anglo-Saxon place-names should correspond chronologically to the land units they define. After the older names, with Celtic or topographic allusions, there appeared the names of dependent settlements, often with a directional or functional prefix. Later came the personal name element, and an occasional instance where a

---

[67]   Faull, "Place-Names and Past Landscapes," p. 44.
[68]   Ibid., p. 46.

personal name was replaced by that of a later landholder. This suggests an additional complication, that the recorded names of some of these villages could be due more to the purposes of administrative identification, than to any common use by their inhabitants.[69]

Barry Cunliffe has proposed a broad outline for early medieval rural development, at least in southern England. He saw population rise as the impetus for manorial and settlement evolution, which he described as a period of unrestricted growth followed by a period of territorial definition. Boundaries were then established, and some degree of territorial reorganization may have taken place. At Chalton, Hampshire, the pagan village site was abandoned, perhaps in the seventh century, and three new settlements begun. The medieval parish boundaries suggest that these vills and their manors resulted from the division of a single large territory based upon the Chalton site.[70]

Cunliffe's *schema* may be appropriate for the Chalton region of southeast Hampshire and west Sussex, but it does not explain the particulars of manorial origin in the Micheldever area, for two reasons. First, it concerns only nucleated settlements; yet Professor Cunliffe noted that more fieldwork was needed to be done on settlement studies and that "it would be wrong to believe that the only unit of rural settlement in the Saxon period was the village."[71] Secondly, the Chalton model is one-directional. It is based upon the single process of fission, by which a great multiple estate fragments into its composite elements. In middle Hampshire, the process was substantially different. Although both areas equally lack evidence of Saxon transhumance, Micheldever differs in having had what appears to be an early Saxon dispersed settlement pattern, and more certainly, a late Saxon tendency to form composite estates out of manors newly connected tenurially.

THE DEVELOPMENT OF THE MANOR IN THE MICHELDEVER AREA

Let us now apply to the Micheldever area, the conditions and structures of the early medieval manor that have been presented in this chapter and

---

[69]   P.H. Sawyer suggests that the change in the personal-name elements of a village name, which appears in some donations, may have been a way of commemorating the donors. See *From Roman Britain to Norman England* (London, 1978), p. 155.

[70]   Barry Cunliffe, "Saxon Sussex: Some Problems and Directions," *The South Saxons*, ed. Peter Brandon, pp. 221-26, 225. But see M. Hughes, "Rural Settlement and Landscape," pp. 72-76, for some amendments to Cunliffe's conclusions.

[71]   Cunliffe, "Saxon Sussex," p. 224.

detailed in Appendices A and B. Patterns of local landholding, we have seen, are based upon hidage assessment groupings and observations of estate characteristics. Placing these in the context of overall Anglo-Saxon manorial development, we may come to some conclusions on the origin and evolution of the manor in middle Hampshire.

The appearance from the sixth century onward of place-names with the element *tun* is thought to mark the founding of habitation sites that were not independent townships, but were parts of a larger entity, an estate that often bore a *ham* name or a topographic name. Personal names soon followed; they reflect the name of a current or recent landowner at the time the manor appeared in the documents, rather than the name of some past war-chief and his followers.

At the beginning of the eighth century all the vills in middle Hampshire appear to have been held as 'folkland,' except those lands around Winchester that had been granted to the bishop and the clergy of his cathedral 'minster.' The Micheldever valley comprised one of the 'folkland' districts, with Micheldever as its royal centre. This was changed in 900, when most of the eastern part of the valley was made over as a grant to the New Minster. More units of 'folkland' were converted to 'bookland' in the tenth century, and the last tracts left royal control in the early eleventh century. By Domesday all the land in the Micheldever valley had come into private hands. The granting of 'bookland' by charter did more than create a permanent, heritable title to the holding: it also removed it from liability for royal dues. Because of this, the ninth century saw the appearance of the 'three common dues' as exceptions to a charter's implied or expressed immunities. With less 'folkland' supplying food-rent, Wessex could still compete with other Anglo-Saxon kingdoms, but without an adequate supply of men for military duty and the maintenance of strategic positions, as specified in the common dues, it could not expect to maintain royal authority, nor effectively resist Mercian pressure.

The appearance of the three common burdens in late Anglo-Saxon charters, in opposition to what must otherwise have been the general assumption of royal rights by landowners, certainly marks the firm establishment of the early medieval manor.[72] The permanent transfer of lands and rights was not an abrupt step, but rather a further shift in a series of developments in the evolution of the manor. The properties involved, moreover, were long established. Charter boundary clauses usually show

---

[72] This argument is at the core of Eric John's *Land Tenure in Early England* (Leicester, 1960).

that the land-units were of some age; new land divisions were rarely created.[73]

At Micheldever, there were several land-units (vills) identical in size and shape to independent manors in the same 'strip parish' series. Identifiable with later tithings, these land-units have external boundaries which appear to date from at least the ninth and tenth centuries. The field systems separated by these tithing divisions were therefore probably already in existence when a block of land units became Micheldever manor in 900. By this time, the shift in settlements had taken place here, indicated by the abandonment of two Middle Saxon sites in the upper Dever valley. The stage in rural development that created the strip pattern of land units at Micheldever could well be that described by Cunliffe as 'a period of territorial definition.'[74]

These blocks of land (the unitary manors and the later tithings) are best identified as 'vills,' comprising a nucleated settlement with its field system, pasture, and woods. Returning to the definition of the manor as a collection of possessions and privileges that had as its economic base the land-unit of the vill, one can say that the manor was present in Hampshire, but its lands were not recorded as such until they were 'booked.' But could they be considered manors even while they remained as 'folkland'? It would seem so. Just as Micheldever manor contained fully-formed vills that never became independent manors, or became so only at the end of the Middle Ages, so too there remained in middle Hampshire a number of vills that were not granted out from royal control by charter before 1100. They were either part of the royal demesne, or were more commonly let to royal dependents for service and/or rent. These lands should be considered manorial; Domesday Book shows that they had everything except a tenant-in-chief.

The origin of the manor ought to be found in the eighth and ninth centuries when the creation of the vills partitioned earlier topographic districts into discrete land-units. Some vills were soon to have place-names with personal elements, reflecting the presence of landowners. The basis for the medieval manor was created when the king first associated particular vills with the support of individuals, and no longer cared for all his warriors from the general revenue. It may be that larger populations and the expanded authority of kingship caused more friction between the kingdoms,

[73]   The *gewrinkeled dic* separating Abbots Worthy from Martyr Worthy ran along the mixed headlands and furlongs of a pre-existing field system. Other ditches and banks are occasionally mentioned (e.g., *fritheling dic*), but there is no evidence that they represent the internal divisions of field systems.

[74]   Cunliffe, "Saxon Sussex," p. 225.

leading to greater need for fighters, who had to be rewarded in land. These men acquired some form of domination over the properties they received, possibly assuming royal authority on a temporary basis. As the Christianized monarchies developed greater jurisdiction over their subjects, to the detriment of the kinship group, the 'booking' of a property made permanent the title to a vill, and also conveyed with it a share of the increased royal authority over its inhabitants.

One of the questions originally posed can now be answered. Manor and vill were nearly simultaneous creations of Anglo-Saxon society. We have attempted to demonstrate that the vill was a socio-economic response to demographic and economic pressures of the eighth and ninth centuries. The heritable, 'booked' manor was an aristocratic response to the concentration of population into the organized workforce of the village, and to the monarchy's willingness to permanently allocate specific vills for the support of its warrior followers. Before the creation of independent properties as 'bookland,' a manor had been perhaps only a loosely defined right to the royal dues from a locality. The evolution of the early medieval manor was as much the process of continual redefinition, as it was the acquisition of new authority over land and its inhabitants.

4

Territorial Divisions: The Parish

The development of early medieval territorial units in Devon was put forward a generation ago by W.G. Hoskins:

> All over the map we detect patterns made by groups of parishes which clearly fit together like pieces of a jigsaw puzzle to form a single block. In this way we can construct original large estates whose age takes us back well into pre-Conquest times and probably into the earliest stages of the Saxon settlement in Devon. These large estates, covering in many instances twenty or thirty thousand acres, were subsequently carved up, especially at their edges. Large areas at the margins were granted away by the lord to lesser men for more intensive exploitation. In due course these marginal areas acquired a church of their own, as the work of colonization proceeded and the population grew, and sooner or later they were elevated to the status of separate ecclesiastical parishes.[1]

In Hampshire, the recognizable patterns of the medieval landscape were made by the institutional divisions of parish and hundred, which replaced the ancient Anglo-Saxon local territorial units. The late Saxon period witnessed the establishment of these two local elements of ecclesiastical and royal administration. This post-Carolingian world was shattered by savage Viking attacks, which came to a crisis in 1016 with the fall of the Alfredian dynasty and the incorporation of England into a Continental empire. The repetition of conquest and incorporation fifty years later permanently ended medieval England's isolation and political independence. Spanning both sides of that great watershed of social and political transformation, the parish and the hundred were to remain integral parts of English medieval life, serving as the instruments by which everyday judicial and religious activities were organized. As such they are instances of continuity between Anglo-Norman institutions and those of the tenth-century kingdom.

---

[1] W.G. Hoskins, "The Making of the Agrarian Landscape," in *Devonshire Studies*, ed. W.G. Hoskins and H.P.R. Finberg, (London, 1952), pp. 289-333 at pp. 294-295.

The origin of the parish, and its place in the development of the Old English church organization, is essential to a discussion of early medieval territorial development. Architectural and tenurial sources supplement the ecclesiastical records to produce the framework of an early parochial system for middle Hampshire. One may compare this outline to previous observations on the Anglo-Saxon church organization in Hampshire, and consider the relationship of such parochial units to other early medieval territories.

Church Organization

When St. Augustine led the Roman Christian mission to England at the behest of Pope Gregory the Great in 597, he introduced to the island the ecclesiastical organization used on the Continent. The missionaries seem to have entered the early Anglo-Saxon kingdoms or tribal groupings only at royal invitation, and to have succeeded in their missions of conversion only with aristocratic consent. As a result, the dioceses of the bishops generally conformed to Anglo-Saxon kingdoms and subkingdoms.[2]

In England, the early church leaders of the papally sponsored organization continued the Continental practice of preferring a former Roman town as the *civitas* for an episcopal see.[3] That for the kingdom of Wessex was originally in its upper Thames heartland, at the Roman town of Dorchester, the equivalent of Canterbury, Rochester, London, etc. After the Mercian conquest of the north bank of the Thames, the Wessex bishopric was moved to the southern royal city, Winchester, ca. 660.[4] The Winchester see originally encompassed the six later counties of Dorset, Wiltshire, Somerset, Hampshire, Berkshire, and Surrey—that is, all the land south of the Thames from Kent and Sussex to Devon. It was later divided, when a bishop for its western territories was established at Sherbourne. This second see was later moved to Ramsbury, then Sarum, and its border with the Winchester diocese remains practically identical to the county division between Hampshire and Wiltshire. Whilst the early bishops of Winchester

---

[2]   Bede wrote that in 604 Augustine installed Mellitus in London because the king of Essex and the *provincia* had converted, *HE* 2.3, *ASC, s.a.* 604. Noted in William A. Chaney, *The Cult of Kingship in Anglo-Saxon England* (Manchester, 1970), p. 159. Chaney argued that the success of the Roman mission was due to the overlordship of Aethelberht of Kent.

[3]   *Civitas* was the term applied to a cathedral city by at least the ninth century. See R.E. Latham, *Revised Medieval Latin Word-List*, British Academy (London, 1965), p. 89.

[4]   *ASE* 122.

enjoyed the appropriate powers and revenues of their office, the episcopal
church may have had no special authority (beyond a spiritual primacy) over
the other churches, the so-called 'minsters.'[5]

Equivalent to the early medieval baptismal churches of the
Continent, the Anglo-Saxon minsters had responsibility for specific
geographic districts called parishes, in contrast to the Celtic Church, which
had no parishes.[6] The English churches of the eighth and ninth centuries
were typically staffed by a community of clerics that was hardly
distinguishable from a monastery (hence the name 'minster' *monasterium*).
Situated at a royal vill or 'kingstun,' a minster served a territory of
jurisdiction probably identical to that administered by the royal ealdorman
or reeve from the same center, an arrangement that has been described as
"England garrisoned with spiritual *burhs*."[7] They were for centuries the
only permanent religious institutions, and as such claimed to hold the right
to baptize and bury throughout their *parochiae*. Later, when manorial
chapels and village churches appeared in numbers, the ancient foundations
came to be called 'old minsters,' or mother churches.

Certain rights of the minster were defined by royal legislation in
Ine's law code of the late seventh century, the time when the 'minster
system' had matured. Further legislation appeared in the tenth and eleventh
centuries when the rights of the minsters were threatened by the increasing
numbers of churches founded and controlled by individual lords,
corresponding to the rise of private manors and the spread of 'bookland.'
These private churches soon acquired some of the rights of the minsters,
reckoned as the five customs sanctioned by royal law: tithe, church scot
(first fruit), soul scot (burial), plough alms, and light dues. The ancient
baptismal churches often retained little but their titles of honor.

There is no evidence for the support of cathedrals by their dioceses
in the late Saxon period; Frank Barlow suggested "perhaps from the
beginning the bishop's minster had been on an equal footing with the other
minsters in the diocese drawing tribute only from its own smaller parish."[8]
In the next century, these arrangements would disappear with the
establishment of the medieval parochial system that would be later organized
by rural deaneries, a transition extensively documented by John Blair, who

[5]   Frank Barlow, *The English Church 1000-1066: A History of the Later Anglo-Saxon
Church* (London, 1979), p. 179.
[6]   John Godfrey, *The Church in Anglo-Saxon England* (Cambridge, 1962), p. 312.
[7]   Ibid., p. 316.
[8]   Barlow, *English Church*, p. 179.

maintained that the demise of the secular minster church took place after a brief period of favour under the Normans.[9]

The late Saxon laws ranked the churches hierarchically: a 'head minster' was the bishop's seat; a *medemia mynster* was an earlier missionary center, while a 'lesser minster' was a village church, and a 'field church' was a chapel with limited ecclesiastical rights. Three classes of churches continued into the Norman period, as William's legislation regulated fines for the violation of a cathedral or monastic church, a *matrix ecclesia parochialis*, and a chapel.[10] Placing responsibility for Christian worship upon the minsters of a diocese was standard Anglo-Saxon practice, and was in fact the basis of the early medieval parochial system in England. It is not however directly comparable to the later medieval parochial system, because the Anglo-Saxon arrangements continually underwent major changes.

The private or manorial churches, which became common during the tenth century, are more likely to have generated the modern parochial system than are the older mother churches.[11] Although the pagan origins of private churches are debatable, it appears that some private churches existed in some form, soon after the Conversion.[12] No doubt more were created during the eighth and ninth centuries, often where a cross had been set up for public worship at a convenient spot (e.g., a ford or crossroad) or a site of pre-existing local importance (e.g., a pagan burial mound or meeting place). The practice of converting crosses into village churches was to continue into the eleventh century, and on a limited scale even later. The extent of local churches is imperfectly revealed in the Domesday Book; the old minster system—decayed by that time—probably had been wrecked by the Danish wars of the ninth century, which looted the minsters and

[9]   Ibid., p. 183; John Blair, "Secular Minster Churches in Domesday Book," in *Domesday Book: A Reassessment*, ed. P. Sawyer (London, 1985), pp. 104-142.

[10]   Godfrey, *Church in Anglo-Saxon England*, p. 321.

[11]   Daphne H. Gifford, "The Parish in Domesday Book: A Study of Mother Churches, Manorial Churches and Rural Chapels in the Late Saxon and Early Norman Periods" (Ph.D. Thesis, University of London, 1952), pp. 34, 61. She cites Edgar's legislation which provided that a thegn share his church revenues, and the *Rectitudines Personarum* for the use of a church to define thegnly status.

[12]   Gifford, ibid., pp. 36, 38. Godfrey found that on the Continent, the city clergy served chapels and oratories in the countryside, but in Francia the rural churches were more commonly private institutions than in Italy. He noted that in 541 Justinian encouraged landowners to build chapels by giving them the right of presentation (*Church in Anglo-Saxon England*, p. 313). See also J.H. Bettey, *Church and Community: The Parish Church in English Life* (London, 1979), pp. 14-19, particularly for pagan Roman and Celtic origins and influences. G.H. Cook's *English Mediaeval Parish Church* (London, 1954) is a sound introduction that emphasizes architecture.

scattered their collegiate communities. In the vacuum created by the half
century of pillage and war, the small rural church, the 'lesser minster,' was
probably joined by many former rural chapels in assuming the religious
responsibilities and rights that had belonged to the *medemia minster*.[13]

The new rural churches were seigneurial, built and controlled by a
lord. A church was often a manorial component, an attribute of an estate.
Such an asset the Anglo-Saxon Church had no desire to, or was unable to,
refuse the increasingly powerful aristocracy. It may be that Church leaders
thought private churches better than no churches at all, or that by acceding
to the 'manorialization' of the village church, they were winning valuable
allies and protectors. The spread of village churches parallels the growth of
seigneurial power in the late Saxon period. Protective legislation appeared
in the tenth century, particularly a law forbidding dismissal by the church's
proprietor.[14] Claiming that "by 900 private ownership of churches and
ecclesiastical property was universal," John Godfrey compared the early
medieval manorial church to the mill, each worked by a specialist at the
pleasure of the lord, who could buy, sell, bequeath, or divide such
assets.[15]

Eleventh-century conditions in middle Hampshire can be seen in the
Micheldever and Candover valleys, where only six churches were recorded
in Domesday Book. Of the six, only one was given a value, that held by
Mauger at Stoke Charity and valued at 15s.[16] That the Domesday
surveyors treated churches as part of the manorial resources confirms

---

[13]   Godfrey, *Church in Anglo-Saxon England*, p. 379.

[14]   Ibid., p. 320.

[15]   Ibid., p. 319. The trend toward the 'privatization' of churches, including some of
the former mother churches, is evident in the Domesday record. There, churches are listed
among the other manorial assets, often with an assigned valuation. Daphne Gifford suggested
that the use of the term *valet* was applied to an episcopal manorial church when it was held
away from the manor by a named person, or when the bishop held a church on another
manor. Churches with *reddit*, she believed, were specifically vicarages, showing the amount
actually paid to the bishop by the priest ("Parish," pp. 257-259).

It is quite possible, however, that only the churches that were attached to manors
and were clearly defined as manorial assets, came within the purview of the Domesday
Survey. A large-scale comparison of the Domesday churches, moreover, is unlikely to be
rewarding, because the values assigned to churches vary greatly in different parts of the
survey. For the hundred as the basis of major inconsistencies in the Hampshire Domesday
survey, see E. Klingelhöfer, *Settlement and Land Use in Micheldever Hundred, Hampshire,
700-1100*, Transactions of the American Philosophical Society, vol. 81 pt. 3 (Philadelphia,
1991), pp. 115, 118-119. But see also Gifford, "Parish," p. 254; *DBB* 444; and John Blair,
"Secular Minster Churches in Domesday Book," in *Domesday Book: A Reassessment*, ed.
Peter Sawyer (London, 1985), pp. 104-142.

[16]   *DB Hants* 2, 14 (40 c).

Godfrey's comparison with the mill. The Micheldever figures are typical of those for Hampshire. The limitations of the Domesday entries obscure rather than reveal the true value or extent of the local churches that were such a dominant part of early medieval life.

ADDITIONAL EVIDENCE: ARCHITECTURAL AND TENURIAL

A necessary step in recreating the early medieval parochial system is to locate the pre-Conquest churches. Those church buildings that do survive are all late Saxon in date; none go back to the time of the 'minster' system. Despite differing opinions on the development of the Anglo-Saxon church architecture (and therefore on construction dates and broader influences which may have accompanied stylistic changes), the spiritual territory of the local church is accepted to have been that of the estate on which it was built.[17] Consequently, evidence for the existence of a pre-Conquest church may be evidence for an Anglo-Saxon manorial center. Domesday Book remains the major source of information on early medieval parochial arrangements, but it can be supplemented by two other sources: the architectural and archaeological evidence for the church structures themselves, and the documentary record of the right of patronage—the advowson—of the churches, plus any other special association between church and manor or church and church.

The evidence for Anglo-Saxon architectural remains in middle Hampshire is not extensive, but enough is known to make some observations. Although no early medieval structures survive in the Micheldever and Candover valleys, there are churches in the Somborne, Itchen, and Tichborne valleys that exhibit pre-Conquest architectural characteristics. Three churches (Somborne, Headbourne Worthy, and Hinton Ampner) show late Saxon architectural details typical of the late tenth and early eleventh century. A fourth (Tichborne) may have been built, or rebuilt, shortly after the Conquest. Evidence of Anglo-Saxon carved stonework, moreover, appears at several other churches in the area: Alresford, Steventon, and Wherwell, while Whitchurch retains a Saxon grave slab. Archaeological research elsewhere has shown that Anglo-Saxon

---

[17]   Gifford ("Parish," p. 349) noted that the proportion of churches on royal manors that are possible former minsters is strikingly high. William Page showed that pre-Conquest landowners frequently had churches near their residences. See Page, "Some Remarks on the Church of the Domesday Survey," *Archaeologia* 66 (1915), 61-101.

and Norman stone churches usually replaced earlier stone and wooden structures.[18]

The middle Hampshire group of pre-Conquest church buildings shows a shared style of decoration, typically Anglo-Saxon, denoting a greater familiarity with wood than with stone construction. With the exception of a few royally funded enterprises (e.g., Old Minster, Winchester, rebuilt ca. 1020; and Westminster, London, built ca. 1060), these great churches may not have had the wealth to embark upon major construction programs until after the Norman Conquest.[19] Therefore, the late Saxon trend to stone church construction may indicate a regional economic prosperity, as the agricultural regime matured. Evidence of manorial wealth was displayed in this way more perhaps by local landowners, who financed much of the work, than by the great lords and ecclesiastical institutions, who had other demands and interests.

Outside of some recorded dependencies of the Winchester Old Minster, there exists no ecclesiastical list (e.g., of early medieval customary dues) for groups of churches in middle Hampshire. But there is information on the later medieval ownership of the advowson, or presentation, of middle Hampshire churches. An advowson was tenurially heritable and caused churches to become attached to particular manors or churches. After the twelfth century, the right of advowson is generally well recorded. In some instances it was established after the Conquest, but in cases lacking such definite documentation, it could reflect conditions going back to the late Saxon period.[20] The advowson records usually reveal conditions of dependence, but occasionally they show other situations: a church divided between two owners, special obligations or dues, or the presence of subsidiary chapels. The right of presentment was often held by the lord of the manor, but when this was not the case, groupings of such special privileges and extra-parochial authority may indicate the presence of former minsters.[21] Using the material assembled in Appendix C, we can arrange

---

[18]   See Bridget Cherry, "Ecclesiastical Architecture," in *The Archaeology of Anglo-Saxon England*, ed. D.M. Wilson (Cambridge, 1976) pp. 151-200.

[19]   Earl Odda's handsome chapel (ded. 1056) close to the important Anglo-Saxon church of St Mary, Deerhurst, Gloucestershire, may be the work of a great lord and royal kinsman, but there is no evidence for the widespread construction of royally-associated structures. See H.M. Taylor and Joan Taylor, *Anglo-Saxon Architecture* (Cambridge, 1980), pp. 193-194, 209-210.

[20]   For example, Cheriton and Whitchurch, which have Anglo-Saxon place-name elements referring to Christian sites, and are identified here as the sites of early minsters.

[21]   This is in the basis for P.H. Hase's study, "The Development of the Parish Church in Hampshire, particularly in the Eleventh and Twelfth Century," (Ph.D. Thesis, Cambridge University, 1975).

the middle Hampshire parishes by river valley to locate the likely early minster centres and territories (see Figure 4.1).

The parochial development of the Dever valley parishes generally followed the descent of the manors there. Micheldever itself was a rectory until 1302, having subsidiary churches at East and West Stratton, Popham, and Northington, its Domesday manorial dependencies. The bishop held Wonston church, which was given jurisdiction over the villages of Cranbourne and Sutton, while Norton, a royal manor, seems never to have had a church of its own. Hunton was a chapelry dependent upon the episcopal manor at Crawley, and Bullington church was held by Wherwell Abbey. The bishop held Stoke church, though in 1086 Mauger held (or farmed) the living. The diffuse pattern of parochial associations or groupings suggests that an early ecclesiastical center at Micheldever retained authority over the eastern valley, while a parallel center at Wonston had authority over a few parishes in the western end of the valley. The bishop's early possession of Wonston manor may have enabled or encouraged him to push its claim to spiritual superiority over the villages not included in the New Minster's 'hundredal' manor of Micheldever.

The Candover parishes show little evidence for grouping by advowson. Northington, as noted above, was attached to the church at the manorial center of Micheldever. Brown Candover possessed a chapel at Woodmancott. Such ecclesiastic particulars must reflect tenurial relationships of the late tenth and early eleventh-century, because these manors were not associated until shortly before the eleventh century, and Brown Candover and Woodmancotte were separated soon after 1066. Other advowsons belonged to their respective manors, and cannot be traced back to an ancient mother church. Abbotstone church followed the manor held by the descendants of the Norman, Hugh de Port. In the thirteenth century Swarraton church was controlled by the Abbot of Waverly, Wield was held by the Bishop, and Southwick Priory had been given the church at Preston Candover. In 1291 the lords of the manor presented the livings at Chilton Candover, Farleigh Wallop and Herriard.

The Alre valley shows a preponderance of episcopal churches. Domesday Book records three churches attached to the bishop's manor of Alresford, of which one would have been at Alresford, another was probably a dependency at Medstead, and the third could have been on the site of New Alresford, as an unnamed vill, or perhaps at the early place-name 'Lanham' in eastern Alresford parish. The other three churches were held by private lords. That at Bishops Sutton was given by the son of Eustace, count of Boulogne, to Merton Priory, along with its dependent chapel at Ropley. Bighton too was a manorial church, the advowson of which belonged to Hyde Abbey (the New Minster).

The Tichborne valley had a high proportion of associated churches. Of the six churches in the valley, four were ecclesiastically linked. The advowson of Tichborne was held by Cheriton church, to which were attached the chapelries of Beauworth and Kilmeston. Only Bramdean and Hinton Ampner were manorial churches. Cheriton was probably the site of the mother church of a *parochia*, as is suggested by its place-name *cyric-tun* ('church-ton').[22]

The churches of the upper Itchen valley were strongly affected by the proximity of the Winchester episcopal see. The bishop of Winchester held churches at Littleton and Avington, and Domesday Book recorded two for him at Easton (the second perhaps being a dependent chapel at Yavington). The advowson of Ovington seems to have been acquired by the bishop in the thirteenth century. St. Swithun's Cathedral held the churches at Martyr Worthy and Headbourne Worthy, while the advowson of Kings Worthy followed its manor. Abbots Worthy may never have had its own church. Those at Itchen Abbas and Itchen Stoke were held in the thirteenth century by their respective manorial lords, St. Mary's (Nunnaminster) of Winchester, and Romsey Abbey.

Of the parishes of the upper Test valley, several were held by the bishop: Overton, Whitchurch, Oakley, and North Waltham. Whitchurch was a Saxon foundation, and had its own dependency at Freefolk. In 1086, Whitchurch was held by the priest Alvric. Overton had a dependency at Tadley, some distance to the north, which could well be a later medieval annexation, as Overton was then becoming a rural town. The advowson of the churches at Wooton St. Lawrence, Laverstoke, Dean, Ashe, and Steventon followed the descent of the manor. Ashe and Laverstoke churches were noted in the Domesday Survey, but Steventon church was not recorded until 1238.

In the middle Test valley, the foundation of Wherwell Abbey in 1002 initiated a rearrangement of manorial and parochial relationships. The living of the church at Wherwell, with its chapel at Tufton, was a abbey prebend, a benefice assigned to a member of the chapter as a stipend. So were the churches of Middleton, Goodworth, and Bullington. Leckford, however, was a prebendary advowson of St. Mary's Convent, Winchester, the lord of the manor, and Longstock was among the parish churches given to Mottesfont Abbey ca. 1200 by the Briwere family. Of the other churches in the group, Fullerton seems to have had no church until the fourteenth century, and the advowson of Barton Stacey and its chapel at Newton Stacey was given to Llanthony Priory by the son of the Earl of Gloucester in the

---

[22]   *ODEPN* 100.

twelfth century. The living of Chilbolton, an episcopal manor, was in the hands of the bishop.

The churches of Somborne valley were dominated by Mottisfont Abbey in the later Middle Ages, but their earlier associations are not known. Soon after 1200, the brothers John and William Briwere (Brewer) gave to Mottisfont Abbey the churches of Kings Somborne (with its chapel at Upper Eldon), Little Somborne, and Ashley. Before then, the advowsons of these churches probably followed their manors, which were acquired in the late twelfth century by the Brewer family. As the manorial grouping was a recent creation, the Briwer's collection of advowsons is unlikely to represent some ancient association. Elsewhere, the chapel at Upper Somborne was a seigneurial presentation, as was the church at Farley Chamberlaine where Hyde Abbey (the New Minster) was lord of the manor. Sparsholt was one of the nine churches of Winchester Cathedral's Chilcomb manor; the Bishop held both manor and church at Crawley.

The evidence collected in Appendix C reveals that there were only a few non-manorial advowsons in each locality. Nevertheless, the results of the survey are not ambiguous or contradictory. At the end of the early Middle Ages, certain churches had spiritual superiority over adjacent districts, and (except for tenurially associated manor churches) these 'superior' churches ought to represent the ancient minsters and their *parochia*.

Figure 4.1 depicts churches that are first recorded as having advowsons held separately from the manors they served. William Page noted that the Domesday churches in Hampshire show both the developing medieval parish system and the older pattern of 'mother churches.'[23] Although churches here are not recorded in ecclesiastical documents as having the title *matrix ecclesiae*, there are several examples of ecclesiastical centres of that type, and typically they bear the name of the hundred, or a place-name indicating an early Christian establishment (e.g., Whitchurch and Cheriton).

In the Tichborne valley, Cheriton was the center of four churches, and in the Alre valley, Alresford had three Domesday churches. The Candover and upper Itchen valleys, however, show little sign of an earlier ecclesiastical arrangement. Brown Candover and Easton each had a dependent church in the eleventh century, but in neither case is this enough to postulate the site of an ancient missionary church. At the same time, it should be noted that the fabric of the late Saxon church at Headbourne

---

[23] Page, "Church of the Domesday Survey," 73, 76-77. But John Blair urged caution in using Domesday Book, which he felt was a poor guide to minsters but good for the important churches of 1086: "Secular minster churches," p. 112.

Worthy includes a monumental stone sculpture. It may be proof of the antiquity of Headbourne Worthy as the religious center for the upper Itchen valley, but the sculpture could equally represent the artistic and spiritual pretensions of the Old Minster for a possession that lay only a few miles from the city, on the approach road from London and central England.

There is evidence for other minsters in middle Hampshire. The Test valley churches with advowsons held as prebends of Mottisfont Abbey do not indicate an ancient *parochia*, because their association was created by the late twelfth-century accumulation of manors by a local landowning family. Rather, Kings Somborne should be considered a mother church, because it was a hundredal center and possessed two subsidiary chapelries. Wherwell is probably another, even though its dependencies can be traced back no further than the eleventh century. On the upper Test, the place-name favours Whitchurch over Overton as an ancient missionary foundation; each church had one dependent chapelry. And in the Dever valley, most of the parishes were divided between two ecclesiastical centres: Wonston which had three dependencies, and Micheldever which had three or four, and had spiritual responsibility for other settlements without a church.

Middle Hampshire therefore offers a fair proportion of early medieval mother churches. In four of the eight valley-delineated groups of parishes (Somborne, Alresford, Wherwell, and Micheldever),[24] a church with attributes of an ancient spiritual superiority over the surrounding territory, was located at a hundredal manor. In two other cases (Whitchurch and Cheriton), it had a place-name indicating the site of an early Christian foundation, perhaps with an origin in the missionary activities of the seventh century (see Appendix B). Evidence for the minster system appears in some places and not in others. It is present at Alresford, which became 'bookland' in the eighth century, and at Kings Somborne where most manors were alienated from the Crown only after the eleventh century. In both locales, the settlement pattern is little different from the rest of the region. But we noted above that in both cases, the typical transformation of landholdings into separate, small manors did not take place. There would have been less demand here for new, independent churches. In several cases, a remnant of royal 'folk' land had its own ecclesiastical arrangement, independent of relationships in the rest of the locality. Sutton held Ropley, Barton Stacey held Newton Stacey, and Wonston claimed a superiority over Sutton Scotney, Norton, and Cranbourne. And royal churches, no matter how minor or late in date, received spiritual allegiance from the few royal

---

[24]   Brown Candover is a likely candidate for a fifth church with a valley-group name.

manors that had not been alienated. The presence of such examples of 'secondary' parochial centres suggests that early land grants did convey some ecclesiastical rights, and that the creation of 'bookland' removed a locality from both the royal administration and the 'minster' system.

The ancient parochial system seems to have survived into the early tenth century. After Micheldever was granted to the New Minster in 900, the churches in the western half of the Dever valley that were not attached to the New Minster, were subsequently regrouped around the less important Wonston. But after the 909 grant of Hunton, as an attached holding of the bishop's Crawley manor, Hunton church did not stay under the authority of Wonston (later an episcopal manor and church), but became a chapelry of Crawley. Of course in all these considerations, it was the bishop who ultimately approved such arrangements, and the cathedral scribes who recorded them. These officials stood to gain much if they bore no witness to an earlier parochial system, in which the bishop's minster had no rights superior to those of any other minster. The destruction of the pre-Alfredian, early medieval 'minster' system may be attributed to the Danish wars and to the growth of the private church. The paucity of written evidence for the early medieval parochial system, however, could well be due to an episcopal and cathedral disinclination to preserve documents undermining the legitimacy of the manorial church. And in middle Hampshire, most manorial churches came to be owned by the bishop or the cathedral clergy.

PREVIOUS OBSERVATIONS ON THE HAMPSHIRE PAROCHIAL SYSTEM

The findings presented here must take into account three previous reconstructions of ancient Hampshire *parochiae*. William Page, Rosalind Hill, and P.H. Hase examined different aspects of the mother church arrangements, that together lead in the direction of my more encompassing reconstruction. Nevertheless, differences of interpretation do exist, and these are best discussed by presenting the individual contributions in chronological order.

William Page contended that Domesday Book entries revealed the identities of early medieval mother churches. That churches "recorded at hundred boroughs or manors or other administrative centres [were] frequently the only churches entered into the survey under such hundreds" was convincing in theory but only partially successful in practice.[25] Record collecting on the part of the Domesday survey teams varied from hundred

---

25   Page, "Church of the Domesday Survey," p. 66.

hundred to hundred, and the presence of a church was one of the items often left unreported. In Hampshire, there is a further complication in that, by 1086 many hundreds were based upon recent tenurial relationships, and were made up of disparate holdings widely scattered about the shire. These hundreds reflect eleventh-century seigneurial rights of jurisdiction over the local court, and do not correspond to the administrative units upon which the Anglo-Saxon system had been based (see Figure 5.1).

Consequently, there is no support for Page's claim that long-term links existed in Buddlesgate Hundred between the south Hampshire 'ancient minster' at Nursling and the bishop of Winchester's central Hampshire manorial churches at Chilbolton on the Test and Stoke Charity on the Dever. His attachment of the church at Worthy to a mother church at Meonstoke missed the Domesday Book scribal error that failed to record the hundred in which Worthy lay. Moreover, Page's expectation that frequently only the churches at hundredal centres were recorded by the Survey, must be qualified by the presence of minor churches in Hampshire Domesday entries. In *Eselie* (Ashley, later Sutton) Hundred, not only was the hundredal manor church of Bishop Sutton recorded, but also the church in the tiny hamlet of West Tisted.

Excepting the Hampshire hundreds, Page's observations were usually well-founded, and his research remains a valuable pioneering effort. Other scholars have noted the inadequacy of the hundredal equation here (whereby the late eleventh-century hundred *caput* was equated with a seventh or eighth-century ecclesiastical and administrative center), and in recent years attempts have been made to correct in part, or entirely, Page's reconstruction of the early medieval minster system in Hampshire.

In 1976 Rosalind Hill presented a brief account of her research into the local history of Hampshire's Test Valley, in particular, the strategic north part of Kings Somborne hundred.[26] She examined its ecclesiastical divisions, the eight parishes of the later Middle Ages, and identified the four Domesday churches as Kings Somborne, Little Somborne, Houghton, and the chapel at North Houghton. She concluded that Kings Somborne church was a *matrix ecclesia* with dependencies at Little Somborne and Stockbridge, the latter a newly formed settlement that would develop into an important regional market center in the later Middle Ages. The reason why Stockbridge never had an independent parochial church, Hill proposed, was that Kings Somborne church was an early 'chief minster':

[26]   Rosalind Hill, "Some Parish Boundaries in Hampshire," in *MSCC* 61-65. The northern part of the Domesday hundred comprised the parishes of Houghton, Longstock, Kings Somborne, Little Somborne, Leckford, Ashley, and Farley Chamberlaine.

at which the entire population living on the eastern bank of the Test from Stockbridge Down southwards to Farleigh Mount paid its ecclesiastical dues and sought sanctuary when need be. The territory has a sort of convenient geography. To the north and south it is bounded by high ridges of downland, to the west by the river and the complicated marshes which fringe its banks, to the east by the woodland which in the eleventh century were taken into the king's forest.[27]

Rosalind Hill wondered whether Kings Somborne achieved its position because of a powerful local religious tradition, or because the north part of the Kings Somborne Hundred formed an early territorial holding concentrated in the hands of one owner, who built the church near his hall. Because it was, as far as is known, always a royal manor, one can assume that such a sole owner was in fact the king himself.

The geographic unity of Hill's proposed early territorial holding and ecclesiastical district is similar to the use of geophysical data in this study. The conclusions are somewhat different, however, as she used only the late eleventh-century hundred (though not its southern part); by contrast, I would propose a Somborne valley group of vills based upon the coincidence of manor/parish boundaries with the watersheds separating drainage basins in middle Hampshire. Professor Hill did note the impressive topographical features of Stockbridge Down and Farleigh Mount, which do indeed mark the north and south limits to the Somborne drainage basin, but which do not necessarily correspond to the Kings Somborne Hundred of Domesday, because Leckford lies on the far side of the ridge. Furthermore, the full topographical unit includes the parish of Houghton on the west side of the Test, and the wooded upland parishes of Crawley and Sparsholt. Nevertheless, Miss Hill's attempt to recreate the ancient *parochia* based on Kings Somborne represents a decisive step beyond Page's use of the Domesday Book to locate mother churches.

Also in the 1970s, P.H. Hase completed a notable contribution to the history of early medieval parishes in Hampshire. His research led to series of observations: (1) in the seventh and eighth centuries a mother church was established at each *villa regalis*; (2) in the tenth century, the reorganization of the Old Minster led to the division of the large Winchester *parochia*, and the same period saw the division of *parochiae* in northwest Hampshire into small parishes; (3) it was not until the eleventh century that the large *parochiae* of south Hampshire were fragmented into medieval parishes. Hase disputed Page's contention that each hundred contained originally only one church, because "completely independent churches

---

[27] Ibid., pp. 64-65.

always existéd in the interstices of the mother church *parochiae*."[28] He concluded that manorial churches were *not* founded by manorial lords, but evolved from the prebendal field churches serving the mother churches. Claiming that thegns paid the mother churches for certain ecclesiastical rights in their manorial churches, and that a division of revenues would not have been normal otherwise (because it was canonically illegal to alienate a church endowment, and the rector was in no position to lose much income), he also rejected Gifford's efforts to equate the Anglo-Saxon village church with the Continental *Eigenkirche*.[29]

Dr Hase also investigated the relationship between ancient mother churches and royal vills. He concluded that in Hampshire all examples of mother churches were in the advowson of the king, earl, or ecclesiastical institution, and furthermore that the majority were royal. In the thirteenth and fourteenth centuries, the mother churches remained wealthier than the average parish church, and they had notably large, amorphous parishes, the result of independent parishes splitting off from the original *parochia*, so that often what was left looked like a slice of bread from which several bites had been taken at random. Hase noted that every well-established case of a mother church was located at a royal hundred center, or at an ecclesiastical hundredal manor. He used the Domesday hundreds as the basis for organizing his material, though not as closely as Page, for he was wary of the effects of beneficial hidation. Tracing the dissolution of the ancient *parochiae*, he hoped, "should show how the hundred grew out of early royal head-manors."[30]

Finding, however, no overall pattern to parish size and mother church frequencies, he proposed that the parish system had developed differently in different parts of Hampshire, but did not explain the differences by such contributory factors as ethnicity, population density, or political and natural geography. His reconstruction of a *parochia* system was more successful in southern Hampshire than in the north, perhaps because the scattered Domesday hundreds and ubiquitous cathedral and episcopal estates of northern Hampshire yield only the most tenuous patterns. The difficulty in locating discrete minster districts no doubt led Hase to theorize the existence of independent Anglo-Saxon churches at parochial interstices. His efforts to recreate the minster system were ultimately frustrated by his use of the Domesday hundreds, which were often only a collection of tenurially associated Hampshire manors, served by a common court that had attained hundred status.

---

[28]   Hase, "Parish in Hampshire," p. 40.
[29]   Ibid., pp. 3-6, 26, 31-34.
[30]   Ibid., pp. 37-39; quote taken from Preface, n.p.

The reconstruction of two minster *parochiae*, Micheldever and Winchester/Chilcomb, reveals the problems of interpretation. Although four churches were dependent upon Micheldever church, Hase was uncertain if it had been a mother church before it was granted to New Minster. He saw "some evidence that a major estate had been fractured here at some time."[31] He suggested that perhaps Micheldever and the Candover 'microscopic hundreds' of Bermondspit and Mainsborough were originally a single territorial unit. Yet the resulting *parochia* would have been centred upon the wooded watershed between the Dever and Candover valleys, high ground that was then heavily wooded and little populated. Such underdeveloped lands are unlikely to have comprised the heart of a viable territorial unit in the early Middle Ages.

The Cathedral's Chilcomb estate, plus certain episcopal manors, Hase identified as an ancient *parochia* with the Old Minster as its *matrix ecclesia*. He suggested that this seventh-century ecclesiastical estate came to be divided upon Ethelwold's reform of 964, with the Old Minster obtaining most of the lands to the west of the Itchen to form Buddlesgate Hundred (with a meeting-place inside the gate of the Cathedral Close), and the bishop receiving most of the lands on the east bank to become Fawley Hundred (with a meeting place on Fawley Down overlooking Chilcomb).[32] Hase's chronology of the development of the Chilcomb estate is likely to be correct, but his reconstruction of an original Winchester territory as a large block of parishes extending from Bishop Stoke to Martyr Worthy and from Hursley to Cheriton, was determined by the jurisdictions of eleventh and twelfth-century hundred courts and by the landed possessions of ecclesiastical institutions, which more often than not were late accumulations unrelated to ancient territorial divisions.

The existence of ancient "coterminous tenurial, judicial and ecclesiastical units" can certainly be accepted, even if some of Hase's reconstructions can not. He found difficulties in applying some of the Hampshire evidence to his theories of parochial development; there were no areas in northern Hampshire where the early medieval 'minster' parochial system was completely satisfactory, and "in areas with franchisal estates, the original boundaries cannot be given at all."[33]

---

[31] Hase, "Parish in Hampshire," p. 219.
[32] Ibid., p. 264.
[33] Ibid., p. 309.

Summary of Parish Origins

Before the parochial system typical of the later medieval period, there was another method of organizing the clergy. This was the 'minster' system, whereby a community of priests at a single district church, similar to the continental 'baptism' church, served an area that would later be covered by five to ten medieval parishes.

It is generally assumed that the minsters would have been situated at royal vills, and their *parochiae* the same as the local administrative units. Attempts to define the *parochiae* geographically have not succeeded on the whole, largely because the Domesday hundreds provide inadequate boundary lines. This is confirmed in Lincolnshire, where David Roffe concluded that even though tracing early parishes by soke boundaries "is likely to indicate eleventh-century estates where they are associated with private churches, the resultant boundaries do not necessarily express ancient divisions of the landscape."[34] On the other hand, the large parish of Rivenhall, Essex, is believed by its investigators to represent an example of estate continuity, tracing its descent from the Roman villa estate.[35] Further north, the careful research on Warram Percy, Yorkshire, has suggested that the two Saxon manors making up a bipolar settlement may have each been served by a proprietary church. Furthermore, Warram Percy parish (comprising five townships) is thought unlikely to have been formed before the Conquest, its irregular shape spreading across both a hundred boundary and a watershed divide. The details of Warram Percy parish are, however, unlikely to be comparable to ecclesiastic developments in Hampshire. Warram's first stone church is of the twelfth century, while middle Hampshire has stone parish churches one or two centuries earlier, suggesting a difference in wealth, resources, religiosity, or concentration of power in the hands of the lord. More important, the church, village, and all tenurial arrangements had been subject to 'Scandinavian reorganization,' which the Hampshire communities were luckily spared.[36]

---

[34]   David Roffe, "Pre-Conquest Estates and Parish Boundaries: A Discussion with Examples from Lincolnshire," in *Studies in Late Anglo-Saxon Settlement*, ed. M. Faull (Oxford, 1984), pp. 115-122.

[35]   W.J. and K.A. Rodwell, *Rivenhall: Investigations of a Villa, Church, and Village, 1950-1977*, C.B.A. Research Report 55 (London, 1987); but see the review by C. Hayfield, *Medieval Archaeology* 32 (1988), 322-324.

[36]   These Warram Percy findings were presented on pp. 88-92 and especially figure 3, in J.G. Hurst, "The Warram Research Project: Results to 1983," *Medieval Archaeology* 28 (1984), 77-111. This has recently been supplanted by R.D. Bell and M.W. Beresford, *Warram Percy: The Church of St. Martin*, Society for Medieval Archaeology Monograph 11 (London, 1988).

By using architectural and tenurial evidence to supplement the ecclesiastical, we have tried to locate the ancient minsters of middle Hampshire, and reconstruct their *parochiae*. The early medieval parochial system displays the same distinctive pattern of later parish groupings that we have observed for manors: groups defined by valley catchment areas. There are some instances of secondary parochial centres, which are attributable to manorial division, but there is no case here of two ancient minsters in a single catchment area. One may conclude that, just as the dioceses formed soon after the Conversion were based upon the Anglo-Saxon kingdoms, so the early medieval *parochiae* mirrored the smaller political units.

5

Territorial Divisions: The Hundred

By the middle of the ninth century, the contest between Mercia and Wessex for domination of southern England had eliminated the smaller kingdoms of Essex, Sussex, and Kent. The ensuing Danish wars destroyed the East Anglian, Mercian, and Northumbrian royal dynasties. Thus, by the end of the ninth century, only one Anglo-Saxon kingdom survived, its dynasty and political institutions intact. Although initially removed from the brunt of Danish attacks, Wessex used an admirable organizational ability to first repel, then subdue its enemies. Simply stated, each of the three kings successively victorious over the Danes added a new element to the government of their expanding realm. King Alfred instituted the burghal system, whereby military obligations were attached to strategically located quasi-urban defended centres. Attracting and protecting populations, most of the *burhs* had markets and mints, and were often the origin of English medieval boroughs. Disregarding the defunct pre-Danish political divisions, Edward the Elder imposed upon the Midlands a system of equal-sized administrative units, the 'shires.' Each took its name from the *burh* that was its administrative centre, with an assembly-court (moot) under a 'shire-reeve' (sheriff). In the second quarter of the tenth century, Athelstan issued legislation concerning the unit of local government, the 'hundred' division of the shire. The 'hundred-moot' was a popular assembly and court run by the 'hundred-reeve.' Responsibilities for law and order were divided among local groups of ten men, 'tithings,' who were authorized by the hundred to form *expeditiones* to catch criminals and retrieve stolen goods. These three royally created institutions represented the backbone of the Old English administration, and with minor changes by the Normans, remained the basis of English government throughout the Middle Ages.[1]

[1] The conclusions of H.G. Richardson and G.O. Sayles about the pre-Conquest origin of English local government in *The Governance of Medieval England from the Conquest to the Magna Carta* (Edinburgh, 1963), pp. 42-69 are accepted here, but not necessarily their views on early medieval central government and military service. For a more recent study of Anglo-Saxon administration, see H.R. Loyn, *The Governance of Anglo-Saxon England 500-1087* (London, 1984), esp. pp. 131-171.

Wessex Administration

The ultimate origins of these three components of late Anglo-Saxon government have been much debated. Combined, they represent a structure that with the central bureaucracy of the Court, Frank Barlow called 'Neo-Carolingian.'[2] Certainly there are similarities between the Anglo-Saxon shire and the Carolingian *pagus* and *comitatus*, and between their subdivisions, the hundred and the centena.[3] Alfred's burghal system may have been partially adopted from the Danes' own creations (the Five Boroughs of the East Midlands). It has recently been claimed that the Danes (and in part, Alfred) inherited a network of burhs created by Offa of Mercia at the end of the eighth century, in response to a presumed Carolingian 'marketing system.'[4] A debt to the documented mid-ninth-century regional program of strategic fortifications undertaken by Charles the Bald is more likely, especially considering the dynastic connections between the late Carolingians and the House of Wessex.[5]

The kingdom of Wessex had long experience in administering discrete political units; it had ruled for generations the once independent kingdoms of Kent, Sussex, and Cornwall. For an even longer time it had attached to itself provinces of other states (e.g., Surrey and Devon). West Saxon frontier groups with names ending in *saet* (e.g., *Wilsaet, Sumorsaet*) were often the basis for units of administration that are later found in the shire system. A loosely defined relationship between an ethnic or settlement region and the 'kingstun' that became its political centre appears to have been formalized and regularized in the ninth century. This development incorporated some earlier arrangements (*Sumorset* and *Sumerton*), but other name changes may reflect the growing importance of the shire town or

---

[2]   Frank Barlow, *The English Church 1000-1066: A History of the Later Anglo-Saxon Church* (London, 1979), p. 30.

[3]   Helen Cam, "Suitors and Scabini," in *Liberties and Communities in Medieval England: Collected Studies on Local Administration and Topography* (Cambridge, 1944), pp. 49-63.

[4]   Jeremy Haslam, "Market and Fortress in England in the Reign of Offa," *World Archaeology* 19 (1987), 76-93. Haslam uses charter references to military duties, including fortress building and bridge building, to propose a system of fortified markets throughout the Mercian territories.

[5]   The Wessex borough construction can be viewed as part of a western European movement in strategic fortification. Alfred's stepmother was Judith, daughter of Charles the Bald, and Alfred himself spent some time in Francia with his father during the 854-57 journey to Rome. Alfred later brought St. Grimbald to Wessex as a teacher, and his daughter married the Count of Flanders, while his granddaughters married into the Carolingian, Saxon, Robertian, and Burgundian houses. See *ASE* 44-46.

borough (*Wilsaet* and Wilton, later Wilt[on]shire, and similarly, Ham[pton]shire).[6] It is not until the early decades of the tenth century, though, that a regular network of English boroughs brought with it the extension and development of the West Saxon shire system, whilst the hundred system first appeared in the following generation.

The Hundred System

The hundred system first appears in a legislation, 'The Hundred Ordinance,' which Dorothy Whitelock dated to the reign of Edmund (939-946). Dr Whitelock commented:

> There were certainly courts which met every four weeks before the time of this ordinance, and the places at which the hundreds held their meetings often have names which prove them to have been meeting-places from very early times. There is evidence from very early times, too, of the assessment of the county in round figures of a hundred or multiples of a hundred hides, but no early evidence for administrative areas called hundreds or assessed at a hundred hides. While several of the midland counties are made up of hundreds which have this assessment, there is no such neat correspondence in the southern districts. It seems probable, therefore that the institution of hundreds in the Midlands either was on a different principle from that current in the South, or took place at a much later date, when any original correspondence between the name and the assessment had in the South been obliterated by later development.[7]

She attributed this legislation to the general reorganization of the Midlands by the kings of Wessex, and considered it possible that the name 'hundred' may have been applied then to unequal-sized districts in the South solely for uniformity of terminology.

Following Dr. Whitelock's argument, the hundred may have had its origins in Wessex, but like the shire, it lacked the regularity of its transplanted form in the Midlands. An earlier Wessex local district, of whatever name, combined the royal administrative functions embodied in the reeve and his responsibilities for revenue collection at the royal vill, with the popular function of the moot, as assembly and local court. But the connection is unclear, as Dr. Whitelock pointed out, between such

---

[6]   But not Berkshire, which kept its geographic name, and did not become 'Readingshire.' See Loyn, *Governance*, p. 55; and David Hinton, *Alfred's Kingdom: Wessex and the South 800-1500* (London, 1977), p. 13; both accept an early existence of the traditional shire.

[7]   *EHD* 1: 393.

traditional arrangements of local government in Wessex, and their systematic application in the Old English kingdom by ordinance directives and regularized territorial units. One thread of continuity may have been picked up by Helen Cam, who suggested that the late tenth and eleventh-century private hundreds were not new and dramatic creations of a failing monarchy, but rather a legalizing formalization of *de facto* local conditions. Noting that the Winchester see (bishop and cathedral) possessed nine hundreds in Hampshire, Miss Cam concluded that it was "highly probable that from very early times endowments of bishoprics carried with them rights which in the course of time crystallized into titles of hundreds."[8]

This condition would however not apply to the New Minster, which far from being an ancient bishopric, was in fact established by King Alfred's testament. Set beside the Old Minster cathedral in the centre of the 'capital' city, it was planned perhaps as a royal chapel, certainly as a royal burial place.[9] The New Minster's great estate at Micheldever was a foundation gift on a scale appropriate to an episcopal church, and it came to bear title to a hundred. This early tenth-century grant might then represent the middle ground between the ancient possessions of the old minsters, which had no documentation at all, and the eleventh-century concern for the documentation of all jurisdictions, as seen in the details of Domesday Book and similar surveys, and in their continued use.[10]

The Ship Hundred

In the late tenth century, the English monarchy sought to create and maintain a fleet, using 5-hide units as the basis for building and manning 60-man ships. The resulting 300-hide 'ship-sokes,' are documented under Ethelred (978/9-1016), but attributed by Richardson and Sayles to the reign of Edgar (959-975). They estimated that his navy (for which there is some tradition), comprised 1200 men and 20 ships in a squadron for each coast, or 60 ships in all.[11] The 60 ships would have required the service of 180 hundreds, perhaps one-fourth the original forces of the country. The new 'ship-hundred' system of military mobilization and supply may have been

---

[8]   Helen Cam, "The Private Hundred before the Norman Conquest," in *Studies Presented to Sir Hilary Jenkinson*, ed. J. Conway Davis (Oxford, 1957), pp. 50-60 at 55.

[9]   See Martin Biddle, ed., *Winchester in the Early Middle Ages*, Winchester Studies 1 (Oxford, 1976), pp. 449-469. It was independent of the Old Minster in Winchester, as Westminster would be independent of St. Paul's in London.

[10]   See Sally Harvey, "Domesday Book and Its Predecessors," *English Historical Review* 86 (1971), 753-773.

[11]   Richardson and Sayles, *Governance*, pp. 42-44.

organized on a rough territorial basis, but more importantly, these were not under the direct administrative of a sheriff. The man or institution held responsible for the proper functioning of each ship appears to have been rewarded with the profits from its respective jurisdiction or soke. The system was no doubt conceived as a more effective instrument of central government, but by bypassing the busy sheriffs, it was soon co-opted by powerful men and institutions during the difficulties of Ethelred's rule. Like other early medieval political and administrative instruments, the ship-hundred system involved the blending of royal bureaucracy with seigneurial license, and military obligations with ecclesiastical privilege.[12]

The appearance of the multiple ship-hundreds at the end of the tenth century occurred at the same time that aristocratic privilege was re-establishing itself over the bureaucracy of the Old English state. The hundred system, part of the carefully integrated administration of the English kingdom, along with the shire and the borough, was thus to lose its direct ties to the Crown. It may have been military expediency on the part of Edgar or Ethelred, but the alienation of royal authority to figures in the church reform movement corresponded to a similar alienation of royal properties to those same privileged clerical leaders.[13] It was also in that period that hundredal privileges were claimed by churches, and forgeries were produced to support these claims. In middle Hampshire, the Micheldever charter (S360) was probably rearranged and rewritten just to incorporate the important claim to the hundred court of Micheldever and the financial rewards of its judicial fees. There is no reference to hundredal authority in the authentic refoundation charter of the New Minster of 966 (S745). Though admittedly it did not deal with specific estates, it does refer to secular authority over its possessions, i.e., the three common burdens, *expeditione, pontis arcis[q]ue constructione*.[14] The forgery claiming to be a 903 grant of Edward the Elder (S370) lists the several manors associated

---

[12]   The best documented of the ship-sokes, the Liberty of Oswaldslow, shows that the Bishop of Worcester had full jurisdiction over the triple-hundred, and gave out 5-hide blocks of land in leases for three lives in service tenure, to obtain the 60 warriors he needed. For Stenton's views, see *ASE* 485-486, 681-682; refuted in part by the analysis presented in Eric John, *Land Tenure in Early England* (Leicester, 1960), pp. 80-161.

[13]   Nearly as much land in Hampshire was alienated during the 16 years of Edgar's reign (959-975), as had been during the previous 36 years (924-959), as shown in F.G. Aldsworth, "Toward a Pre-Domesday Geography of Hampshire: A Review of the Evidence" (BA Dissertation, Department of Archaeology, University of Southampton, 1974), Figs. 20, 21. There is some duplication of estates in these figures, because Aldsworth included confirmations, re-grantings, and forgeries among the charters he used.

[14]   *Liber Monasterii de Hyda*, Rolls Series 45, ed. Edward Edwards (London, 1866), p. 200.

with Micheldever in Domesday Books, along with their hidage and churches. This probably late eleventh-century fabrication began the list by specifically claiming the hundred: *do quendam fundum quem indigenae Myceldeufer appellant cum suo hundredo et appendicibus, habens centum cassatos et ecclesiam.*[15]

The tenth and eleventh centuries were a time of rapid institutional change, which may have been catalyzed by the second wave of Scandinavian invasions that led directly to the Danish Conquest of 1016 and indirectly to the Norman Conquest of 1066. The political status of the shire system was to change in the eleventh century with the creation of earldoms for Canute's 'jarls.' The system was subsequently affected first by the development of the earldoms into the great territorial 'principalities' of the late Anglo-Danish state, and secondly by the increasing disassociation between earldom and shire under the Norman dynasty. Previously, the hundred system had been transformed from Athelstan's combined royal and popular instrument of law-and-order, into Ethelred's ill-fated procedure for allocating supplies and men for the navy. The policy whereby authority over the new 'triple-hundreds' was given to ecclesiastical figures does reveal the strong ties between the Anglo-Saxon church and state. However, it may also show a too great dependence upon church leaders by Edgar and Ethelred, a limitation of the late Saxon kingdom. Because the administration of its new defence system was shared between royal officials and religious lords, their less than co-operative efforts and lack of prompt concern for military mobilization undermined the national resistance to the Viking invasions.

The Late Saxon ship-hundreds may have caused more dislocation of the normal shire administration than they added to the defence of the country. They created a barrier between the hundred and the king, and so contributed to the rise of territorial lordship. The largest step in that direction, however, took place under the Anglo-Danish dynasty. By the mid-eleventh century, the earls of England had amassed huge estates composed of *comitales villae*, manors associated with the earldoms.[16] Some of this 'comital' land was alienated royal property, and may have carried with it full juridical rights. By this time, earls also received the 'third penny' (one third the profits of justice) from the shire courts in their territories, and in many cases from hundred courts, or groups of them.[17] The earls were not reluctant to treat these holdings as personal property.

---

[15] *BCS*, 602; *KDC* 336; *Mon. Angl.* ii, 437-438, no. 4.
[16] *DBB* 167-168.
[17] Ann Williams, "Land and Power in the Eleventh Century: The Estates of Harold Godwinson," *Proceedings of the Battle Conference on Anglo-Norman Studies* 3, ed. R. Allen Brown (1960), pp. 171-187.

Thus, in 1066, the (Nether) Wallop manor had descended to Countess Gytha from Earl Godwin; to it were attached the 'third pennies' of six hundreds, and free pasture and pannage in the woodland belonging to those hundreds.[18] At the same time, Kings Somborne manor had control over the jurisdiction (*soca*) of two hundreds, and by the thirteenth century the manor of Basingstoke held the returns of six hundreds.[19] The creation of multiple hundreds was thus a pre-Norman development, one that continued and even flourished in later medieval, feudalized England.

The Origin of the Hundred

The later evolution of the hundred can be followed, but what were its antecedents? We have noted that Dorothy Whitelock assigned the origin of the hundred to pre-Viking Wessex, where, like the shire, it lacked regularity. The Midland shires were equal-sized, taking their name from the fortified *burhs* that were their administrative centres. The Midland counties had hidage assessments that corresponded to the number of hundreds they contained. Many of these were assessed at 100 hides, while those with 50 or 200 hides were described as 'half-hundreds' or 'double-hundreds.'[20]

The hundred had several functions: judicial, financial, administrative, police, and ultimately, military. As a royal officer, its leader, the hundred reeve, transmitted directives from the shire court government to the locality, and revenues and requests in the reverse direction. In the eleventh century and perhaps earlier, the men of the hundred were recognized as the authority on the proper assessment of manors; it was they who affirmed or corrected the information gathered by the Domesday surveyors.[21]

A local unit of administration existed in Wessex before the Danish wars, though one cannot claim that it bore the name 'hundred.' Sir Frank Stenton summarized the late Saxon evidence for the origin of the hundred: many hundreds were financially associated with ancient royal manors, and hundreds often bore the same names as the manors to which they were attached. Further, some royal manors received not only profits of justice from the hundred, but also payments representing former food-rent from the

---

[18]   *Domesday Book: Hampshire*, ed. J. Munby (Chichester, 1982), 38c. This edition translates *pasnagium* here and throughout the text as 'pasturage' rather than 'pannage.'

[19]   *DB Hants* 38c, note 1.44. See also Cam, *Liberties*, pp. 99, 100.

[20]   *ASE* 298, 299.

[21]   R. Welldon Finn, *Domesday Book: A Guide* (Chichester, 1973), pp. 5-16, doubts if the Inquest clerks visited each hundred. Rather, they remained in the shire town, and the hundred-men reported there.

local inhabitants. Occasionally, a royal manor received the profits of justice from a whole group of hundreds. Nonetheless, frustrated by the paucity of earlier evidence, Stenton branded the origin of the hundred to be one of "the most difficult problems in Anglo-Saxon history."[22] Indeed, the efforts of many historians have, by increments, made it only somewhat less enigmatic.

The strong connection between hundreds and the early Saxon administrative centres of the royal vills was first investigated by H.M. Chadwick, who concluded that the hundred district had a Danish origin and that preceding it was an ancient local territory rendering dues at a place that evolved into a king's *tun*.[23] Helen Cam later drew together the evidence for the hundredal manor and the practice of grouping hundreds. She defined the antecedent of the hundred as:

> a ninth century or older unit of government, a district centring in a royal *tun* and administered by a royal reeve, valued at one hundred hides, but older than the territorial hundred so called, and very possibly described in the laws by the vague name of *manung* - jurisdiction. ... [It was] emphatically an administrative district, organized from above, with a royal rather than popular basis.[24]

Maitland distinguished between manorial dues associated with the *feorm*, and the jurisdiction of the hundred. He thought that the community court meeting, or moot, was the original element, and that the hundred's antecedent was a community of the folk.[25] We have seen that Page, and more recently, Hase examined the connection between original mother churches and the ancient royal manors that were hundred centres. Both scholars found a strong correlation to suggest that these district churches were uniformly established at such centres, and they tried to identify and reconstruct the territorial units that were controlled spiritually and politically from these sites. Their relative lack of success may have been due to their assumption that the Domesday hundreds reflected Anglo-Saxon territorial units. Unfortunately, a century of jurisdictional alienation had resulted in the artificial rearrangement of both manors and hundred divisions. The late eleventh-century Hampshire hundreds bore little resemblance to the West Saxon district or 'manung' of Helen Cam.

---

[22] *ASE* 298, 300.

[23] H.M. Chadwick, *Studies in Anglo-Saxon Institutions* (Cambridge, 1905; New York, 1963), pp. 239-262.

[24] Cam, *Liberties*, p. 90.

[25] *DBB* 236-241.

THE ARCHAIC HUNDRED IN HAMPSHIRE

Before the late Saxon period, the territorial divisions of middle Hampshire were physically defined by valleys and catchment areas (see Figure 5.1). Such topographic considerations are increasingly recognized as fundamental determinants for social and political entities.[26] Upon the assignment of 'bookland,' these districts were split up into individual manors, the geographic groupings of which serve as the basis for reconstructing the pre-manorial territorial units. The watershed divisions closely correspond to some important manorial boundaries, and very often hundred boundaries follow the same topographic lines. Royal authority recognized and used these pre-manorial districts, apportioning their hidage assessment in blocks of 100 hides. Where the original assessment seems not to have been 100, it was 50 or 150. The upper Test and the Test upland areas may even have been a single district of 200 hides assessment without subdivision; it would be the equivalent to the late Saxon 'double-hundred.'

These valley units may be best described as 'archaic' hundreds. Representing a half-way stage between a unit of Germanic tribal society and the territorial jurisdictions of the hundred, vill, and manor, the details of its transformation are discussed below. Figure 5.2 illustrates the territorial division of Hampshire (save for the extreme northeast, the New Forest and the Isle of Wight) into the eight valley groups of middle Hampshire, plus other similarly topographically-based manor groups that are described in Appendix D.

We have reviewed how the physical components of the political and ecclesiastical administration may reflect early medieval conditions. In middle Hampshire, this documentation points to the division of the landscape into topographically-based land units. Each one of the archaic hundreds had a known royal and/or hundredal manor. Each one also had a *matrix ecclesia*. Archaeology supports the identification of these locations as ancient royal centres; in Hampshire north of the Solent, there are thus far nine sites of

---

[26]   See R.J. Chorley, "The Drainage Basin as the Fundamental Geomorphic Unit," and C.T. Smith, "The Drainage Basin as an Historical Basis for Human Existence," in *Water, Earth and Man: A Synthesis of Hydrology, Geomorphy and Socio-Economic Geography* (London, 1969), pp. 77-99; pp. 101-110, respectively. For Hampshire, F. Aldsworth observed a valley-based Anglo-Saxon settlement pattern, and proposed that early territories were also based on the valleys: F.G. Aldsworth, "Towards a Pre-Domesday Geography of Hampshire: A Review of the Evidence," (BA dissertation, University of Southampton, 1974), p. 179.

major pagan Saxon cemeteries and/or important early settlements.[27] All nine were discovered in the vicinity of royal manors identifiable as hundred and/or ancient parochial centres, most likely the foci of the valley units (see Figure 5.2).

The most ancient type of toponyms are prevalent among the archaic hundred centres (see Appendix B).[28] Topographic place-names were often repeated in a valley group, and those associated with water resources (stream names, 'ford,' etc.) are strongly represented among these centres. Place-names did sometimes change, as conditions and general settlement patterns altered over time. Two names, Basing and Itchen, had a dependent settlement nearby, a 'stoke,' which took the larger settlement name as a prefix. The first example has a personal name element more typical of the Thames valley than of central Hampshire, and in fact lies on the watershed between the two. The second, Itchen, is a river name, and perhaps the original name for the archaic hundred there. As the obviously Christian-named 'Whitchurch' replaced an earlier name for that settlement, so a royal centre at 'Worthy' (meaning 'enclosure, compound') may have replaced 'Itchen.'

It is appropriate here to treat in some detail the one district in the Hampshire chalkland that has been identified as a sub-Roman territorial unit - the Winchester area of the middle Itchen valley. The lands around Winchester have been viewed as the *territorium* of the post-Roman city, transferred in the seventh century to the Church, and similar *territoria* have been proposed for Silchester and Cirencester.[29]

Most of the area around the city for several miles was part of the ancient, huge manor of Chilcomb. It was the prize possession of the Old Minster, and the prime example of 'beneficial hidation,' as the Chilcomb

[27] The nine early Saxon burial sites, according to Audrey Meaney, *A Gazetteer of Early Anglo-Saxon Burials* (London, 1964): Micheldever, Winchester, Kings (Abbots) Worthy, Alton, Droxford, Portsdown, Southampton, Farnham. Major early settlement sites are Chalton, Porchester, Southampton, Winchester, and Cowdery Down, near Basingstoke. See David Hinton, "Hampshire's Anglo-Saxon Origins," in *The Archaeology of Hampshire*, ed. S.J. Shennan and R.T. Schadla-Hall (Winchester, 1981), pp. 56-65.

[28] See Margaret Gelling, *Signposts to the Past: Place-Names and the History of England* (London, 1978). She notes that in some areas topographical settlement names "are regularly used for the main settlement in large conglomerate estates" (p. 123).

[29] For Silchester, see M. Biddle, "Hampshire and the Origin of Wessex," in *Problems in Economic and Social Archaeology*, ed. G. Sieveking et al. (London, 1976) pp. 323-341. For Cirencester, see Katherine Barker, "Institution and Landscape in Early Medieval Wessex: Aldhelm of Malmesbury, Sherborne and *Selwoodshire*," *Proceedings of the Dorset Natural History and Archaeological Society* 106 (1984), 33-42. The antiquity of the Silchester bounds, however, was challenged by D. Hinton, "Hampshire's Anglo-Saxon Origin," p. 57.

hundred, with many estates, was assessed at only one hide. The Old Minster claimed that Chilcomb was given in its foundation grant by King Cenwalh in the mid-seventh century, and Martin Biddle has suggested that these lands represent a post-Roman *territorium*.[30] Maitland examined the tradition of Chilcomb and its supporting documents. As for the hundred hides of Chilcomb, he declared: "It is to be feared that these charters tell lies invented by those who wished to evade their share of national burdens," but for lack of a better explanation he accepted that "the first Christian king had bestowed mile after mile upon the minster."[31]

H.P.R. Finberg also examined the tradition of the Old Minster's Chilcomb estate, as part of his effort to find elements of truth behind the many spurious documents produced by Winchester Cathedral. He noted a late tradition that Cenwalh had given the church three manors: Downton in Wiltshire and Alresford and Worthy in Hampshire. Finberg argued that the tradition is credible. He identified Worthy to have been at an early date "a single large estate comprising the four medieval Worthy villages." He considered it probable that Cenwalh's gift included in 'Worthy' the whole ring of hamlets around the city, and concluded that the large manor of Chilcomb was an original, integral grant from the days of the Conversion, and that it was known by one tradition as 'Worthy.'[32]

This study need not be drawn into the complexities of the Chilcomb diplomatics, but there is no reason why a seventh-century estate necessarily had the same boundaries as that recorded in the late Saxon period. In light of the late tenth- and eleventh-century efforts by the Old Minster to obtain both hundredal jurisdiction and beneficial hidation for a large number of manors, some of which lay in southern Hampshire, it may be prudent to consider the Chilcomb manor a late Saxon composition or reassembling of holdings, and accept the very real possibility that contradictory documents were expunged from the Cathedral archives.

Finberg himself noted how the hundred of Chilcomb (later known as Fawley from its meeting-place on Fawley Down) was "an aggregate artificially put together by combining Chilcomb with eight other villages around Winchester and with a ninth, Avington, which had only belonged to

[30]   Biddle, *Winchester*, 256-258.
[31]   *DBB* 496-498.
[32]   H.P.R. Finberg, *The Early Charters of Wessex* (Leicester, 1964), pp. 214-248. He did not refer to Little Worthy, *alias* Abbot's Barton, which the New Minster acquired from the bishop's estates as part of the arrangements for its move to the Hyde site, ca. 1110. This 'Barton' probably took the Worthy name by association with its neighbour, Headbourne Worthy, in the later medieval period.

the minster since 961."[33] If Avington had been added only a generation or so before the forgery was composed, how can we be sure that the rest of the estate was created as early as the seventh century?

The tradition could be true - in that Cenwalh did grant the manor of Chilcomb to support his newly founded episcopal minster. But the original extent of Chilcomb may have simply been the lands of the vill bearing that name. A fertile side valley of the Itchen southeast of Winchester, Chilcomb had the extensive arable, downland pasture, and riverside meadow for a productive agricultural unit, and was clearly a suitable economic base for the early church establishment. The charter confirming its beneficial hidation in fact refers to the holding as a valley (*vallis illuster Ciltecumb appellata*).[34] Ordinarily, it may have been valued at, say, twenty hides; it is the same size as Bighton, which had that assessment. If the original grant was of the valley called Chilcomb, what then do we make of the late Saxon hundredal manor?

Topographically, Winchester lies in the centre of a valley unit similar to those considered here the earliest identifiable stage of medieval landscape use and landownership. As with those units, the Winchester district is composed of medieval manors/parishes that fall within a natural catchment basin, either as a single tributary valley, or as a topographic zone of a larger river system.[35] Most manors of this middle Itchen valley group were included in the late Chilcomb estate and hundred. Most of the village churches, too, were in the possession of the Old Minster, and there is no evidence for an ancient *parochia* based upon a mother church at Chilcomb. We have seen that episcopal minsters probably had *parochia* indistinguishable from those of other minsters, and the churches of the middle Itchen valley group were no doubt originally dependent upon the Old Minster.

The conflicting views of the lands surrounding Winchester may in fact represent two competing and coexisting territorial units: a folk group based upon the Winchester segment of the Itchen valley basin, and a post-

[33]   Ibid., pp. 230-233.

[34]   It is discussed in *DBB.*, 496, referring to K.342. The document is an eleventh-century possible interpolation of a 909 Edward confirmation. (S376).

[35]   The northern edge of the Winchester unit was formed by the southern boundaries of the upper Itchen valley group, and by the eastern boundaries of the Somborne valley group. These lines follow the ridge from Cheesefoot Head and Telegraph Hill to Easton Down, across the Itchen to Abbots Barton, Teg Down, and west to Farley Mount. The boundary passes along the parishes of Owlesbury, Morestead, Chilcomb, Winnal, Abbots Barton, Weeke, and Hursley. To the south, the topography suggests a line from Hursley to Otterbourne Hill. There the topography changes as the geography passes from the north Hampshire chalk hills to the south Hampshire clay lowlands.

Roman ecclesiastical and administrative *territorium* incorporating much of the same area, but with some different boundaries. Perhaps Leutherius, a Gaul, and the other early bishops of Winchester included a post-Roman *territorium* in their program for establishing Venta as a proper episcopal *civitas*. Generations later, the manor of Chilcomb grew to encompass for all practical purposes, the physical and jurisdictional extent of the middle Itchen valley archaic hundred.

The Devolution of the Archaic Hundred

The correspondence between topographic 'valley' units and manorial groups is the basis for identifying the archaic hundreds of middle Hampshire. Evidence from several sources reinforces this identification: the locations of royal/hundredal manor centres, the sites of ancient mother churches or 'minsters,' the major pagan Saxon burials and settlements, and the archaic toponyms born by the centres of the valley units. These archaic hundreds may have served the needs of the early West Saxon monarchs, but they could not survive the tenurial and political changes of the late Saxon period. It is possible to trace the devolution of archaic hundreds in certain places.

The east half of the Micheldever valley contained the ninth-century moot hall, so recorded on the charter of 900 (S360). Micheldever itself remained the site of the hundred court and the mother church for the eastern half of the valley. The western half lost its judicial integrity, and was divided between several hundreds in 1086. The bishop's holding at Wonston assumed an ecclesiastical superiority over the churches of the western valley. The same transfer of authority took place at Alresford, which was both a hundred centre and a mother church. Some time after it was given to the bishop and the Old Minster, the remaining royal manor of Sutton (by its place-name 'south-tun,' originally a dependent vill) became the centre of a tiny hundred, and also had a limited spiritual superiority (one chapelry).

An archaic hundred centre must have been located in the western portion of the upper Itchen valley. Kings Worthy was the site of a *villa regalis*; in adjacent Abbots Worthy lies a major pagan Saxon cemetery. We have noted the monumental sculpture of the church at Headbourne Worthy, and Easton appears to have been a secondary mother church. As all these villages lie in an approximate half mile radius, it is apparent that this locale had been the traditional political and religious centre of the archaic hundred, but various facets of that authority came to be dispersed among individual villages and manors.

In the middle Test valley, Wherwell was the mother church and centre for Wellford Hundred at Domesday, but Barton Stacey (again, a place-name indicating a dependency; *beretun* = 'barley farm') was also a

Domesday hundred centre and one of the royal manors that still received revenue from the ancient *feorm* (food-rent) in 1086. And in the upper Test, Whitchurch was the site of an early minster, with dependent churches and a surviving late-Saxon gravestone. After it became an ecclesiastical manor, the hundred centre seems to have been moved to Overton (another secondary place-name), which also came to be held by the Church, though the hundred remained under royal control.[36]

From Archaic Hundred to Hundred

The Hampshire archaic hundreds were geographic units into which settlement divisions naturally fell. These territories were post-Roman, pagan 'Saxon' in origin, and owed little to the Romano-British organization of the landscape. Their boundaries followed Roman landscape features only when the latter coincided with a topographical division. In middle Hampshire, there is no evidence to claim that the valley-based archaic hundred descended from a pre-Roman territorial unit. Indeed, the settlement evidence appears to contradict such a view, since Celtic occupation and communication routes were normally restricted to the chalk uplands, and Saxon habitation sites and the roads joining them developed along the valleys. It is possible that the early sub-Roman settlement pattern here was dispersed, in scattered farmsteads and hamlets, but the early medieval population rise and agricultural 'boom' created here a strong riverine pattern of vills and manors, which is recorded in the ninth century, but is indirectly attested to in the eighth.[37]

Though the valley units probably coalesced into self-defined territories with folk-moots during the sixth century, as British or sub-Roman influence finally disappeared, their recognition as districts of particular tribute assessment (an arbitrary 100 hides) may have been formalized only around 700. This likely occurred after the Christian kings of Wessex had consolidated their power to a certain degree, and before they started to alienate to the Church blocks of land as 'bookland,' usually assessed in simple fractions of one hundred hides.[38]

---

[36] The 909 confirmation by Edward is spurious (S378), but the lack of any alternate documentation may in fact suggest that Whitchurch was an early grant to the Old Minster. But see O.S. Anderson, *The English Hundred Names: The Southwestern Counties*, Acta Universitatis Lundensis (Nova Series), Band 35 (Lund, 1939), p. 195.

[37] For details of the Late Saxon settlement study, see Eric Klingelhöfer, *Settlement and Land Use in Micheldever Hundred, Hampshire, 700-1100*, Transactions of the American Philosophical Society, vol. 81 part 3 (Philadelphia, 1990), pp. 75-81.

[38] Chilcomb, if an original foundation grant to the Old Minster, was earlier, but there is no record of the hidage it may have held, presumably because such figures had not been formulated ca. 650.

In each archaic hundred, the food-rent from the hundred hides was received and stored at one of the settlements, which was administered by a royal agent, a reeve (*gerefa*). This holding developed into a specifically 'demesne' royal manor (*villa regalis*) when the other lands in the archaic hundred were granted out as alienated 'bookland' or leased out as 'folkland.' When royal influence upon local justice increased, the royal vill took in the profits of justice from the local court or 'moot,' and with the spread of Christian institutions, the collegiate minster established at the 'kingston' enjoyed ecclesiastic privileges throughout the archaic hundred, which became its *parochia*. Exceptions to this original union of folk-group, royal district, and church missionary area, began to appear in the eighth and ninth centuries. It was then that the shift in the location of hundred centres and mother churches, and the creation of secondary hundred and parochial centres, was most likely initiated by alienation of the ancient *villae regales*.

During the tenth century, a standard form of hundred was imposed upon the rest of England, with its law-and-order responsibilities spelled out by royal ordinance. However, the growth of lordship by the end of the century meant not only the removal of lands from the authority of the reeve at the hundred moot, but the successful claim by middle Hampshire major landholders to the profit - and control - of the hundred court itself. The late Saxon formation of new great estates brought with it the creation of new hundred divisions, often made up of non-contiguous holdings. By the eleventh century, the hundred system in Hampshire had been largely broken up into a patchwork of jurisdictions, few of which remained in the hands of the king. Just as heritable, private manors replaced 'folkland,' so seigneurial immunity as expressed in liberties, sokes, and private hundreds brought an end to the Old English hundred. Even royal hundreds were often gathered together by dominant comital families in the eleventh century, as royal power was eclipsed by the rise of the great earldoms, the English equivalents of the territorial principalities of the Continent.

The steps that marked the reversal of the administrative precocity of the late Saxon monarchy also marked the rise of lordship in England. Its growth was the last major stage in the transformation of the ancient world, drawing upon the heritage of the Romans, Celts, and Germans, into the medieval synthesis - a responsive solution to the realities of a defensive and depopulated post-Roman West. The subsequent legal conversion of all holdings into fiefs was in comparison a minor institutional adjustment of the late eleventh and twelfth centuries. Under Norman feudal tenure, all land was held from the king, by a military obligation that was soon defined as specific knights' fees from each holding. At the base of Anglo-Saxon landholding was a similar, but less rigorously defined military obligation, from the original warrior holdings of 'folkland' to the late Saxon creation of quasi-feudal 'ship-sokes,' with their 300 hides supplying 60 military men, a ratio that was often adopted by the practical Norman administrators as a useful guideline: one knight for five hides. The continuity between the Anglo-Saxon state and the Anglo-Danish, and after that the Anglo-Norman, was a slow process by which valuable institutions or procedures were generally retained, the others passing into oblivion.[39]

[39]   The general observations put forward here are not contradicted by the specifics of Sawyer's detailed argument concerning 'concealed lordship.' See P. Sawyer, "1066-1086: A Tenurial Revolution?" in *Domesday Book: A Reassessment*, ed. P. Sawyer (London, 1985), pp. 71-85.

6

Early Medieval Territories

In middle Hampshire, the ancient valley territory has strong claims to be the origin of not only the hundred, but also the parish and manor. What is the supporting evidence for this territory, and what is its broader historical context?

TERRITORIAL DEFINITIONS

Sir Frank Stenton acknowledged that "one of the anomalies of Anglo-Saxon history is the extreme rarity of early references to fundamental [political] institutions."[1] Until recent advances in toponymics and medieval archaeology, this fact limited research on early medieval political units to the scanty references in documents and religious works.

The English writers of the eighth century, according to Stenton, recognized only one type of unit smaller than a kingdom. Repeated references to *regiones* and *provinciae* appear in the Anglo-Saxon literature, but neither, he claimed, was a technical term, and there was little evidence to show what English word lay behind them.[2]

Early medieval references to Surrey, however, do suggest at least one term. Bede's Latin refers to the later shire as the *regio Sudergeona,* and the Old English text has *Sudrig*(e)*na land*.[3] In this case, the *regio* of Surrey was the equivalent of 'Surrey-land.' Among other uses, 'land' was considered by Eilert Ekwall to have often been prefixed by names denoting either a district (Cleveland, Hartland, Holland), or a large estate (Rutland). A closer look at the citations, however, suggests that this was a use particular to the North of England, one that continued to be used into and beyond the period of Scandinavian settlement.[4] It is possible that the

1   *ASE* 298.
2   *ASE* 293.
3   *HE* 4.6.
4   *ODEPN* 222, 245, 397, 453.

Northumbrian Bede, or his translator, employed a dialect idiom that equated *regio* with 'land.'

What Bede and others commonly used for territories were the names of tribes, and as a 'technical' term, *maegth*, meaning 'kindred' and by extension 'folk, people.'[5] For J.E.A. Jolliffe, Bede's *regiones* and *provinciae* were represented by *maegth* and *theod* ('tribe,' 'people').[6] The English kingdoms were always referred to by their folk-names, not their territorial names, e.g., 'West Saxons' rather than 'Wessex,' and *Merce* 'Mercians,' rather than 'Mercia.' This was true for smaller political units as well.

There exists one substantial administrative document to survive from the pre-Viking period, the 'Tribal Hidage.' It is a tribute list of the peoples controlled by the Mercian kings, with hidage assessments of the various components, and has been attributed to the period 670-690.[7]

In this complex and controversial document, many if not most of the names are difficult to identify (in the forms given by later copyists). Most refer to what were small groups of peoples normally included among the Middle Angles of the east Midlands. Some can be identified by their appearance in Bede's *Historia*. Wendy Davies has identified three types of peoples' names: proper names like the *Hwicce* of the Severn valley (or the *Gewisse* of Wessex); those ending in the element -*saetan*, meaning 'inhabitants,' 'settlers'; and those that have a plural ending -*inga*, or -*inga*-onto a personal or topographic name.[8] To Davies's types, one could add the element -*wara* ('defenders,' 'inhabitants') that forms part of *Cantawara* 'Men of Kent,' with their capital *Cantawaraburig* (Canterbury). Elsewhere, the *wara* element also appears in *Dornwaraceaster* (Dorchester) the capital of the *Dornsaete* of modern Dorset. In this case, it would appear that the *Dornsaet* and the *Dornwara* were interchangeable terms. *Saet* was used for groups in southern and western England, perhaps in areas that came under

[5]   *ASE* 293.

[6]   J.E.A. Jolliffe, "The Era of the Folk in English History," in *Oxford Essays in Medieval History Presented to Herbert Edward Salter* (Oxford, 1935), pp. 1-32. Related to *theod* is *theodum* ('lord,' 'ruler'), *theodland* ('district,' 'country'), and *theodisc* ('language'): John R. Clark Hall, *A Concise Anglo-Saxon Dictionary*, (New York, 1916, rev. H.D. Merritt, 1962), pp. 357, 358.

[7]   Wendy W. Davies and H. Vierck, "The Contents of the Tribal Hidage: Social Aggregates and Settlement Patterns," *Frühmittelalterliche Studien* 8 (1974), 223-293.

[8]   Ibid., p. 229. Paul Courtney points out that tribal-based place-names were given by people *outside* tribal areas and are found on the borders of environmental zones or ecotones: "The Early Saxon Fenland: A Reconsideration," in *Anglo-Saxon Studies in Archaeology and History*, ed. D. Brown, et al., British Archaeological Reports, British Series 92 (Oxford, 1981), pp. 91-102.

Anglo-Saxon control only in the late sixth and seventh centuries, and it may have retained to some degree a sense of 'settlers,' inhabitants of a frontier. The *Wilsaet* of the Wyle valley in Wiltshire and the *Tomsaet* of the Tame valley in the Mercian west Midlands would probably fit this criteria.[9] The *Tomsaeta* appear in the Tribal Hidage, as do the *Elmetsaetan*, among others. Elmet was the sub-Roman British kingdom in the south Yorkshire marshland that separated the Angles of York from the rest of their kin in central England. It was conquered in the early seventh century, when the last British king, Certic or Cerdic, was expelled.[10]

The circumstances accompanying the *saetan*, then, suggest that they represent the later phases of the Anglo-Saxon expansion, and although the term may have been in use in eastern England, it seems not to have been applied to the population groups that coalesced before the great movement westward into depopulated British lands following the Yellow Plague of the mid-sixth century. It may be that *wara* was an older term, one more connotative of an earlier age.[11] In southeast Hampshire, the inhabitants of the Meon valley were not known as the *Meonsaet*, but as the *Meonwara*.

Jolliffe suggested that the suffix -*wara* marked the folk basis of the Kentish 'lathe,' the unit of local administration that preceded the hundred in Kent.[12] In Domesday Book, Kent was divided into six such districts, which can be identified with ancient people-names formed by a topographic name and the element *wara*, i.e., Limenwara (Lymne R.), *Wiwara* (Wye R.), *Burgwara* (Canterbury), and a probable *Tenetwara* (Isle of Thanet).[13] The term *wara* may therefore mark a regional difference between Anglo-Saxon peoples, as it does not seem to have been used in Anglian areas, and is most frequent in districts traditionally considered to have been settled by Jutes—Kent, the Isle of Wight, and southern Hampshire. In the eighth century, Romney Marsh near the Sussex border was occupied by the

[9]   There is little evidence for organized Anglo-Saxon territories in western England before the late sixth century. See J.N.L. Myres, *The English Settlements*, The Oxford History of England, 1B (Oxford, 1969), pp. 162-172, 185.

[10]   *ASE* 33, 74, 80. Bede called the British king of Elmet 'Cerdic,' the same name as the founder of the West Saxon dynasty, which is the Celtic 'Ceretic.'

[11]   Clark Hall, *Anglo-Saxon Dictionary*, p. 397. *Wara* is genitive singular of *waru* 'shelter,' 'guard,' 'defence.' By extension, could it have had the connotation of 'military zone'?

[12]   Jolliffe, "Era of the Folk," p. 4; and "The Origin of the Hundred in Kent," in *Historical Essays in Honour of James Tait*, ed. J.G. Edwards et al. (Manchester, 1933), pp. 155-168.

[13]   For lathes, see H.M. Chadwick, *Studies on Anglo-Saxon Institutions* (Oxford, 1905), p. 249. For *wara* names, see *ASE* 284.

Merswara and was called *regio Merscwarariorum* in 811.[14] The use of *regio* with *wara* shows that in Kent, at least, the land occupied by a *wara* was considered a *regio* in the middle Saxon period.

Another term used to define territories was *ge*, related to the ancient German district, the *gau*. One instance of its use is Surrey, referred to as *Suthrige*, *regio sudergeona*, and *sudrig[e]na land*. This *ge* or *gau* was that part of the London-based Middle Saxons' territory lying south of the Thames. The different references reveal that the *gau* was identified with a 'land' and a *regio*. The other important examples are Ely, as *Elge*, the 'eel district,' and Eastry, an area in Kent east of Canterbury, recorded as *Eastorege*, *regio Eastrgena*. In the case of *ge*, the territorial term was primary, and the folk-name was a later development or alternative use.[15] The Tribal Hidage does have some names with what must be this territorial term. The *Unecung ga* was perhaps that part of Berkshire between Goring and the Thames loop. The other names, *Nox gaga* and *Oht gaga*, which clearly contain scribal errors, were probably on the Wessex borders, perhaps in Surrey, which does not appear on the list.[16]

Davies and Vierck's impressive study of the Tribal Hidage identified the units composing the list, and explained their political and social relationships.[17] By examining the post-Roman archaeology, geography, and toponymics of the Midlands, they established discrete 'settlement areas,' to which they were often able to assign one of the tribal groups. In comparing the Anglo-Saxon tribes with Continental equivalents, they found an Old Saxon *Sudergo*, the same formation as the Surrey *Suthrige*.

Davies and Vierck recognized that "*Gouwe/gewe* in Old High German, *ga/go* in Old Saxon, as *ga-awja* 'settlement area by water,'" was a primary aspect of Anglo-Saxon settlement.[18] And just as the past identification of early English hundreds did not succeed because of a too great dependency upon the jurisdictional boundaries of later date, so too were scholars frustrated in their attempts to identify early districts in

---

[14]   *ODEPN* 392.

[15]   *ODEPN* 158, 166, 458. The genitive plural use is thought to have been a derivative form corresponding to the Gothic *gauja*, meaning 'inhabitants of a *gawi* (district)'.

[16]   Davies and Vierck, "Tribal Hidage," pp. 230, 285. The most logical explanation is that these entries have been hopelessly miscopied, and that *Noxgaga* was the *north[ra]-ge*, and *Ohtgaga* was the *suth[ra]-ge*, of the Middle Saxons, simply divided by the Thames. Thus Surrey was not omitted from the Tribal Hidage. The preceding entry, *Wihtgara*, ought to be placed between north Hertfordshire of the *Hicca*, and Middlesex. Could it refer to St. Albans?

[17]   But for another interpretation of the location of the tribes, see Cyril Hart, "The Tribal Hidage," *Transactions of the Royal Historical Society* 5th ser. 21 (1971), 133-157.

[18]   Davies and Vierck, "Tribal Hidage," p. 287.

Germany by the compiling of "relevant place-names given in historical documents, supplemented by the mapping of ecclesiastical and legal divisions which were held to coincide more or less exactly with the old *gau*-boundaries."[19] But when place-names are plotted onto physical maps, patterns of 'dendritic distribution' appear. These reveal settlement areas that encompassed both sides of a river, but were usually closely confined to it by unfavourable geography. Vierck argued that this same pattern governed settlement areas and political units in early England, and could be closely correlated to Davies's work on the early group-names. It may well be that the riverine pattern of manors and vills of middle Hampshire is related to this German model of settlement areas. A broader study of Wessex may be able to define the geographic extent of such tribal entities, named and unnamed.

There is, however, one further Anglo-Saxon term for a territorial unit, which has particular relevance for Hampshire: *scir*, later 'shire,' a word with an accepted origin as a 'portion,' a 'cutting' of a larger entity.[20] It seems that the poetic form of *folk-scearu* appearing in *Beowulf* was recognized by Joliffe as the early use of 'folk-shire.'[21]

In Yorkshire, Granville Jones has convincingly reconstructed the boundaries of the late eleventh-century Burghshire (*Borgescire*), a wapentake of 300 hides.[22] Yet he assumed that its boundaries were identical to a presumed original Anglian *scir*, or even of a Celtic predecessor. There were several other northern 'shires' made up of a few hundreds, e.g., 'Wilpshire'

---

[19]   Ibid.

[20]   *Scir* is generally assumed to be related to *sciran, scieran* 'to cut, to shear,' but it could also have had an original sense of tribal identity in the adjectival form *scir* 'pure, unmixed, bright.' The verb *sciran* has both meanings: 'to make clear, declare, decree' and 'to clear from, get rid of.' See *ODEPN* 407; and Clark Hall, *Anglo-Saxon Dictionary*, p. 296.

[21]   Jolliffe, "Era of the Folk," p. 4. But Clark Hall, *Anglo-Saxon Dictionary*, p. 123; and *Beowulf, with the Finnesburg Fragment*, ed. C.L. Wrenn, rev. W.F. Bolton (1973), p. 100, n. 73, have this term referring to 'common pasture.' H.R. Loyn, *The Governance of Anglo-Saxon England 500-1087* (London, 1984), p. 34, translates it as "'folkshare' (presumably the ownership of allodial lands)." The term is problematic, and Loyn's translation is probably the strongest, but the context in the poem is important, in that Hrothgar did not control this folkshare. Could not a share of folkland convey with it folkrights, including participation in a local autonomous political assembly, which may have taken its name from such shared authority? There are dangers, however, in trying to read to much into one word, and that found once in a single poem. It is more likely that *scir*, as 'office, authority, district,' was simply the entity that would *sciran* ('to make clear, declare, decide, decree') to the general populous: Clark Hall, *Anglo-Saxon Dictionary*, p. 296.

[22]   G.R.J. Jones, "Multiple Estates and Early Settlement," in *MSCC* 15-40.

in Lancashire.[23] The few examples that can be found in the far north of England, their identification with wapentakes, and their possible pre-Anglian origin, however, are not necessarily relevant to early district terms for southern England, in particular the traditional usage in Wessex. On the other hand, there is good reason to believe that the units of 300 or so hides, which went by the name *scir* in Yorkshire and Cornwall, do represent the application of an Anglo-Saxon term to originally Celtic territorial divisions.[24] Use of this term certainly had taken place by the late ninth century, when King Alfred's will mentioned Triggshire in Cornwall, and it probably dates back to the conquest of these lands at the beginning of the century.[25]

At the other end of the island, early territories in Scotland have been examined in depth by G.W.S Barrow, who came to similar conclusions. Following Jolliffe's suggestion that the key to tracing early institutions may lie in the soke jurisdiction, Barrow first found evidence in England to associate the Saxon thegn with the Domesday 'sokeman,' concluding that they were "pretty much the same animal ... a class of ministerial freemen."[26] He located examples of soke districts that he identified as ancient territories, the *regiones* of Bede: Tottenhamshire in Middlesex, Walthamshire in Essex, and Hallamshire (Sheffield) and Howdenshire. In Northumbria, Barrow looked for such *scirs* and thanes, employing there and beyond the Firth the technique of locating royal vills with an ancient church centre, indicated by the toponymic *eccles*, *kirk*, or *passelec*. Barrow noted that in a few examples, the sokes retain the old *scir* size, but by Domesday most were obscured by the movement of their *caput* or church. He saw evidence of shires and thanedoms as Anglian influence, with the thegn as a royal agent administering the *feorm*, but clearly earlier than the late ninth-century date that Loyn attributed to the appearance of the thegn.[27] Barrow went on to suggest that the Anglian names were simply applied for administrative convenience to older, Celtic territories, then perhaps coming under more direct royal control, a theme carried further in Driscoll's work

[23] *ODEPN* 521.

[24] O.S. Anderson, *The English Hundred Names: The South-Eastern Counties* (Lund, 1941), p. 151. Anderson notes the Cornish districts of Triggshire, Wevelshire, *Piderscire*, and *Poudescire*.

[25] For Alfred's will, see *Liber de Hyda*, 62 ff., '... on Truconscire ... .'

[26] G.W.S. Barrow, *The Kingdom of the Scots: Government, Church and Society from the Eleventh to the Fourteenth Century* (London, 1975), pp. 17, 27.

[27] Ibid., p. 64.

on Pictland.[28] Other studies have claimed to identify ancient districts in the baronies of Copeland and Gilsland in Cumberland (Cumbria), "on a par with shires in other northern counties."[29]

In the Midlands, Glenn Foard undertook a comprehensive use of medieval soke boundaries to reconstruct the Anglo-Saxon administrative districts of Northamptonshire. Admitting that the hundred pattern in the eastern two-thirds of the county had been imposed after the ninth-century reconquest of the Danelaw, Foard nevertheless hoped to locate the earlier administrative districts, assuming with Loyn that the Danish conquest had little effect on local boundaries. Using both sokes and rural deaneries as the basis for defining territorial associations, Foard tried to juxtapose the jurisdictional elements with the hundred framework. He was able to identify 'central places' rather than the districts they served, and made every effort to seek the origin of those central places—and their function—in a late Roman villa-based system with a seigneurial basis. Foard more convincingly demonstrated that this technique can identify tribal and provincial groupings, particularly those of the Tribal Hidage.[30]

The Shire System

The local *scir* that marked the Anglo-Saxon acceptance and use of pre-existing territories was fundamentally different from the late Saxon shires. The 'shiring' of England took place in the early tenth century, when Edward the Elder imposed a new administrative system upon the territories

[28]   Barrow (ibid., pp. 65-68) questions what terms were used in Scotland before thane and shire, and he suggests that, just as the mair (*marus*) can be identified with 'thane,' a cognate of the Old Irish *cathir* ('city' or 'monastery') or Primitive Welsh *caer* ('fortified centre') might be the element of such 'shire' place-names as Cathermothel and Catherlauenache (Carlownie). It is interesting to note that one of the settlements at Chalton, Catherington, has the *caer* element, and might therefore refer to one of Barrow's district centres, transposed from Scotland to a residual Celtic population in southeast Hampshire. For Pictland, see Stephen T. Driscoll, "Power and Authority in Early Historic Scotland: Pictish Symbol Stones and Other Documents," in *State and Society: the Emergence and Development of Social Hierarchy and Political Centralization*, ed. J. Gledhill, B. Bender, and M.T. Larsen (London, 1988), pp. 215-234.

[29]   See A.J.L. Winchester, "The Medieval Vill in the Western Lake District: Some Problems of Definition," *Transactions of the Cumberland and Westmoreland Antiquarian and Archaeological Society*, New Series 78 (1978), 55-69; and Rachel Newman, "Problems of Rural Settlement in Northern Cumbria," in M.L. Faull, *Studies in Anglo-Saxon Settlement* (Oxford, 1984), pp. 155-176.

[30]   Glenn Foard, "The Administrative Organization of Northamptonshire in the Saxon Period," *Anglo-Saxon Studies in Archaeology and History* 4 (1985), 185-222.

of the former Mercian kingdom.[31] Alfred had spent twenty years organizing and directing a defence of Wessex that included the systematic construction of strategic population centers, *burhs*, and the first area of territorial administrative reorganization was probably Wessex. Somerset, Dorset, and Devonshire represent the incorporation of earlier conquered districts, but Berkshire, Wiltshire and Hampshire comprised the Wessex heartland. The Anglo-Saxon Chronicle referred to Berkshire first in 860 (*Bearrocsir*), Hampshire first in 755 (*Hamtunscir*, from *Hamtun*, Southampton), and Wiltshire in 870 (*Wiltunscir*, but *Wilsaetan* in 800 and 878).[32]

The positive evidence of the Anglo-Saxon Chronicle has led to the belief, expressed by Stenton, that "Wessex was apparently divided into shires before the end of the eighth century."[33] The specifics of the 755 entry, however, do not necessarily support this conclusion. In that year, King Sigeberht was deposed by the Wessex *witan*, and Cynewulf took the throne. Sigeberht was given *Hamtunscir*, which he held until he murdered his last faithful ealdorman, and was driven out into the Weald, where a herdsman killed him at the stream at Privett (*Pryfetesflodan*) on the watershed east of the Tichborne valley.[34] The lengthy narrative of this entry is highly unusual, as is the reference to this ex-royal territory—an eighth-century Elba. A full century passed before the appearance of another shire in the records, and one must seriously question the assumption that the *scir* in 755 was necessarily identical to the shires of the late ninth century.[35] Excluding this entry, all three Wessex shires first appear in the same short period 860-870. Under their respective ealdormen, the levies of Hampshire and Berkshire fought Viking hosts in 860, and Ethelred, Bishop of Wiltshire, was elected Archbishop of Canterbury in 869 (*s.a.* 870). Similarly, the Devon levies fought the Vikings in 851 (*s.a.* 850), when the term used was *Defenascir*, which was based upon *Defnas* the 'men of Devon,' who appeared in the Chronicle in 823, when they fought the Britons and conquered Cornwall.[36] In 837 and 845, the *Dornsaete* appeared, while *Dornsaeteschire* was not recorded until the 940s.

---

[31] See *ASE* 335-338.

[32] Asser says *Berrocscire* was named after *Berroc Silva*, a forest name that linguistic scholars believe to originate in a hill, *Bearruc* of British origin (*barro* = summit): *ODEPN* 39; W.H. Stevenson, *Asser's Life of King Alfred*, (Oxford, 1904), p. 1.

[33] *ASE* 293.

[34] *ASC s.a.* 755.

[35] David Hinton considered this entity to have been artificially created, and not one of the original territories, "Hampshire's Anglo-Saxon Origins," in *The Archaeology of Hampshire*, ed. S.J. Shennan and R.T Schadla-Hall (Oxford, 1981), pp. 56-65; 63.

[36] See *ODEPN* 46, 47, 148, 430.

The evidence, such as it is, suggests that ca. 850 the term 'shire' was applied to major components of the West Saxon kingdom, and the standard Wessex shires appeared within a singularly brief period. The 'shiring' of Wessex occurring at this time was therefore related not to Egbert's short-lived expansion of Wessex to dominate all England south of the Humber in 829, but rather to the circumstances following his death in 839. Then, his son Ethelwulf succeeded to Wessex and his son Athelstan (who died a few years later) to Kent, Surrey, and Sussex. After major battles every other year throughout his reign, Ethelwulf journeyed to Rome in 855, marrying the daughter of Charles the Bald on his return. The appearance of *Defnascir* in 851 preceded any 'shiring' that might have taken place after his return in 858. A 'shire system' of some form is therefore likely to have been in place ca. 850, before Ethelwulf's departure for Rome, and would not have been imitative of other administrative systems he was exposed to on his travels. On the contrary, the new 'shire' was probably a direct response to Viking raids—a division of the kingdom into units responsible for raising the local levies and conducting regional defensive operations. These new shires of the ninth century replaced earlier West Saxon territories, as the tenth-century English shires replaced the former sub-kingdoms and tribal units of Mercia.

The Origin of Hampshire

The reference to *Hamtunscir* in the mid-eighth century has no apparent relationship to the ninth-century Wessex shires. An alternative identification is the *scir* we have seen in Northumbrian and West Country examples, in particular the Cornish *scir* recorded in the ninth century, a small territory later divided into three hundreds. If the pre-Viking *Hamtunscir* was similar to the Cornish 'Triggshire,' what part of later Hampshire did it occupy? Two things may be deduced: 1) *Hamptunscir* was based upon, and included *Hamtun, Hamwi[c]h* (later Southampton); and 2) it probably did not include Sigeberht's refuge at Privett, which was considered part of the vast Weald forested area stretching from eastern Hampshire to southern Kent. Privett, the '-stead' place-names north of it, and Wield parish itself, near Candover, all mark the western end of the Weald. Sigeberht's territory may not have included the Meon valley, because no reference was made to its accepted eighth-century identification, the tribal name *Meanwara*.[37] The New Forest was still known in the early eleventh century as *Ytene*, which Stenton has shown to be a genitive plural of a late Saxon *Yte*, identical to the *Iutae*

---

[37]   *HE* 4.13.

of Bede.[38] The Isle of Wight and the south shore of Hampshire were both considered Jutish territory. If Sigeberht had retained them, mention would have been made of their folk name, as was customary in the pre-Viking period. He did not, therefore, become a 'king of the Jutes.' Similarly, it is highly unlikely that Sigeberht held onto Winchester, the ancient royal city, the episcopal see of the West Saxons, and the locale of highest status in Wessex.

By the process of elimination, the *Hamtunscir* of 755 was most likely restricted to the area surrounding Southampton at the mouth of the Itchen. Following a different line of research, Patrick Hase proposed just such an Anglo-Saxon territory. He convincingly identified the later manors of North and South Stoneham, and the jurisdiction of Mansbridge Hundred, with the extent of the ancient *parochia* of St. Mary's, which was the mother church of the eighth-century commercial centre of *Hamwic* or *Hamtun*.[39] The predecessor of late Saxon and medieval Southampton nearby, Hamwic was the major trading centre on the south coast, perhaps monopolizing commerce between central southern England and the Seine river at Rouen. Thus, while the limited geographic territory proposed here for the *Hamtunscir* of Sigeberht's 'rump' kingdom might first appear to have been a confined, Elba-like territory, it actually contained the wealthiest part of the kingdom of Wessex—its port of *Hamwic*—certainly an acceptable reward for abdication.[40]

The origin of the district of *Hamtunscir*, like the Cornish *scirs*, may have been different from the origin of a *saet* or a *wara*. Perhaps the Cornish *scirs* were units controlled by the Crown by right of conquest and treated differently than the rest of Wessex. Could the former Jutish territory at the mouth of the Itchen be an earlier example? Alternatively, one may hypothesize that the unique development of the entrepot of Hamwic would not have been ignored by the West Saxon kings, and it is in just such special circumstances as these that one would expect to see the introduction of new terminology, or the adaptation of an existing vocabulary to fit the new conditions.

It may be that the term *scir* was gaining popularity in the eighth and ninth centuries as an expression of territorial kingship, while the *maegth, wara,* and *saete* were falling out of administrative use, as less appropriate to changing concepts of political power and royal authority. Originally

[38]   See *ASE* 23.
[39]   P.H. Hase, "The Development of the Parish Church in Hampshire, particularly in the Eleventh and Twelfth Century" (Ph.D. Thesis, Cambridge University, 1975), 150 ff.
[40]   David Hinton presents a good overview of the mid-Saxon emporium of Hamwic, in *Alfred's Kingdom: Wessex and the South 800-1500* (London, 1977), pp. 3-8.

applied to small divisions of a few hundred hides, the *scir* would later be adapted to the needs of the monarch, first of the West Saxons, then of the English. Jollife reasoned that the antiquity of the poetical form *folk-scearu* implied an ancient Anglo-Saxon 'folk-shire.' If this were true, then *scir* had its origin in a tribal or ethnic concept, only becoming an administrative term after the 'folk' was rendered obsolete by the growth of monarchy.

Summary of Territorial Definitions

This brief review of the terminology used by Anglo-Saxons to identify political, administrative, or tribal units has revealed a multiplicity of available forms. Some, perhaps most, may have been interchangeable. A *regio* could be a *ge* (gau), but it could also bear a purely folk name; *saete* and *ware* may have been identical. *Wara* districts lay adjacent to *scir* districts; on the Hampshire south coast were the Meon valley inhabitants (*Meanware*) to the east, the land around Southampton at the mouth of the Itchen (*Hamtunscir*) in the centre, and the 'New Forest' land of the Jutes (*Ytene*) to the west.

The general tribal groups of Anglo-Saxons often distinguished themselves by direction (e.g., East Anglians, Middle Saxons), and within these major groupings were more specific divisions, sometimes very broad, like Norfolk and Suffolk, but usually on a smaller scale, e.g., the five rapes of Sussex or the six lathes of Kent.[41] It was this level of territorial division that was called a *ge*, a *wara*, or a *saet*, even though the names of specific locales sometimes seem to have been later extended to larger territories (e.g., Surrey, Dorset). There was certainly variation in the size of these territorial units; terminology may have had more to do with political status than with size. The *scir* probably originated as a folk-group term, but its meaning and use underwent a series of evolutionary changes in the Anglo-Saxon period. The *scir* entered recorded history in the eighth century as a small territorial unit, perhaps even with the concept of a great estate, or personal domain, but in the mid-ninth century the term was applied to large divisions of the kingdom set up as military zones, by which Ethelwulf attempted, with some success, to defend Wessex. That the kingdom survived Viking attacks long enough for Alfred to refurbish its defences, may be due more to the strength of a pre-existing 'shire system' than has been hitherto recognized.

---

[41]   This is not to suggest that the lathes and rapes of Domesday were intact ancient territories. Like the Hampshire archaic hundreds, they were much altered in geographic extent and hidage assessment. See Dennis Hazelgrove, "The Domesday Record of Sussex," in *The South Saxons*, ed. Peter Brandon (Chichester, 1978), pp. 190-220.

EARLY SAXON TERRITORIAL UNITS

No specific Anglo-Saxon territorial and tribal terms can definitely be applied to the districts of central Hampshire. The Winchester West Saxons were known as the *Gewisse*, but otherwise there are no known tribal names. *Gewisse* was a term similar to many known from the Tribal Hidage and elsewhere, e.g., the kingdom of the *Diere*, part of Northumbria; or the kingdom of the *Hwicce* in Gloucestershire, Warwickshire, and Worcestershire.[42] Within the kingdom of the *Gewisse*, the districts probably had a variety of nomenclatures. Some would have been considered valley folk, like the *Meanware* of the Meon valley of south Hampshire, or the *Wilsaet* of the Wiley valley in Wiltshire. Others may have had, or later developed, an identity around a specific settlement site, taking a name like *Hamtunscir*.[43] The preponderance of river and valley names used for the *capita* of archaic hundreds in middle Hampshire suggests that like Meon, the valley names were commonly the identifying part of the territory/folk name, with *saet, wara,* or *scir* as the second element. Perhaps those archaic hundreds that did not bear a valley name had a different group name—a locational name similar to the *sweord ora* ('Sword Bank') of the Tribal Hidage, or an '-*ing*' name like the Sonning of eastern Berkshire.

A potentially important observation on the place-names of Hampshire is the toponymic difference between north-central Hampshire and the lands lying beyond the Test and Itchen valleys (see Appendix B). The

---

[42] On the meaning of *Gewisse*, see T.W. Shore, *Origin of the Anglo-Saxon Race* (London, 1906), pp. 210-214. Stevenson, *English Historical Review* 14 (1899) proposed that it was related to Gothic *ga-wiss* 'junction,' or *gewiss* 'assured, certain.' Joseph Bosworth, *Anglo-Saxon Dictionary* (Oxford, 1898), has these references, but also gives *gewissend* 'ruler, preceptor, rector.' Clark Hall also has *wisse*, as a pret. sing. of *witan*, 'to guard, to keep': *Anglo-Saxon Dictionary*, p. 413. In this case, a meaning of 'guardians' might refer to an original role as fifth-century troops. A meaning of 'confederates, allies' is thought to represent the disparate elements of Hampshire's Germanic population, while a meaning closer to 'rulers' might indicate their dominant position over a Celtic servile population. On the other hand, the view of sub-Roman Hampshire presented by Martin Biddle would suggest a new meaning to 'confederates'—a political union of Roman, Celtic, and Germanic elements: "Hampshire and the Origin of Wessex," in *Problems in Economic and Social Archaeology*, ed. G. Sieveking et al. (London, 1976), pp. 323-341.

[43] It may be that this was a special case, because in the ancient districts of southern England, the towns are generally named from the tribal unit, with the surviving Roman towns being the exception, e.g., Winchester, Exeter, Cirencester.

watershed to the north and east marks a linguistic boundary, whereby certain toponyms common to one area appear rarely or not at all in others, e.g., 'stead,' '-ing.' This linguistic anomaly probably reflects tribal origins of the Germanic occupants of middle Hampshire that were different from those of the settlers to the north, and even those to the south as well. This ethnic boundary fits the topographical model of early medieval territorial units in Hampshire, and corresponds well with the presumed territory of the *Gewisse*, based upon Winchester and defined roughly by the recorded tribal groups of the Meon and Avon/Wiley valleys.

The variously named, early Anglo-Saxon folk units, however, are much larger than the archaic hundreds, which appear to have been the basic administrative units of the early West Saxon kingdom. Davies and Vierck's detailed study of the Tribal Hidage may bear upon this point. One of their 'settlement area' types is similar to that suggested here for the Hampshire valley-units. As one of its examples, "a small zone clearly defined by surrounding forest around the River Ivel in Bedforshire ... belonged to the *Gifla*."[44] The *Gifla* was recorded at 300 hides, the smallest size unit in the Tribal Hidage. The hidage of this territory is notably similar to those of the early lathes of Kent and rapes of Sussex, and even the *scirs* of Cornwall and Yorkshire.[45]

How do these figures compare with the units proposed for central Hampshire? To obtain a more workable regional scale, let us first extend the assigned hidage figures to other archaic hundreds, reconstructed in Appendix D. Gauging comparable size and geography ought to produce rough estimates of hidage (see figure 5.3). Working southward down the Test valley tributaries, the Hurstbourne valley group, from its large size, was at least 200 hides, the same assessment for the Andover catchment area south of it. The Wallop valley was probably 100 hides, and the same can be assigned to those districts centred at Mottesfont, Wellow, and Romsey. *Hamtunscir* was perhaps 200 hides, although its economic value was growing throughout the pre-Viking period. The Winchester archaic hundred of the middle Itchen was probably 200 hides as well.[46] Bishops Waltham in the wooded, marshy Hamble valley perhaps commanded only 50 hides,

[44]   Davies and Vierck, "Tribal Hidage," p. 279. But note the Tribal Hidage unit comprising a combined Lindesfarne and Hatfield, an instance of an administrative unit combining two tribal or settlement districts.

[45]   The 300-hide unit may have been a natural one for a society employing both the decimal and the duodecimal counting systems. 300 is readily divisible by 2, 3, 4, 5, and 6. Such a territory could be evenly divided into 10 units of 30 hides or 12 units of 25 hides.

[46]   The combination of Winchester and Southampton districts would make a very interesting lower Itchen 300 hide unit, but each may be too large for an individual assessment of 150 hides.

while the Tichfield-Farnham block was another possible 200-hide unit. The rest of the Meon valley groups may not have been highly valued: Droxford at 100 hides, Meonstoke at 50 hides, and East Meon at 100 hides.

The total estimated Test valley catchment therefore comes to 1350 hides, that of the Itchen 750 hides, and the Meon-Hamble valleys at 500 hides. The combined total is 2600 hides. North Hampshire might add a further 1000 hides, and southeast and southwest Hampshire about 700 each. For all mainland Hampshire, then, the rough total comes to 5000 hides.[47]

Territories comparable to this Hampshire estimate are Bede's report of the Isle of Wight with 1200 hides, and the Tribal Hidage assessment of Sussex and Essex with 7000 hides each, and Kent with 15,000 hides.[48] The several *saet* names in the Tribal Hidage vary in size between the *Wrocen saetna* with 7000 hides, the *Chiltern saetna* with 4000, the *Pecsaetan* with 1200, and the *Elmed saetna* and the *Aro saetna* with 600 each.

The estimates for the ancient hidage of Hampshire can be compared to the Domesday figures collated in H.C. Darby's *Domesday Geography*.[49] Sussex has probably the most reliable hidage, because it bore the same eighth-century figure (7000) in both the Tribal Hidage and in Bede's *Historia*.[50] The estimated eighth-century Hampshire figure at 5000, plus 1200 of Bede's Isle of Wight, is 88.5% of the recorded Sussex 7000 hides. How does this compare to the Domesday Book figures? Hampshire in 1066 (including the Isle of Wight) was given at 2860 hides. According to William's surveyors Sussex had only 3193 hides in 1066. The 2860 hides for mainland Hampshire comes to 89.5% of the Sussex total. Assuming a fairly standard reduction of hidage over the three centuries, this remarkable correspondence suggests that the hidage estimates projected from the middle Hampshire valley groups to the rest of the shire, must be substantially correct.

But Hampshire itself was a later creation, probably formed in the mid-ninth century. It is useful here only for comparison, because its hidage

---

[47]   A likely underestimation of southwest Hampshire ought to be balanced by the inclusion of manors that lay over the Wiltshire border in the side valleys of the Test.

[48]   If the *Wihtgar* listed in the Tribal Hidage was an intended reference to the Isle of Wight, was its hidage set at 600 hides, rather than the 1200 that Bede recorded for it, because its lordship was split between Mercia and Wessex? Or as a Mercian ally, had it received 'beneficial hidation'? If the latter were true, then it puts in doubt the reliability of the other hidage figures upon which Davies and Vierck based their identifications.

[49]   The following Domesday figures are taken from the table in H.C. Darby and E.M.J. Campbell, eds., *The Domesday Geography of South-East England* (Cambridge, 1962), p. 618.

[50]   *HE* 4.13.

totals include that for the middle Hampshire region. How do the hidage groupings of the archaic hundreds compare to actual early political units, best defined by the folk groups of the Tribal Hidage? Two points appear from Davies and Vierck's work. First, the smaller groups were assessed at multiples of 300 hides; they found a "four-fold variation...; the multiples of 300 extend to 1200 hides."[51] Davies concluded that the Tribal Hidage concerned the assessment of early Saxon England in a political structure comprising both the few large tribes, the kingdoms, as well as a great many "local social groupings, independently assessable."[52] Secondly, the "settlement areas" that Vierck identified for the local groups are based upon geophysical considerations.[53] These areas roughly corresponded to river valleys, but they were not necessarily confined to them, nor were the larger valleys, at least, occupied exclusively by one folk group. It is consequently hard to apply Vierck's outline of 'settlement areas' to a 'Micheldever model' of Hampshire valley units.

Most of the terrain in central England covered by the Tribal Hidage is dissimilar to that of middle Hampshire, but the Cotswolds between the upper Thames and Severn valleys might be the most comparable, with broad ridges scored by many secondary valleys. This area was part of the kingdom of the *Hwicce*, for which no subdivision is known.[54] In the Thames basin between the Cotswolds and the Chiltern hills northwest of London, Vierck found three other settlement areas separated from one another by "long and narrow belts of forest." The settlements occupied both banks of the Thames, and here he identified the locations of the *Unicung ga* (Oxford and north Berkshire), the *Hendrica* (the middle Thames and east Berkshire), and the *Wixna* (the Thames west of London).[55]

The conclusions of Davies and Vierck, then, tacitly accept the unifying effects of rivers and valleys, but stress the segregating effect of thickly wooded areas, which generally had heavy clay soils. The latter were

---

[51]   Davies and Vierck, "Tribal Hidage," pp. 236, 239; Chadwick, *Institutions*, pp. 241-244, 263-268.

[52]   Davies and Vierck, "Tribal Hidage," p. 240.

[53]   Ibid., pp. 242-248. The techniques used were those developed primarily by Walter Jankuhn.

[54]   See Della Hooke, *The Anglo-Saxon Landscape: The Kingdom of the Hwicce* (Manchester, 1985). Of course the Hwicce controlled several pre-Saxon *civitates*, which probably retained a certain degree of identity, but the external sources (Bede, Tribal Hidage) report no Anglo-Saxon sub-groups.

[55]   Davies and Vierck, pp. 276-279. These tribal units are represented in figure 8, as areas R, V, and W. However, a *Weckling-ga* around St. Albans and Watling Street, and the *Wissa* tribe of Cambridgeshire, were considered by Cyril Hart to be names distorted by copyist errors: "The Tribal Hidage," pp. 143-144, 151.

avoided by the early Anglo-Saxons, and thus formed natural divisions between settlement areas. This observation has direct relevance for the ancient territorial divisions of Hampshire. The most basic geographic divisions for Hampshire are topographically determined catchment zones, but there are other kinds of geographic divisions. Most important for Vierck was the pedological division of soils, the major determinant of the limits to prehistoric and post-Roman forest clearance. Among the ancient wooded districts of Hampshire was that separating the Thames basin from the Test and Itchen catchment areas, and to the east, the Weald of Kent and Sussex extended up to the Meon, Tichborne, and Alresford valleys. It is in southern Hampshire, however, that woodland and soil differences most strongly affected ancient territorial units and must be added to purely topographic features. Here, a thickly forested belt crossed east-west, coinciding with the Tertiary formation of heavy clays and sands that separated the central Hampshire chalklands from the plateau gravel of the Hampshire coastal area.[56] This belt would represent one of Vierck's pedological divisions between settlement areas, and the manorial groupings can be divided along a line following the general course of this geophysical division: the southern border of the archaic hundreds based on East Meon, Meon Stoke, Winchester, Somborne, and Wallop, shown on figure 5.1.[57] This geographic line marks a tribal division; the woodland zone to the south was a frontier separating the Saxon-held lands from coastal areas settled by the Jutes. Furthermore, in southeast Hampshire, the area of the Portsdown chalk upland should mark another Saxon territory, with centers at Portchester and Havant. It was probably formed by a group related to the South Saxons.[58]

The remaining area of central Hampshire can be broken down even further. Between the *Meanware* of the Meon valley and the *Wilsaet* occupying the Wily/Avon region of Wiltshire, was a large area of the Test and Itchen valleys that by the process of elimination must have been the territory of the *Gewisse*. This little-known kingdom whose dynasty supplied members of the West Saxon monarchy doubtless had its royal centre at

[56] See *Domesday Geography of South-East England*, ed. Darby and Campbell, p. 292, fig. 90.

[57] Compare with the lines separating the 'Hampshire Downs' from the 'Hampshire Basin': ibid., p. 358, fig. 103.

[58] Barry Cunliffe has proposed an early Saxon 'federate' territory for the Meon-Porchester district, but this area is not well defined as a geographic unit. See Martin Welsh, "Early Anglo-Saxon Sussex: From *Civitas* to Shire," in *The South Saxons*, ed. Peter Brandon (Chichester, 1978), pp. 13-35, 27. David Hinton would have the Portchester area owing allegiance to the kings of Sussex until the conquest of the entire region by Caedwalla in the late 600s ("Hampshire's Anglo-Saxon Origins," in *The Archaeology of Hampshire*, ed. S.J. Shennan and R.T. Schadla-Hall [Winchester, 1981], pp. 56-65).

Winchester, a Roman cantonial capital, and more importantly the only Roman city within the Test-Itchen chalkland.[59]

How do these groupings compare to those of the Tribal Hidage? We have seen that the upper Meon valley had an estimated 150 hides in the chalk upland; with Droxford further down the Meon and Waltham on the neighbouring Hamble, the total comes to 300 hides. This figure is the size of the most elementary political unit in the Tribal Hidage. Estimates for the Itchen catchment area from Winchester north come to 550 hides, and those for the Test chalkland are 1050, totalling 1600. If the archaic hundreds further downstream were within the territory controlled by the *Gewisse*, the addition of the Romsey and Mottesfont groups brings the total estimate to 1800, and with *Hamwic*, it might be an even 2000 hides.

With the *Meanware* having an estimated 600 hides, and the *Gewisse* having 1800, or perhaps 2000, the two tribal groups of central Hampshire compare favourably with those of the Tribal Hidage.[60] Of the twenty-five groups that were not kingdoms of the Heptarchy, four had 300 hides, six had 600, two had 900, and five had 1200. Above this level, there was no group until the 3500 and 4000 hides of the *Hendrica* and the *Chilternsaetna*, respectively. The Meon valley was equivalent to one of the standard sized groupings that comprised the Mercian hegemony. The *Gewisse* has no comparable unit in the Tribal Hidage, but it does occupy a significantly empty echelon in the hierarchy of political units. It could represent a multiple of 300, at 1800 hides, and therefore correspond to one-half the size of the *Hendrica*, or at 2000 hides, it would be exactly one-half the amount of the *Chilternsaetna*.

Like the earlier comparison based on the Domesday assessments, this crude comparison is one of the few available methods of assessing the value of the estimated hidage figures for the middle Hampshire archaic hundreds. Such as they are, the results are again positive. Yet in one respect this region does display a significant difference to that surveyed by the Tribal Hidage. Contrary to what may have been common in the Midlands, the *Gewisse* of Hampshire probably did not divide up their territory into 300 hide blocks. First, the configurations of the archaic hundreds do not easily permit such 'triplings.' Although Romsey, Mottesfont, and Wellow could possibly have been triple-hundreds, the other units cannot be juggled to fit credibly into a coherent pattern. Further, a 300-hide unit has been claimed for the Kentish 'lathe,' the Northumbrian and Cornish 'shire,' and the small folk groups of the Anglian Midlands. There is no evidence that such a unit

---

[59]   For conflicting views of post-Roman Hampshire, see Biddle, "Hampshire and the Origin of Wessex"; and Hinton, "Hampshire's Anglo-Saxon Origins."
[60]   See Davies and Vierck, 'Tribal Hidage,' p. 235, fig. 3.

was ever an integral part of the political and administrative structure of the West Saxon kingdom. The origin of the hundred in Wessex, in fact, suggests the reverse. The tradition here, it seems, was for tribute, justice, and military service to be administered by the small valley districts. As hundreds, half-hundreds, and double-hundreds, they represent a type of small-scale 'settlement area' proposed by Vierck.

There does not appear to have been any special nomenclature for the archaic hundreds. A sub-Roman unit may have been referred to as the *ager* of Merovingian and early Carolingian Francia.[61] But if hundreds, as the Germans' *centeni* of Tacitus, had entered Britain with the Anglo-Saxons, it is surprising that they existed for five hundred years with no reference to the term.[62] The physical definition of the archaic hundreds gave them a valley, stream-based identity: thus, stream name = valley name = central place (royal vill) name = archaic hundred name. Perhaps the archaic hundreds were too small to receive one of the typical folk suffixes—*saet, wara, ge*, or even *scir*. For the present, it is fruitless to speculate upon what specific group-name element may have been given to a district that Jolliffe might have called a 'folk-shire.' In lieu of a definite appellation, and to distinguish it from other early medieval *scirs*, this term may be suitable for identification purposes. Yet the very absence of folk-suffixes and group-names implies a general use of valley names for Hampshire territorial units. Because of this, and because these units were naturally based small scale 'settlement areas,' the archaic hundred system of Hampshire should be viewed as standardized administrative units applied to the pre-existing local 'folk-shires' of the *Gewisse*. The resulting half-hundreds and double hundreds found in middle Hampshire do not obscure the fact that these were multiples of what was considered the norm, and perhaps the goal of the assessment procedure: the 100-hide territorial unit. This was the origin of the hundred in England.

SUMMARY OF TERRITORIAL DEVELOPMENT

The earliest tangible medieval political unit in middle Hampshire is the *Gewisse*, the West Saxon tribe that controlled the Itchen and Test river valleys. We have seen that the same area is defined by place-name

---

[61] See Françoise Bange, "*L'Ager* et *La Villa*: Structures du paysage et du peuplement dans la région mâconnaise à la fin du Haut Moyen Age (IXe-XIe siècles)," *Annales* 39 (1984), 529-569.

[62] W. Stubbs (ed.), *Select Charters and Other Illustrations of English Constitutional History*, ninth ed. (Oxford, 1913), p. 67.

terminology; a different toponymic usage appears beyond the watersheds of the middle Hampshire basin. The population grouped itself into what may be termed 'folk-shires,' settlement areas based upon the physiography of river valley catchment areas. Perhaps because the introduction of Christianity gave the monarchy access to more sophisticated accounting and recording techniques, the rise of royal authority in the seventh century was closely related to the development of royal administration. As a means of assessing regular tribute, the kings of Wessex assigned to the valley folk-shires standard assessments of theoretical households, at 100 hides, occasionally halves or doubles of 100 hides. Possibly harking back to the prehistoric Germanic *centeni* hundreds recorded by Tacitus, these 'archaic hundreds' were the origin of the hundred districts of later English local government.

In the seventh century, the kingdoms of southeast England underwent significant territorial changes, primarily because of the competing expansions of Mercia and Wessex. In the second half of the seventh century Wessex pushed into Dorset and Somerset; in the next century, Devon was subdued. Before then, the great forest of Selwood on the border between Wiltshire and Somerset had marked the western frontier of Wessex, the diocese west of the forest later referred to as 'Selwoodshire.'[63]   At the same time, however, Mercia steadily expanded, first to the Thames, occupying Dorchester in the 640s, then occupying Berkshire.[64] In the late seventh century, Wulfhere of Mercia even conquered the Isle of Wight and southern parts of Hampshire, including the *provincia Meanuarorum*.

In 685, a new dynasty came to power in Wessex, and with it a shift in national interest. A prince of the royal house of the *Gewisse*, Caedwalla focused his attention away from the West Saxons' Thames toward the *Gewisse*'s homeland around Winchester, reversing Wessex's losses in southeast England. Defeating the king of Sussex, he may have taken from him those lands now forming southeast Hampshire. He eradicated the Jutish royal dynasty of the Isle of Wight and replaced the population there with settlers from the mainland. The island and probably the other Jutish lands of south Hampshire were then directly governed by Caedwalla and his lieutenants. The archaic hundred system might therefore be attributed to the dynamic personality of Caedwalla, but it is more likely a product of the lengthy and important reign of his successor, Ine (689-726). Stenton found the events of his reign 'remarkably obscure,' but considered him one of the earliest statesmen of Anglo-Saxon history, who created, or supported, the

---

[63]   *ASE* 65.
[64]   *ASE* 63 ff.

church organization in Wessex, founding a new see for the western provinces and presiding over its earliest recorded synods.[65] The law code bearing his name was the first for Wessex, and he is the one ruler of the West Saxons who would be expected to create the organized system of hundred-hide units. The same period saw the spreading out of missionary 'minsters' from the original Christian royal foundation of the 'Old Minster' at Winchester, to each of the valley units, which became spiritual jurisdictions as the early medieval *parochiae*.

By the 730's, however, resurgent Mercian power wrested Somerset, Berkshire, and Surrey from West Saxon control. The new frontier became the artificial Hampshire-Berkshire border—running in a fairly straight line for the breadth of Hampshire and bisecting the *territorium*, if not the walls, of the abandoned Roman city of Silchester. This border cut across earlier *parochiae*, permanently altering them. The extreme north of Hampshire was, in fact, one of the areas where Patrick Hase found it impossible to reconstruct the arrangement of mother churches and their *parochiae*.[66] The creation of the Hampshire-Berkshire border does not imply that the lands on either side of it simultaneously became 'shires.' In fact the Mercian king Ethelbald referred to the Kennet-Lodden section of the Thames south bank, not as Berkshire but as the *provincia* of the Sunnings adjacent to the Surrey province. The *Hamtunscir* given to a deposed Wessex king in 755 cannot be assumed to be the later medieval shire; it probably comprised only the vicinity of Southampton.

The formal 'shiring' of Wessex took place in the mid-ninth century. It was probably Ethelwulf who engineered this administrative reorganization to establish regional defence forces against Viking raids. At this time Hampshire came into being, with the Mercian border dividing it from Berkshire, and a new boundary generally following the Avon-Test watershed separating Hampshire from Wiltshire. The north-south line of the Wiltshire border cut across several valley units of Test tributaries, and like the Bershire border, seems not to have incorporated the boundaries of earlier territorial units. Yet interestingly enough, where the boundary ran east-west across the lower Avon valley, it crossed the river near the place-name Charford. This has been identified with a reference in the Anglo-Saxon Chronicle to a sixth-century battle at *Cerdicesford*, which is thought to represent a stage in the conquest of sub-Roman territories by the early

---

[65]   *ASE* 71, 72.
[66]   Hase, "Parish in Hampshire," p. 309. He found difficulties in determining the *parochiae* for Crondall (p. 297), Basingstoke (pp. 313-319), and Kingsclere (pp. 320-322). It may be related to the inconsistencies in the Domesday hundred boundaries depicted on the illustrations for the *parochiae* of Kingsclere and Basingstoke.

leaders of the West Saxons.[67] This portion of the border may well mark an earlier division between post-Roman peoples. As it lies on the geophysical division between the chalkland and the southern Tertiary sands and clays,[68] it may be in fact an extension of the division we have observed further east between the *Gewisse* of central Hampshire and the *Jutae* of the south coast.

The late Saxon period witnessed the imposition of West Saxon institutions upon the rest of England. The ancient territories of the Midlands were redrawn into shires, and the shires were divided into hundreds. A century later these Midland hundreds often retained their assessment of 100 hides, while those of Wessex had already been altered by the powerful forces of private and institutional lordship. The ship-soke of three hundreds was a late tenth-century development that might have preserved previous territorial divisions, but the rise of other forms of private jurisdiction, the hundredal manor, the liberty, and the soke, effectively brought about the physical disintegration of the archaic hundred. At the same time, many more churches had been built, often originally subject to the mother church of the archaic hundred. The Danish wars were the catalyst for abandoning the 'minster' system, and by the eleventh century, its authority was divided between the new village churches and the growing power of the episcopal cathedrals.

After Canute's conquest of 1016, the territorial divisions underwent further alteration. Domesday Book reveals that the authority over and profits from many hundreds had been attached in clusters to special comital estates. These were associated with the rise of the great Anglo-Danish earldoms, equivalent to Continental principalities. In the Norman period, a powerful monarchy eliminated the great earldoms, but the groupings of hundreds continued. By 1100, the territorial divisions of England had undergone four centuries of massive, irrevocable change. The original territorial units had become lost in a palimpsest of new boundaries, drawn and redrawn, as for a dozen generations, manors, vills, and even hundreds passed among the masters of England—first Saxon thegn, then Danish jarl, and lastly, Norman baron.

---

[67]   See *ASE* 22, 23.
[68]   See Darby and Campbell, *Domesday Geography*, p. 567, fig. 160.

7

Summary, Comparisons, and Conclusions

The rural development in the Micheldever region of middle Hampshire is summarized below, followed by a consideration of comparable research. The chapter concludes with a review of the main findings of this study and some observations on their broader historical significance.

SUMMARY OF RURAL DEVELOPMENT

To summarize the sequence of early medieval rural development in the Micheldever region, one must turn to supplementary sources. Celtic names appear among the earliest entries in the West Saxon king list, and most names for rivers in middle Hampshire are of Celtic origin. These surviving elements of pre-Germanic culture hint at a sub-Roman hybrid 'Saxo-British' regional state under the shadowy *Gewisse*, the tribe or dynasty of Winchester. As the sixth-century plague also hastened the collapse of British kingdoms to the west, the conquest of this region, traditionally attributed to the West Saxons, may parallel the Frankish absorption of similar sub-Roman states.[1] Early English toponyms identify the central Hampshire watershed of the Test and Itchen rivers and their tributaries as a distinctive tribal area. These river valleys divide into geographically defined segments; in the Micheldever region there are eight such units. Each valley catchment area was the basis for Anglo-Saxon settlement.[2] In this study the term 'archaic hundred' has been applied to the valley unit antecedent of the late Saxon 'hundred' administrative district. Each territory had a traditional central place with a large pagan cemetery (later a missionary 'minster' church) and a chieftain's or noble's hall (later a royal vill or 'kingstun'), where tribute

---

[1]   Martin Biddle has found sub-Roman fortifications at Winchester and even possible evidence of epidemic death. See "Winchester: The development of an early capital," in *Vor- und Frühformen der Europäischen Stadt im Mittelalter* (Göttingen, 1972), pp. 229-261.
[2]   This substantiates Alan Everitt's observation that early Anglo-Saxon settlement was by river or 'vale' communities; see his "River and Wold; Reflections on the Historical Origins of Regions and Pays," *Journal of Historical Geography* 3 (1977) 1-19.

was collected and which often served as the site of the popular 'moot' assembly.

Early medieval population growth led to an increased food demand that soon surpassed the small-scale post-Roman agricultural base. As early as the late seventh century, the law code of Wessex referred to shared fields, or at least to shared pasture rights, an essential part of the common field system. A ploughteam of six to eight oxen, and the availability of replacement animals, was beyond the means of all but the most wealthy Anglo-Saxon peasants. The cooperative use of plough-oxen was rewarded by the allotment of crops from strips that were intermingled to benefit all farmers equally. At the same time, large teams caused an increased demand for summer grazing and winter fodder, leading to cooperative arrangements over pasturage.[3] Because of the competition for grazing by the ploughteams, similar arrangements were soon extended to sheep and probably swine. The result was the establishment of defined conditions that controlled most aspects of agricultural production, both arable and husbandry, the mixed farming economy of the early medieval period.

The expanded cooperative agriculture required a large, concentrated workforce. The coalescence of small fields into large blocks was accompanied by the population shift from independent farmsteads of the post-Roman period to a nucleated farming settlement, i.e., the village. Early to mid-Saxon settlements that had existed roughly from the sixth to the eighth centuries were abandoned. The village community comprised landholders, their families, and their dependents, all of whom shared, to one degree or another, economic responsibilities and benefits. As the farmers forged new links to create the village community, so earlier links were severed. Villages and their lands were economically independent of the larger territorial unit (the 'archaic hundred') and of each other. The valley-wide land use of arable, pasture, and woodland was replaced by a land use based on the vill.

A nucleated village was a discrete economic entity, and the authority over and revenue from it was more attractive to the warrior aristocracy than was the old system of tribute collected from the archaic hundreds and dispensed at court. Following the Church's lead in obtaining chartered lands in perpetuity from the king and his *witan* (council), however, the nobility also demanded the privilege of taking out of the tribally controlled 'folkland' their assigned estates as chartered, inheritable, 'bookland.' The resulting

---

[3]   Here I would agree with W.O. Ault's view that common grazing rights were part of cooperative agriculture from the beginning, rather than a later development; see *Open-Field Farming in Medieval England* (1972), p. 17. Joan Thirsk proposed the opposite in "The Common Fields," *Past and Present* No. 29 (Dec., 1964), 3-25.

alienation of such lands from the folk effectively destroyed the tenurial integrity of the archaic hundred, while it weakened the disinherited clans and strengthened the inheriting lineage groups. By the ninth century, the grant typically comprised a single vill—the classic medieval manor.

The archaic hundred slowly disintegrated. During the period 800-1000, its civil functions were completely divided among the manor, vill, and hundred. The late ninth-century Danish wars effectively destroyed the archaic hundreds' ecclesiastical counterparts, the early medieval *parochiae*, and emptied the 'minster' churches that served them. Their territories were split between the increasingly powerful cathedrals and the rapidly multiplying village parishes.

In the tenth century, certain families and large religious houses began to acquire many single-vill manors and amass them into large estates. These new large estates were usually centred upon earlier royal grants, to which were attached adjacent or sometimes quite distant manors obtained later. The resulting late-Saxon manorial structure can be identified as the 'multiple estate' described by Glanville Jones and Peter Sawyer. In the late tenth century, the religious reform movement brought about new ecclesiastic foundations. Through bequests and royal grants, these institutions also amassed groups of manors. In the eleventh century, ecclesiastical estate formation was slowed, and even reversed, under the more militant Anglo-Danish and Anglo-Norman governments, though new holdings from both royal and Church land were created by new families like the Godwins.

In the early tenth century, the Alfredian kings of England imposed the judicial and police institution of the 'Wessex' hundred upon the rest of England south of the Humber, but by the end of the century major ecclesiastical landowners began to claim hundredal rights over their lands. This development was probably associated with the Crown's assigning to these same bodies the responsibility for mobilizing local military forces and collecting defense-related dues, later the recurrent 'Danegeld' tribute payment. In the early eleventh century, hundreds came into the hands of lay lords, at the same time that the office of earl replaced that of several Anglo-Saxon ealdormen. By Domesday, many hundreds were nothing more than private courts for an institution's properties, exempt from traditional hundredal authority. Such a hundred was a forerunner of the later medieval 'liberty' or 'soke.'

Changes in the conditions of landholding began to appear shortly before the end of the tenth century. Properties continued to be leased for a life term, or for several lives, but sometimes with conditions of service instead of money rent. The change may reflect a need for retainers during the crisis of the Danish wars and the continued effort of reconquering the north of England. But the broader context might suggest that the continued success of the new agricultural regime and the growing profits from wool exports gave the owners of large manors satisfactory incomes from their demesne operations. Leasing small properties at service tenure supplied them with the services they needed without the upkeep of additional retainers. The conditions of a lease (ca. 1000) of lands in the Micheldever valley were simply that the recipient be loyal in all things, civil and spiritual, in support of which he apparently swore an oath of 'fealty.'[4]

Military service first appears in leases when late Saxon large estates were being formed. The contemporary creation of the ship hundred system of military obligations and mobilization by Edgar or Ethelred made some land magnates responsible for the service of a prescribed number of soldiers, generally one per five hides of land, and they began to lease small manors in return for this military service. The drift toward military tenure may or may not have been halted by the Danish kings, but the immediate importance of William's imposition of Norman feudalism upon England was his exclusion of Englishmen from military tenure. By 1086, however, manors were leased privately—without military service—to Englishmen, in some cases their former owners.[5] Domesday Book rarely notes such instances of farming out; it was not part of the seigneurial conditions that William wanted recorded. For the English, the short-term money lease was the best available way to hold land, and to support a family. For the Normans, it supplied the steady revenues needed to maintain their far-flung and expensive conquests. This late eleventh-century development was a further step in the evolution of an expanding rural economy. It marked the end of the 'classic' demesne manor that had supplied its lord with material, not money, and that in turn marked the end of the early Middle Ages.

COMPARATIVE STUDIES

For the present, the comparability of settlement studies is problematic. Anglo-Saxon settlement studies of differing regions have yielded widely varying results. If these are not due at least in part to poor data or method, one must conclude that local factors largely determined patterns of settlement. Perhaps more immediately pertinent, previous detailed research has been undertaken for areas somewhat smaller than the Micheldever

---

[4]   S1420, the New Minster gives land at Barton and Drayton to Wulfmaer and his wife, for their lives. The text reads: "... *sy freond + hold into them minstre on aeclere stowe aegther ge for Gode ge for worulde*," A.J. Robertson, *Anglo-Saxon Charters* (Cambridge, 1935), p. 144.
[5]   Reginald Lennard, *Rural England 1086-1135* (Oxford, 1959), pp. 105-141.

region of middle Hampshire, and broader investigations have not employed as full a range of sources and approaches.[6]

Some findings of other Anglo-Saxon settlement studies clearly conflict with those presented here. Specific differences concern the economic base of early medieval manors, patterns of settlement, and the nature and origin of the districts in which the manors lay. For example, the surveys made by William Ford in Warwickshire, Alan Everett in Kent, and Glanville Jones in Sussex found instances of detached tracts of woodland tenurially connected to arable holdings. These scholars concluded that livestock transhumance was the operative factor underlying early medieval settlement and land use.[7] Della Hooke, however, observed that attached holdings in the west Midlands are often of late Saxon date and may not represent ancient links of land use and tenure.[8] Nevertheless, she has postulated that intercommoning was the cause for linked territories and that the geographic groupings of these may reveal the extent of ancient "folk-regions" based upon riverine areas.[9] Peter Brandon, however, thought this explanation was inappropriate for the Sussex Weald, and Barry Cunliffe found no evidence for transhumance in the eastern Hampshire/western Sussex area around Chalton.[10] Similarly, there was no tradition of early medieval

[6]   For methodology, see Eric Klingelhöfer, *Settlement and Land Use in Micheldever Hundred, Hampshire, 700-1100*, Transactions of the American Philosophical Society, vol 81 part 3 (Philadelphia, 1991), pp. 12-16, 120-127. David Hinton has recently and successfully reviewed new archaeological information and its contribution to early medieval history in *Archaeology, Economy and Society: England from the Fifth to the Fifteenth Century* (London, 1990), esp. pp. 21-132.

[7]   W.J. Ford, "Some Settlement Patterns in the Central Region of the Warwickshire Avon," in *MSCC* 274-294; Alan Everett, "River and Wold: Reflections on the Historical Origin of Regions and Pays," *Journal of Historical Geography* 3 (1977), 1-19; G.R.J. Jones, "Multiple Estates and Early Settlement," in *MSCC* 15-40.

[8]   Della Hooke, *Anglo-Saxon Landscapes of the West Midlands: The Charter Evidence*, British Archaeological Reports, British Series 95 (Oxford, 1981), pp. 48-53. She also notes that references to fifty-hide units may represent at least part of early, large territories. These views are a modification, not a repudiation, of her observations in "Pre-Conquest States in the West Midlands: Preliminary Thoughts," *Journal of Historical Geography* 8 (1982), 227-244.

[9]   Della Hooke, *The Anglo-Saxon Landscape: The Kingdom of the Hwicce* (Manchester, 1985), pp. 78-84. She contrasts this general pattern of transhumance groupings with the parallel land units (strip parishes) characteristic of some river valleys, e.g. the Stour (see p. 66).

[10]   Peter Brandon, "The South Saxon *Andredesweald*," in *The South Saxons* ed. P. Brandon (Chichester, 1978), pp. 138-159; Barry Cunliffe, "Saxon and Medieval Settlement-Pattern in the Region of Chalton, Hampshire," *Medieval Archaeology* 16 (1972), 1-12.

transhumance practices in central Hampshire; the detached holdings were added to estates in the late Saxon stage of 'fusion.'

In East Anglia, Peter Wade-Martins concluded that the movement of villages throughout the medieval period provides the basis for understanding East Anglian rural development.[11] But in Hampshire, there was little village movement (woodland areas aside) between the tenth century and the fourteenth. Perhaps rural development in Hampshire reached maturity before that of East Anglia, which underwent heavy Danish settlement in the late ninth century.

The search for continuity has long been a factor in early medieval historical research. Glanville Jones proposed a pre-Saxon origin for early medieval territories, which he reconstructed in Yorkshire and Sussex by using boundaries of later medieval manorial and ecclesiastical jurisdictions.[12] Jones's estates and the model of development proposed by Cunliffe for the Chalton area form large blocks of land, but they show no correlation to the geophysical considerations that produced the eight early Saxon 'archaic hundreds' in middle Hampshire and the twenty-three other districts suggested between the Hampshire Downs and Southampton Water (see Appendices A and D). It remains to be seen if this aspect of the Chalton model needs more refinement, or if the southeast area of Hampshire underwent a distinctly different territorial formation to that of central Hampshire. Chalton lies on the far edge of Hampshire, in an area that was perhaps originally settled by Germanic groups of South Saxon ancestry and allegiance. The Micheldever model therefore should represent more closely the type of territorial formation typical of Wessex. Similarly, Patrick Hase demonstrated that the early *parochia* were ecclesiastical replicas of existing civil districts, and the territorial units he reconstructed were convincing in the south Hampshire littoral with its Jutish associations, but were less successful in the Hampshire hinterland, where they do not correspond to the topographically based archaic hundreds.[13]

The archaic hundred is, in fact, the link between the folk territory of the post-Roman period, and the lay institutions present at Domesday—the manor, the vill, and the hundred. The *parochia* of the eighth and ninth centuries were based upon the archaic hundred territory, the centre of which became the location of the royal manor and the 'minster' church. The developing monarchy of Wessex used what was there already, the natural

[11]   Peter Wade-Martins, "The Origins of Medieval Settlement in East Anglia," in *Recent Work in Rural Archaeology*, ed. P.J. Fowler (Bradford-on-Avon, 1975), pp. 137-157.

[12]   G.R.J. Jones, "Multiple Estates."

[13]   See P.H. Hase, "The Development of the Parish in Hampshire, Particularly in the Eleventh and Twelfth Centuries," (Ph.D. thesis, Cambridge University, 1975).

grouping of a farming population in discrete valley catchment zones, as the source of a regularized supply of tribute.[14] This study has compared the hidage assessments of Domesday Book and other eleventh and twelfth-century documents, to figures of *mansae, cassati,* and hides recorded in the earlier grants and leases of the eighty-seven manors of the eight catchment areas of middle Hampshire. The resulting figures, extrapolated for original hidation, yield a noticeable pattern of groups that total at, or close to, one hundred hides, with other totals clustering around fifty, one hundred fifty, and two hundred hides.[15] These eight valley units have proved to be the sole configuration whereby the hidage of the eighty-seven manors would form discrete groups that totalled one hundred hides or its variants, left no manor in isolation, and had mother churches, royal vills, and pagan cemeteries as their 'central places.' Despite the aptness of F.W. Maitland's opinion that "counting hides is repulsive work,"[16] the hidage survey of the Micheldever region has yielded the response to the complaint made thirty years ago by Sir Frank Stenton:

> No one has yet worked out in detail, and for a large area, the relationship between the number of *mansae* assigned to particular estates by tenth-century charters and the number of hides answered for the same places in 1066.[17]

Following the landmark studies of H.P.R. Finberg elsewhere in Wessex,[18] English scholars have continue to explore the subject of early territories. In 1984 Katherine Barker proposed that "a territory largely defined by natural features" was a component of ancient Selwoodshire and the land along the watershed between Cirencester and Lyme Bay in western

---

[14]   In an interesting study of the archaeological evidence for the economies and polities of the early Saxon period, C.J. Arnold argues that by the eighth century, important early Saxon rural settlements "may have lost their 'central persons' who had removed themselves to royal sites," which dismembered the lord/retainer local redistributive economy (*An Archaeology of the Early Anglo-Saxon Kingdoms* [London, 1990], p. 198).

[15]   These figures are comparable to those of Cambridgeshire, where Cyril Hart believed a hundred system was imposed ca. 917. His "initial hundred pattern" had 16 hundreds, of which seven were ordinary hundreds, two were 'hundreds-and-a-half,' and seven were double hundreds. See *The Hidation of Cambridgeshire*, Dept. of English Local History Occasional Papers, 2nd ser., no. 6 (Leicester, 1974), p. 36.

[16]   *DBB* 511.

[17]   F.M. Stenton, *The Latin Charters of the Anglo-Saxon Period* (Oxford, 1955), p. 79.

[18]   See H.P.R. Finberg, *Lucerna: Studies of Some Problems in the Early History of England* (Leicester, 1964).

Wessex.[19] Della Hooke thought that linked landholdings were evidence for river-based 'folk-regions' in the West Midlands.[20] Glenn Foard has considered the role of natural features in the division of land between small territories in the East Midlands.[21] Elsewhere, Margaret Gelling has concluded that before their breakdown into unitary manors, large 'composite' estates existed in many parts of England, a view that is extended by the work of Glanville Jones and G.W.S. Barrow in the north of England and Scotland.[22] The central places of the composite estates frequently bore place-names with topographic elements, examples of which have been noted in Berkshire, Warwickshire, Oxfordshire, and Durham.[23] In Berkshire, Gelling used the boundary clauses of Anglo-Saxon charters to recreate on paper several great estates, which do show a valley orientation, though not a clear equivalency. In short, Gelling has pushed the charter and toponymic evidence as far as justifiable, and has come close to identifying the archaic hundreds of Berkshire.

As noted above, the antiquity of the 'multiple estate' has been claimed by Glanville Jones to have a pre-Saxon, even a prehistoric origin. Dr Gelling has found some support for this contention, in the fact that the rarity of Roman roads as boundaries of such great estates suggests that the boundaries predated the roads. In middle Hampshire, however, there appears to be little or no continuity between Celtic and Romano-British settlement groupings and those of the Anglo-Saxons. Roman features, including roads, rarely coincided with boundaries of the most ancient territorial divisions, and bore no relation to the topographical determinants

---

[19]   Katherine Barker, "Institution and Landscape in Early Medieval Wessex: Adhelm of Malmesbury, Sherborne and *Selwoodshire*," *Proceedings of the Dorset Natural History and Archaeological Society* 106 (1984), 33-42.

[20]   Hooke, *Kingdom of Hwicce*, pp. 78-84.

[21]   Glenn Foard, "The Administrative Organization of Northamptonshire in the Saxon Period," *Anglo-Saxon Studies in Archaeology and History* 4 (Oxford, 1985), pp. 185-222. He is particularly concerned with explaining the numerous detached portions of townships, hundreds, and even counties here, not to mention detached pasture rights and townships split between counties; see fig. 5, p. 196, and fig. 6, p. 197.

[22]   G.R.J. Jones, "Multiple estates"; and G.W.S. Barrow, "Pre-Feudal Scotland: Shires and Thanes," in *The Kingdom of the Scots* ed. Barrow (1973), pp. 7-68.

[23]   Margaret Gelling, *Guideposts to the Past: Place-Names and the History of England* (London, 1978), p. 125. Ford, "Some Settlement Patterns," 181-82, presents evidence that watershed was a factor in territorial division. Given the criticism of the study, however, one must refrain from claiming the Warwickshire results as corroborating the Hampshire findings; see David Hill, *An Atlas of Anglo-Saxon England* (Toronto and Buffalo, 1981), p. 78. But see also E. Watts, "Comment on 'The Evidence of Place-Names' by Margaret Gelling," in *MSCC* 212-225. It is not clear why the "non-habitative" place-names cited by Watts are necessarily those of composite estate centres.

of the ancient valley unit, though they were commonly used as divisions between late Saxon manors.[24] The broad scale of the Berkshire study, however, did not permit the detail of archaeology, drift geology, and topography necessary to recreate the more precise patterns of settlements and territories, and the dynamics by which they evolved. This has since been at least partially covered by Della Hooke's study of localities in Berkshire, where she found evidence for the early presence of medieval settlements and field systems, and for the fission of large, early Saxon tracts of land.[25]

The origin of the manor has been sought in the dissolution of the great estate, otherwise known as the 'federate manor,' 'multiple estate,' 'composite estate,' etc. In middle Hampshire, the 'great estates' of the early Saxon period were valley-based archaic hundreds, and their fission simultaneously produced the individual manor/vills. Thus Maitland's theory that the manor was a late Anglo-Saxon development, a domination of a pre-existing village community, may be correct in a minority of the cases here.[26] Even though territorial lordship did acquire many of its later medieval attributes in the late Saxon period, the origin for this lordship must be sought in the grants and leases of lands from 700 onward. For Maitland, the development of the manor could be traced in the growth of the demesne, and in rents and services.

As the rights of independent farmers coalesced into the cooperative village economic unit, so their duties to a local authority (the archaic hundred) were brought together as seigniorial obligations to a lord of the manor. The manor, described above as the aristocratic response to the vill, was an institutional adjustment to economic and social change. That Sir Paul Vinogradoff's 'tun' or village, as "the rural community of ancient and independent growth,"[27] was the fundamental unit of early England, is therefore true from perhaps only the ninth century onward. Before then the fundamental unit was the archaic hundred.

T.H. Aston's theory of an original unity of lordship and settlement that was later obscured by the spread of 'discrete estates,'[28] reflects one part of the evolution of the manors of middle Hampshire. In the late Saxon

---

[24] See Klingelhöfer, *Settlement and Land Use*, pp. 60-84.

[25] Della Hooke, "Regional Variation in Southern and Central England in the Anglo-Saxon Period," in *Anglo-Saxon Settlement*, D. Hooke, ed. (Oxford, 1988), pp. 123-151.

[26] *DBB* 322.

[27] Sir Paul Vinogradoff, *The Growth of the Manor* (1905; repr. New York, 1951), p. 235.

[28] T.H. Aston, "The Origins of the Manor in England," *Transactions of the Royal Historical Society*, 5th ser., 8 (1958), 59-83.

period, new great estates amassed and absorbed the individual manors that represented the fragmented pieces of the ancient, valley-based territories. But the unitary manor was not an original Germanic institution; it was first created by the alienation of royal/tribal lands and by the subsequent leasing of church lands (and perhaps private lands) to individuals for the duration of several lives. Aston's manor was indeed obscured when ecclesiastical institutions created the new 'discrete estates' of the tenth and eleventh centuries, and acquired the hundred courts that came to accompany large landholdings.

At the same time, the Micheldever findings also partially corroborate Peter Sawyer's conclusions that the great estate incorporating several settlements was "the basic unit of rural organization" in seventh-century England, and that it was the fission of this estate that formed the later medieval village manors.[29] This process, however, did not originate from a multiple estate formed of detached holdings, nor was there a single evolutionary direction from a wide territory to a single-vill manor.[30] The new composite estates of the tenth century absorbed smaller holdings and obscured the previous arrangements of landholding—manors in groups defined by valleys and watersheds. In Hampshire, and probably throughout much of Wessex, these late Saxon multiple estates are unsuitable models for earlier landholding, just as the hundred organization recorded in the Domesday Book was far removed from the mid-Saxon archaic hundred.

There is less ground for comparison between the Micheldever study and research on the Continent. As in Britain, local studies with comparable goals are usually concerned with the broad patterns of larger areas, or with the later medieval period.[31] Moreover, the Continental surveys address different historical problems. For instance, only in Germany and Scandinavia do scholars of Western European agrarian history treat an agricultural and tenurial change that was contemporary with the transformations of societies from pagan to Christian, and governments from tribal kingships to royal administrations. In many respects, England has a unique position, one that includes both the elements of continuity of the

[29] P. H. Sawyer, *From Roman Britain to Norman England* (London, 1978), p. 164.

[30] See Glanville R.J. Jones, "The Multiple Estate as a Model Framework for Tracing Early Stages in the Evolution of Rural Settlement," in *L'Habitat et les paysages ruraux d'Europe*, Les Congrés et Colloques de l'Université de Liège, vol. 58, ed. François Dussart (Liège, 1971), pp. 251-67.

[31] e.g., Léopold Genicot, *L'Economie rurale namuroise au bas Moyen Age, 1199-1429* (Louvain, 1943); and René Noël, *Quatre siècles de vie rurale entre le Semois et le Chiers, 1050-1470* (Louvain, 1977). Much comparative material has been assembled by Genicot in *Rural Communities in the Medieval West* (Baltimore, 1990), esp. pp. 12-29.

sub-Roman successor states, and the independence of culture that existed in the northern Continental lands and the further British Isles.

For Continental scholars, the territorial units of the *pagus* (rural district, canton), the manor, and the manse have been topics of particular importance and extended debate.[32] Rural settlement patterns are a subject of increasing interest, though in the past less effort was given to identifying pre-manorial 'tribal' units because Francia did not have the same pagan centuries of isolation as England. Recent studies in France have in fact suggested a similar time span—beginning in the ninth century and ending by the eleventh, during which the *nouvelle enceullement* of parish and village dissolved and replaced the previous, larger unit of the *ager* and its villas.[33]

Continental studies have emphasized, rather, social and economic history. Following the lead of Georges Duby, the early medieval rural economy has until recently been considered one of technologically backward, subsistence-level farming.[34] This deduction contrasts strangely with the sophistication and detail of the Carolingian estate records used to support this theory. Contemporary conditions in the less advanced

[32]   e.g., M. Auguste Le Prévost, "Anciennes divisions territoriales de la Normandie," *Mémoires de la Société des Antiquaires de Normandie*, 2nd ser., 11 (1840), 1-59; Jean-François Le Marignier, "La dislocation du 'Pagus' et le problem des 'Consuetudines' (Xe-XIe siècles)," in *Mélanges d'histoire du Moyen Age dediés à la mémoire de Louis Halphen* (Paris, 1951) pp. 404-410; David Herlihy, "The Carolingian *Mansus*," *Economic History Review*, 2nd ser., 13 (1960), 79-89; F.L. Ganshof, "Manorial Organization in the Low Countries in the Seventh, Eighth and Ninth Centuries," *Transactions of the Royal Historical Society*, 4th ser., 31 (1949), 29-59.

[33]   Yet rural settlement has been examined with increasing scrutiny; for example, W. Jannsen, "Zur Differenzierung des früh- und hochmittelalterlichen Siedlungbildes im Reinland," *Die Stadt in der Europäischen Geschichte: Festschrift Edith Ennen* (Bonn, 1972); J.B. Ward-Perkins, "Central authority and patterns of rural settlement," *Man, Settlement, and Urbanism*, ed. P. Ucko, et al., (London, 1972), pp. 867-890. Recent research in France shows an increasing interest in early medieval settlements and pre-Carolingian territorial units. Some noteworthy examples of such research are Robert Fossier, *La Terre et les hommes en Picardie jusqu'à la fin du XIIe siècle* (Paris and Louvain, 1968); Frederic Cheyette, "The Origins of European Villages and the First European Expansion," *Journal of Economic History* 37 (1977), 182-206; François Bange, "L'ager et la villa: structures du paysage et du peuplement dans la région mâconnaise à la fin du Haut Moyen Age (IXe-XIe siècles)," *Annales* 39 (1984), 529-569; and Elizabeth Zadora-Rio "Archaéologie du peuplement: La Gènese d'un terroir communal," *Archaéologie Médiévale* 17 (1987), 7-65.

[34]   Georges Duby, *L'Economie rurale et la vie des compagnes dans l'Occident médiéval* (Paris, 1962). For alternate views, see A. Dopsch, *Wirtschaftsentwicklung der Karolingerzeit, Vornehmlich in Deutchland* (Weimar, 1912-1913); and M.M. Postan, *The Agrarian Life in the Middle Ages*, The Cambridge Economic History of Europe, 2 (Cambridge, 1966).

Anglo-Saxon kingdoms were certainly quite different.[35] Jean Chapelot and Robert Fossier noted the different conclusions drawn from the English archaeological sources, but they continued to share Duby's *pessimisme*, viewing the Carolingian rural economy as technologically primitive and accompanied by oppressive poverty at the village level.[36] The Duby viewpoint has been more strongly challenged by Raymond Delatouche, who condemned it for having been based upon a serious misreading of the sources.[37] His careful re-examination of Carolingian documents found that there was in fact no evidence for a scarcity of iron, and that the crop yields of the ninth century were the same as those of the thirteenth century, the apex of medieval agricultural productivity. Of course, the Carolingians were farming the best soils available, compared to the secondary and even marginal land that was to be cultivated in the late thirteenth and fourteenth centuries. The addition of these lands lowered the average crop yield from the levels of productivity that improving techniques and equipment permitted on more fertile fields. Nevertheless, the new view of the Carolingian world does have a logical foundation, that a limited population would enjoy an abundance of hitherto unused resources.

The differences between the approaches and findings of English and Continental scholars are more apparent than real. Just as there are strongly differing views on the Carolingian economy, so there is no unanimity of opinion on the level of economic development in pre-Conquest England. And just as Delatouche has challenged the economic thesis of a generation of Continental scholars, so Peter Sawyer has argued that the late Anglo-Saxon countryside was fully exploited. In Hampshire, the Micheldever region underwent a dramatic change in settlement and land use in the eighth and ninth centuries, and from then on enjoyed a steady expansion of arable production, with perhaps little pre-Conquest reduction in husbandry. It is likely, therefore, that in economic level, if not in

---

[35]   There is, for example, extensive evidence for wide-spread Anglo-Saxon iron production. See David M. Wilson, "Craft and Industry," *AASE* 253-281. For Wessex, see Jeremy Haslam, "A Middle-Saxon Iron Smelting Furnace at Ramsbury, Wiltshire," *Medieval Archaeology* 24 (1980), 1-68. For the industrial activity at Hamwic, see the preliminary conclusions on excavations there in Philip Holdsworth, "Saxon Southampton: A New Review," *Medieval Archaeology* 20 (1976), 26-61, updated in Holdsworth, "Saxon Southampton," in *Anglo-Saxon Towns in Southern England*, ed. J. Haslam (1984), pp. 331-341.

[36]   Jean Chapelot and Robert Fossier, *Le village et la maison au Moyen Age* (Paris, 1980), p. 24.

[37]   Raymond Delatouche, "Regards sur l'agriculture aux temps carolingiens," *Journal des Savants* (1977), 73-100. Earlier reservations were expressed also by Renée Doehaerd, *Le Haut Moyen Age Occident*, La Nouvelle Clio (Paris, 1971).

agricultural detail, England and the Continent were substantially equal by the late Saxon period, and in both cases the strength of rural development was the most important fact of the early Middle Ages.

CONCLUSIONS

The course of rural development in one area of southern England from 700 to 1100 is one of steady economic and institutional evolution in spite of, or perhaps spurred by, such negative factors as the endemic conflict among the Anglo-Saxon kingdoms and the devastation of the late ninth-century Viking attacks.

The Manor

There are two significant findings concerning the manor. First, the origins of the manor in middle Hampshire are found to lie not in a village community, nor in a Celtic or Roman territorial district, the elementary choices of the 'Germanist' and 'Romanist' traditions of historical scholarship. Rather, its ancestry lies in the ancient folk territorial grouping, the archaic hundred, over which the king of Wessex exercised general authority and from which he drew tribute. The kings were able to increase their personal retinue by assigning discrete portions of this folk-group to individual nobles. The noble became the lord, and the landholding became the manor.

Secondly, manorial development did not take place here in the linear movement from a large primitive early· Saxon estate to the individual vill/manor of the later Middle Ages. In middle Hampshire, there was dissolution, amalgamation, and re-dissolution before 1100. Further, in other parts of England early land-units may have had detached holdings for traditional transhumance, but there is as yet no evidence for it in Hampshire. All the detached holdings observed here were late Saxon creations. The complex sequence of fission, fusion, and fission was undoubtedly part of a larger developmental pattern of tenurial and economic stability, which in Anglo-Saxon Hampshire may have corresponded to periods of dominance by ecclesiastic institutions over the lay aristocracy.

The Vill

The process of village creation is another element of early medieval rural development. In middle Hampshire, a seventh and eighth-century movement of population from dispersed sites to more nucleated settlements along the banks of the streams resulted in a 'strip parish' pattern comprising narrow village lands, among which every land-type was evenly distributed. The strips ran up from the well-watered valley bottoms to the dry pasture 'downs' and woods along the valley watersheds. The establishment of vill communities and the layout of new, open-field systems by the ninth century coincided with the emergence of a new rural economy of cooperative agricultural techniques associated with the heavy plough with mould-board, and its large 'medieval' plough-team. Most villages here were established in the eighth and ninth centuries; they were neither part of the original Germanic settlement nor the result of seigneurial pressures in the post-Viking period.

The Hundred

The hundred jurisdictional district of the late Saxon kingdom now appears to have developed from the entity identified here as the 'archaic hundred' to distinguish it from the Germanic prehistoric hundred described by Tacitus, and the late Saxon national hundred system of Athelstan. An elementary territorial unit, the archaic hundred was the vehicle of transformation from a folk group into a royal administrative district. The arachic hundred topographic units were in fact catchment areas defined by the watersheds of small side valleys or sections of larger river valleys. A catchment area typically measured eight miles by five miles, and contained, on average, eleven medieval manors, as the eight valley units of middle Hampshire encompassed eighty-seven manors. A catchment area took its name from the one-hundred-hide tribute assessment imposed upon it by the developing monarchy of Wessex. The archaic hundred had natural boundaries, which were not necessarily followed by later institutional territories. Its presence was later obscured by the effects of property changes and the spread of private jurisdictions, which created the late Saxon 'multiple estate' and the patchwork pattern of Hampshire hundreds of the Domesday Book.

The Shire

In examining the range of Anglo-Saxon terms for territorial units, this study contrasts the shire of the late Saxon kingdom to the earlier and less known *scir*. An early reference to the shire has been claimed for the entry in the Anglo-Saxon Chronicle for 755, which refers to *Hamtunscir*. However, the earliest entries for other Saxon shires appeared within the short time span of twelve years in the middle of the ninth century, when the first sustained attacks upon Wessex by Vikings occurred. At the same time, there was an alternate tradition recorded in Wessex for a Cornish *scir* of a few hundred hides, and the eighth-century 'Hamptonshire' was most likely a small territory of several hundred hides around the thriving entrepot of Hamwic, or Hamtun.

This early use of *scir* was probably a general term for 'district' or 'domain,' and not a particular system of territories. The true shire system of Wessex did not appear until the middle of the ninth century, when an administrative reorganization was needed to address the crisis of sustained Viking attacks.

To summarize, the dynamics of rural development fuelled the evolution from Anglo-Saxon tribal society to medieval 'feudal' society. With no Roman or Celtic origin, the archaic hundred was the early political and economic unit of the *Gewisse* 'Saxons,' and was used by the monarchy as the basis of tribute assessment (one hundred hides per valley unit). The early Saxon hundred broke down when the agricultural change of the open-field system created the village, over which the aristocracy imposed the manor as a source of more permanent wealth and power. The hundred lost its original identity as a valley folk-unit, and became an administrative district, the lines of which followed jurisdictional and manorial boundaries.

Despite the national political collapse leading first to the Danish Conquest of 1016 and secondly to the Norman Conquest of 1066, English rural development had achieved such an enviable strength and stability that Anglo-Saxon local institutions continued to be the basis of medieval English government. For centuries, productivity and population growth had been tempered by the civilizing influence of Christianity in building the prosperity and institutions of the late Saxon 'neo-Carolingian' society. Later medieval achievements—the commercial and urban development of the twelfth century—might well be considered its necessary and inevitable consequence.

Appendix A

Hidage and Manors of Middle Hampshire

In this appendix, a summary of early medieval tenurial history is followed by a presentation of the documentary evidence for each manor of middle Hampshire and a reconstruction of its original hidage figure. It traces their descent before 1100 and tries to reconstruct their original hidage values. It demonstrates that not only are the extents of the early medieval manors of middle Hampshire closely related to and in part defined by valley catchment zones, but each manor falls into a topographically determined grouping. It will also be shown that the original hidage totals for these groupings do not reflect the precise geographical dimensions of the manor groups. The manor groups lack the variation of hidage assessments that results from natural determinants. Rather, their assessment totals display an artificial regularity, with all figures at or close to 50, 100, 150, and 200 hides. Most groups are at the 100-hide figure, which suggests an arbitrary assessment of 100 hides for a standard valley unit.

Tenurial History

The earliest known grant (S360) of lands in the Micheldever valley was the large tract, amounting to nearly one half the valley, that Edward the Elder gave to establish the New Minster in accordance with his father's will. This was the core of the Micheldever manor, comprising the vills of Micheldever-Northbrook, Weston Colley, East and West Stratton, Popham, and Burcot. By Domesday (and probably by ca. 1000), the Micheldever estate had absorbed Southbrook Tithing, thus controlling the entire eastern half of the Dever valley. In the western half, the early place-name Cranbourne was retained by a small manor given to New Minster and added to the Micheldever estate. Originally dependent settlements at Norton and Sutton (Scotney) remained royal properties, though the latter did come into the hands of the Godwin family before the Norman Conquest. Wonston and Stoke Charity lay between the two manorial groups. The first was a tenth-century acquisition of the Old Minster (S381), and the second became an episcopal property before 1066. At the far end of the topographic valley unit was Bullington manor, spanning the Dever stream. It was granted by Ethelred to Wherwell Abbey in 1008 (S904).

Most of the Candover valley manors were granted out of royal possession in the tenth century. The earliest grant was the Micheldever charter of 900 (S360), the boundary of which extended as far as the Candover stream, at a point likely to be the later medieval manor of Totford. Swarraton appears on the spurious charter of 903 (S370), and had been acquired by the New Minster before the forgery was made in the early eleventh century. At that time, Abbotstone appears on a list of Old Minster properties, where Chilton Candover is also found, reflecting the earlier bequest of land to the church by a thegn. The division of property between the cathedral and the bishop gave the latter Chilton Candover, and apparently Wield, which he held in 1066. A strip of Brown Candover had been acquired by the New Minster before the late tenth century when it was added to the original Micheldever charter. By the early eleventh century, all of Brown Candover had come into the hands of the New Minster, because it, too, appears on the '903' forgery. Brown Candover was manorially associated with Woodmancott in 1066, but its tenth-century assessment of 10 hides shows that it had been given originally without Woodmancott. Bradley was included among the lands of Preston Candover, which was retained by the Crown in 1066—or at least by the royal family—as it had six small manors, of which four were held from King Edward, one from his queen, Edith, and one from her brother, Earl Harold. The less fertile upland north of Preston Candover remained royal land. The manors of Farleigh Wallop, Nutley, Ellisfield, Herriod, and *Sudberie* were all still held from the king at Domesday.

The manors of the Alre valley are easily followed. A large, 40-hide estate comprising the later manors of Alresford and Medstead was granted to the Old Minster, reputedly by Cenwalh in 701, and later confirmed by Egbert and others. The large size of the estate and the lack of tangible documentation are good indicators of an early date. A smaller manor, Bighton, was given to the New Minster in 959. Sutton was included in the later parish of Ropley and probably remained royal land until the eleventh century when Earl Harold owned it. In 1086, Count Eustace held it from the king.

The complex development of the manors of the Tichbourne valley begins with a large estate based upon Tichbourne. The monks of the Old Minster owned it in the ninth century. Most of its land was leased to the bishop in the early tenth century, and the boundaries given for these lands comprise the manors of Cheriton and Beauworth. Upon the bishop's death in 958, the leased land went to a kinsman, rather than reverting back to the Old Minster. Later they were restored to the reformed cathedral, as common revenues for the newly installed monks. In 991, Ethelred gave Hinton Ampner to the Church of St. Peter in Stoneham, Hampshire, but the manor must have reverted to the Crown or was exchanged, for in 1045, Edward the Confessor gave it to the Bishop of Winchester. The only manor in the Tichbourne valley to remain under royal control was Bramdean, which was held by four men in 1066, and by two royal servants in 1086.

The south bank of the Itchen valley seems to have been an early source of royal grants. Easton was in the bishop's hands ca. 875, and probably had been so for a long time. In 900, reference was made to the gift of Ovington to the Old Minster by an ealdorman's grandfather, an event that had probably taken place in the third quarter of the ninth century. Edgar confirmed the Old Minster's possession of Ovington, and in 961 he gave it Avington as well. On the north bank, the history of the Worthys is complicated by forgeries. The Old Minster claimed that ca. 710 Cenwalh had given it lands at Headbourne Worthy and that Egbert gave it Martyr Worthy ca. 840. Ethelwulf did grant Martyr Worthy to a thegn ca. 870, and he may have restored Headbourne Worthy to the Old Minster, which held both in 1066. In 961, Chilland was confirmed in the possession of the Old Minster, which had probably received it from the thegn to whom Athelstan had given it in 939. Canute granted Abbots Worthy in 1026 to the Bishop of Crediton, who passed it to the New Minster by 1066. Littleton, Itchen Stoke, and Itchen Abbess have no pre-Conquest credentials, but they were no doubt recent donations to the Old Minster, Romsey Abbey, and St. Mary's Abbey of Winchester, respectively. Finally, Kings Worthy was never granted out before the Conquest and was part of the king's revenue in 1066.

The upper Test valley was another area where the monks of the Old Minster claimed to have received large estates before the early tenth century. King Edward reputedly confirmed in 909 the bishop's title to the manor of Whitchurch, which included the adjacent vills of Freefolk and Whitnall at Domesday. He is further claimed to have confirmed in 909 the monks' title to Overton with its detached holding at Bradley (a wooded area north of the Test, and not the Candover manor of the same name). These five estates were later confirmed by Edgar. In 940 Edmund and in 956 Eadwy granted Quidhampton to certain thegns, who later gave it to the Old Minster. The remaining royal land of the upper Test valley was at Polhampton, which was given in 1033 by Canute to Earl Godwin. His son Tosti held it in 1066, but William then confiscated all the property of the Godwinson family, and it was once again royal land in 1086. King William did return to the New Minster its manor of Laverstock, which had been held of the abbey by a Saxon lady until her death after the Conquest.

In the northeast upland of the Test watershed, most of the lands remained under royal control. Deane, Oakley, Steventon, Dumner were still royal property in 1066. Ashe had been acquired by Earl Harold, but it was reclaimed by the king in 1086. Winchester Cathedral did have some properties here, though. Ethelred granted Wooton St. Laurence in 990 to a priest, from whom it passed to the Old Minster. North Waltham had long been attached to the monks' Overton manor, recorded in the reputed confirmations of 909 and 961 as well as in Domesday Book.

The earliest recorded grant in the middle Test valley is that of Chilbolton, which was given to the Old Minster in 934. Eadred gave Leckford in 947 to a priest, who bequeathed it by 955 to the New Minster and St. Mary's (Nunnaminster) of Winchester. Edgar booked Middleton to himself in 968, and he must have given or left it to his wife, the foundress of Wherwell, which possessed it in 1066. The territory of Middleton then included the vills of Forton, Middleton, Longparish, and Aston. Tufton was also acquired by Wherwell Abbey before 1066. Lands at Drayton and Barton Stacey were leased to a thegn by the abbot of New Minster ca. 1000, so they had been acquired in the tenth century.[1] More lands were taken out of Barton Stacey, even though the core of the property was part of the royal *feorm* in 1066. Edward the Confessor seems to have given the Old Minster

---

[1]   During the Danish wars, Drayton manor was lost to the New Minster, but after Canute had given it to a noble (perhaps the son of the recent lessee), he reversed himself and restored it to the New Minster (S956).

in 1045 a small tract of land at Barton Stacey, as well as the vills of Bransbury and Forde. Newton Stacey, a daughter settlement, first appears in a forgery of eleventh-century date.

The final group of manorial descents to summarize is that of the Somborne valley. It underwent less alienation of royal lands than is found elsewhere in this survey. Crawley was an Old Minster manor, acquired before the 909 Edward confirmation charter was forged at the end of the century. Across the Test, Houghton was probably the *Horton* in the ca. 970 Edgar confirmation of Old Minster lands (S827); it was held by the bishop in 1066. The remainder of the Somborne valley was royal land.

THE HIDAGE OF MIDDLE HAMPSHIRE

Middle Hampshire is divided into eight topographic units: the Micheldever, Somborne, Middle Test, and Upper Test zones of the Test River drainage system; and the Candover, Alre, Tichborne, and Upper Itchen zones of the Itchen River drainage system (see figure 3.1). The manors within these areas are presented in geographic order, ascending or descending the valleys. Information for each manor/village unit is presented in the following order: pre-1100 documentary references, hidage assessments, and discussion of manorial extents. The charter references are to Peter Sawyer, *Anglo-Saxon Charters*, and descriptions of the documents are drawn from Sawyer and from H.P.R. Finberg's *The Early Charters of Wessex*. The hidage figures are taken from grants, ecclesiastical lists, and the Domesday figures of 1066 and 1086, as presented in Munby's 1982 edition.[2]

The combined results serve as the basis for first, reconstructing each Anglo-Saxon manor's territory, and secondly, grouping the manors within topographic units. For each group, a summation of the findings covers the territorial unit and any irregularities, the estimated hidage total and alternate figures, and an explanation of the results and their local significance.

Charter references are S = Sawyer, *Anglo-Saxon Charters*. Other abbreviations are OM = Old Minster; NM = New Minster; DB = Domesday Book; numbers following the abbreviations refer to the sections and entries as recorded in *Domesday Book: Hampshire*, ed., J. Munby; TRE = *Tempus Regis Edwardi*: (1066); AJ = *Archaeological Journal*, several volumes in which G.B. Grundy published his study "Saxon Land Charters and Place-Names of Hampshire."

---

[2]   More detailed discussion of individual charter bounds can be found in "Micheldever," especially pp. 583-619.

The Itchen River Drainage System

THE TICHBORNE VALLEY

Tichborne
S385: (899-909) Edward and cathedral clergy to Bishop Denewulf for three lives, reverting to the church of Winchester, 20 hides at *Ticceburnan*. The bounds are those of Cheriton and Beauworth.[3]
S444: Athelstan to Old Minster, 25 hides at Tichborne, including 5 h. at *Beowyrth*. All to remain in episcopal domain. Bounds.[4]
S1491: Will of Bishop Aelfsige (955-958). Divides up episcopal estates. *Tioceburnan* to Wulfric Cufing, with remainder to OM.
S687: Eadgar to thegn Wulfric for 20 mancuses of gold. Restitution of lands, including Tichborne, which Wulfric had forfeited.
S826: Eadgar confirms to OM title to 60 *cassati* at Tichborne, Beauworth, and Ovington.
S818: Eadgar summarizes and confirms charters to OM. Lands are restored to the church, to be administered by the Bishop, as common revenues for the maintenance of the monks, replacing canons' prebends.
S1820: Cathedral list of the lands belonging to Chilcomb estate of 100 hides. Tichborne 25 hides, Ovington 5, Kilmeston 5, Avington 5.
DB: no entry.

Cheriton
Included in Tichborne, above.
DB: no entry.

Beoworth
Included in Tichborne, above.
DB: 2,1 (Fawley H.) Alresford 51 hides, now 41. Included are 6 hides of Beauworth.

Kilmeston
S693a: (961) Edgar grants thegn Ethelwulf 10 *mansae* at Kilmeston, at annual rent payable to church of Winchester with reversion to OM Bounds: Kilmeston, 8 acres of meadow, messuage in town, and land at Millbarrow.[5]
S693b: 961 Bishop Brithelm and clergy OM to Ethelwulf, Kilmeston for 3 lives.
DB: 2,2 (Fawley H.) Bishop hold K. 5 hides.
2,2 Aldred holds K. from Bishop, 5 hides.

---

[3]   *AJ* 78 (1921), 150-156.
[4]   Ibid., 156-159. These bounds are not exactly the same as those presented above, which is prpbably related to the increase of the estate from 20 to 25 hides.
[5]   *AJ* 78 (1921), 159-161; 83 (1926), 155-162.

Hinton Ampner

S942: (990-992) Ethelred to St. Peter and All Saints, Stoneham, 10 *mansae* at *Heantun.*[6]

S1007: (1045) Edward to B. Aelfwine, 8 *mansae* in Hinton.[7]

DB: 3,18 (Mainsborough H ?) 8 hides, TRE and now pays for 5.

Bramdean

No charter; royal land.

DB: 68,7 (Ashley H.) Miles the Porter held B. from K.

TRE 3 manors of 1 hide, 2.5 virgates.

Now nothing.

69,3 Odo thegn holds, Leofwine held from K.E. 1h. 1v.

    The development of the manors of the Tichborne valley is difficult to trace, because the major estate, that of Tichborne itself, became part of the immense Chilcomb estate of the Old Minster, and was not assessed in Domesday Book. The landmarks of the bounds of the lands 'at Tichborne' (S385) show that this tract actually consisted of Beauworth and Cheriton parishes. The hidage reported in the OM inventory of Chilcomb lands (S1820), records 25 for Tichborne, and 5 for Kilmeston. The Kilmeston grant by Edgar to a thegn for 3 lives (S693) is for 10 hides, not 5. This document is accurate, because it is supported by a lease defining the term of the grant as the lives of three successive tenants. The Domesday account gives two manors of 5 hides each. Presumably, Kilmeston estate had been divided before the OM inventory was drawn up, and only one of the manors was included in the Chilcomb holdings of the OM.

    It seems from the documentary evidence, (a portion of which is spurious material), that a 20 hide estate at Tichborne had been held by the clergy of the OM in the ninth century, who leased it to the Bishop of Winchester ca. 900, for three lives. Athelstan later acknowledged the grant to the church of 25 hides at Tichborne, including 5 at Beauworth. Bishop Aelfsige, however, bequeathed an estate at Tichborne, ca. 958, with remainder to the OM. The heir, a Wulfric Cufing, forfeited all his land for some misdeed, but by paying a penalty to King Edgar, he was confirmed in his holding after 960. According to Winchester Cathedral documents, King Edgar is purported to have confirmed the OM in its title to 60 *cassati* (hides) at Tichborne, Beauworth, and Ovington. The 60 hides of this questionable confirmation have every appearance of being the sum of all the documents available to the Old Minster scribes: the 20 hides of the Edward lease, the 25 hides of the Athelstan grant, plus the 10 hides of Kilmeston and a 5 hide-estate at Ovington. That the Edward and Athelstan documents concerned the same lands was a point apparently overlooked by the author of the Edgar forgery, while the early eleventh-century Chilcomb land list accurately reports Tichborne at 25 hides and Ovington at 5 hides.

---

[6]   *AJ* 83 (1926), 139-142.

[7]   Ibid.

Cheriton was a part of Tichborne throughout the early medieval period, while Beauworth was attached to it, as we have seen, in the tenth century. By 1066, however, six hides at Beauworth were held from the Bishop by a layman. The present size of Beauworth might suggest an estate more on the order of 10 or 11 hides, though the southern part of the parish could have been a later medieval addition, as it lies outside the valley in an unpopulated upland that is poorly defined in Saxon charters, and may have been developed only after the Conquest. In this case, the original estate of 5 or 6 hides may have extended only as far as the Tichborne valley watershed.

Beauworth and Kilmeston were in the bishop's Fawley Hundred, as was the Chilcomb manor of Tichborne. Hinton had been granted by Edward the Confessor to the Bishop of Winchester as 8 hides in 1045. By Edward the Confessor's death, the 8 hides were still there, but they had been beneficially reduced to a 5-hide payment. Hinton's hundredal associations are obscure. It has no separate heading in the Domesday Book, leaving open the assumption that it lay in Mansbridge Hundred, the hundredal designation for the manor of the preceding Domesday entry. But this hundred was in southern Hampshire, near Southampton, and it would be most unusual for the bishop to put, or permit the placement of, his manor in a court that was held halfway across Hampshire. It is much more likely that this is an example of an omission of hundred identification in Domesday Book. As Hinton was later in Fawley Hundred, it was probably originally in this particular hundred that included much of the land east of the upper Itchen.

Bramdean was royal land and thus did not receive a charter. The Domesday survey found two small holdings there; the total hidage came to only 2 hides, 2½ virgates, though William later reduced one of the assessments to nothing. The landholders were a royal servant and a king's thegn. These types of individuals often, perhaps usually, received beneficial hidation from the king, and it is likely that the true hidage of Bramdean had once been larger, as the size of the parish suggests. Bramdean was in the tiny hundred of Ashley (later Bishop Sutton), which contained only West Tisted and Bishop Sutton. West Tisted straddles the watershed and is logically associated with East Tisted of the Selbourne valley.

The recorded hidage of the Tichborne valley manors is Tichborne, Cheriton, and Beauworth 25 hides, Kilmeston 10, Hinton 8, Bramdean 2, totalling 45 hides.[8] But there is also a discrepancy in the charter figures. The hidage of the Edward lease was 20 hides, and that of the Athelstan's grant or confirmation was 25 hides, 5 of which were at Beauworth. Examination of the charter bounds prohibits the assumption that the 5 hides of Beauworth were added at that time. Boundary landmarks indicate, rather, that Beauworth and Cheriton were the original 20 hides. The 5 hides must have been added to the west side of the estate, from the east side of present Tichborne parish. Sevington Farm, an early settlement-name, and the only recorded property division, forms a narrow strip that accurately matches the 5 hide allottment. Here I follow Grundy's suggestions, noting his

[8]   This does not include the extra fraction of virgate at Bramdean.

appropriate caution about the many unidentifiable landmarks.[9] One must conclude that little of present Tichborne parish was included in the "25 hides at Tichborne." The question is, what was the remainder of the Tichborne manor proper?

The answer is not readily forthcoming, as Tichborne was soon absorbed into the Cathedral's hundredal manor of Chilcomb, the supreme example of beneficial hidation, with a single hide assessed for the entire hundred. It is easier to gauge the hidage of Tichborne by comparing it to manors of similar size. It has approximately the same area as the five hides that the boundary marks show belonging to the Sevington area of Tichborne. The remainder, then, including Tichborne village, may have had an assessment at a similar figure, probably also 5 hides. This would bring the Tichborne group of manors up to a full total of 50 hides, a surprisingly even total for the valley unit.

THE ALRE VALLEY

Alresford

S242. (701) Ine to OM, 40 *mansae*, bounds of Old and New Alresford, and Medstead parishes. *A.J.* 78 (1921), 69-77.

S284. (n.d.) Egbert to OM, restitution of 40 *mansae* in Alresford. Bounds same.[10]

S1287. (879x909) Edward confirmation of OM's title, after Alfred's forfeiture and Denewulf's gift of a gold bowl to the king. B. Frithestan and sucessors forbidden to lease church land to laymen.

S598. (956) Eadwig to thegn Aelfric, 40 *mansae* at *Alresforda*. Same territory as above.[11]

S814. (n.d.) Edgar to OM, for Ethelwold, restoration of 40 *cassati* at Alresford. Cites original gift by Cenwalh, restitution by Egbert, lease by Denewulf, Alfred's forfeiture, Denewalh's recovery at a price, and Alfred's son's possession. The king now annuls the charter issued to the son, presumably Aelfric.

S1821. List of Winchester Cathedral lands. Alresford 40 hides.

DB (Fawley H.) Bishop Walkelin holds Alresford. TRE 51 hides, now 42, 40 ploughs. Include 4 hides in Soberton and 6 in Beauworth.

Bighton

S660. (959) Eadwig to NM for clothing. 10 *mansae* at *Bicingtun*, in exchange for 60 *mancuses* of gold. Bounds given are those of the present parish.[12]

DB (Chutely H.?) NM held 10 hides, now 7, 8 ploughs.

---

[9]   *AJ* 83 (1926), 158. This does seem the only reasonable conclusion.

[10] Ibid.

[11] Ibid.

[12] Ibid., 106-108.

Bishop's Sutton

S1507 (873-88) Possibly the *Suttune* given by Alfred to Edward the Elder in his will.

DB; 20,1 (Ashley H.) Count Eustace holds from king. Earl Harold held 25 hides. Now answers for 10, so did TRE, as hundred states. 50 ploughs.

20,2 (Neatham H.) Count Eustace holds 5 hides in Headley. TRE 3. Earl Godwin held, and it is accounted for in Sutton.

The Alre valley was divided into three main estates: Alresford, Sutton, and the smaller Bighton. The 40 hides at Alresford appear to date back to a grant in the eighth or ninth century, perhaps by Egbert in the second quarter of the ninth century, though tradition has it that Alresford was bestowed upon the Old Minster by Cenwalh in the mid-seventh century.[13] The 40-hide estate contained the present parishes of Old and New Alresford and Medstead, but probably excluded Wield parish, contrary to Grundy's opinion.[14] By Domesday, it was in the hands of the bishop, rather than the cathedral clergy.

In the rest of the Alre valley catchment basin lay Sutton, an estate valued at 25 hides TRE, but which answered for only 10. It seems never to have been granted to the Church. A *Suttune* was bequeathed by Alfred to Edward the Elder, and Domesday Book records that Earl Harold, then Count Eustace, held it from the king. It had probably remained a royal manor until the eleventh century. The Domesday survey valued the estate at 25 hides, but found land there for 50 ploughs, which strongly suggests that the original hidage assessment was 50 hides. It was probably reduced to 25 hides when Godwin received the estate, and by 1066 it was further reduced to answer for 10 hides. This sort of reduction is not uncommon and here it explains the absence in the early medieval records of the large parish of Ropley, adjacent to Sutton on the east. The combined parishes of Sutton and Ropley would contain enough land for 50 ploughs, which by a rough equivalency would bring the original assessment of *Suttune* to 50 hides.

Lying between these two large estates was the more average-sized manor of Bighton, granted at 10 hides in 959 by Eadwig to the New Minster, and immediately leased out to a king's thegn, a common practice before the Ethelwold/Edgar reformation of the mid-tenth century.[15] The Domesday entry for Bighton omitted its hundredal association; it has been assumed that Bighton was associated with the New Minster estate in Chutely Hundred in north Hampshire that preceded it in the Domesday Book.[16] But this was the little (5 hides) manor of Worting, and there is no parallel to an insignificant and distant manor controlling the judicial arrangements of a larger estate only a few miles from Micheldever.

---

[13] *ECW* 215.

[14] *AJ* 78 (1921), 69-71.

[15] This practice is specifically condemned in the Edgar confirmation grant of the Chilcomb privileges (S817), and must have been fairly widespread, at least in the Hampshire area.

[16] *DB Hants*, chapter 6, entry 3.

Bighton was later in Bishop Sutton Hundred, the late medieval name of the Domesday Ashley Hundred. This is another case of omission on the part of the Domesday Book scribe, who seems to have had great difficulty with the New Minster section of the Hampshire entries.[17]

The 50 hides of Sutton (and Ropley), the 40 hides of Alresford (and Medstead), and the 10 hides of Bighton bring the total early medieval hidage of the Alre valley to an even 100 hides. One may conclude that the Alre valley drainage basin was the unit of assessment and revenue collection that here preceded the later hundreds. It had territorial unity, economic integrity, and was a hundred-hide contributor of royal dues. The relative importance of the place-names suggests that this territorial unit was based on Alresford, and not on the former outlier of Sutton.[18]

THE CANDOVER VALLEY

Abbotstone

S1821. List of Winchester Cathedral lands. Includes *Abbodestun*, 10 hides.
DB: 2,23 (Bountisborough H.) Hugh de Port holds A. from Bishop. 9 hides. Bounds.[19]

Swarraton

S370. (903, sp.) King Edward to New Minster. List of gifts includes 3 hides, 1½ yardlands at *Swerwetone*.
DB No entry. Apparently included with Micheldever lands.

Wield

No charter.
DB: 2,21 (Bountisborough H.) Durand holds Wield of Bishops. TRE two free men held it. 10 hides. Bounds.[20]

Northington

S360. (901) Edward to NM 6 hides at Candover added.
S370. (903, sp.) Confirmation of Micheldever estate, includes 6 hides at Northington.
DB: 6,16 (Micheldever H.) Micheldever manor of 106 hides includes separate holdings, one of 6 hides held by Alfsi, whose father had held it.

---

[17]   *DB Hants*, entries of chapter 4, entry 1 and chapter 6, entries 13-17 were inserted directly after chapter 4.

[18]   Margaret Gelling considers the 'ford' names among early toponyms that could be the center of a conglomerate estate: see *Signposts to the Past: Place-Names and the History of England* (London, 1978), p. 123. For the other valley names, see Appendix B.

[19]   *AJ* 78 (1921), 70.

[20]   Ibid.

Candover

S1507. (873-888) Will of King Alfred. Leaves to second daughter *Cleran* and *Cendefer*.

S360. (901) Edward to NM Includes addition of 6 hides at Candover. Bounds.[21]

S370. (903, sp.)Edward to NM Confirmation of Micheldever and 10 hides at Candover.

S1524. Will of Ordnoth to OM 10 hides at *Cendefer*.

S1821. List of Winchester Cathedral lands. Includes *Endefer* (sic) 10 hides.

DB: 6,13 (Mainsborough H.) NM held TRE for 20 hides. Hugh de Port holds 2½ hides. Alfsi holds Woodmancott, 6 hides 2½ virgates. The 20 hides of this manor now answer for 13 hides and 2½ virgates. (Brown Candover).

2,19 (Mainsborough H.) Godwin and Leofwin held from Bishop TRE, two manors 5 hides each. 10 hides. (Chilton Candover).

21,2; 23,30; 29,13; 35,7; 69,6; 69,8 4 small estates held directly from King Edward, 1 from Earl Harold, 1 from Queen Edith. The largest is 5½ hides, the smallest is 1 virgate. The total is 19 hides, 2 virgates. (Preston Candover).

Farleigh Wallop

No charter.

DB: 69,14 (Bermondspitt H.) Siric the Chamberlain holds from the king; Wulfeva held from King Edward; 4 hides, now 3.

Nutley

No charter.

DB: 56, 3 (Bermondspitt H.) Henry the Treasurer holds, four men held from King Edward. 5 hides, now 2½. Geoffrey the Marshall holds ½ hide of the manor as the Hundred estate.

Ellisfield

No charter.

DB: 23,59 (Bermondspitt H.) among the lands Hugh de Port holds from the Bishop of Bayeux. Auti held from King Edward. 8 hides.

Herriard

No charter.

DB: 23,29 (Bermondspitt H.) Lands of Hugh de Port. Erling held from King Edward. 5 hides.

[21] Ibid., 140-142.

'Sudberie' [22]

DB: 69,13 (Bermondspitt H.) Ednoth and Edwy held from King Edward. After his death they also died. Cola, a kinsman, bought the land from King William. 2½ hides.

The bounds of Abbotstone reveal that the Saxon manor had the same extent as the later parish. Without a boundary description, Swarraton is less easy to define, however, and its original territory may have extended further east than the parish boundary, as far as the Abbotstone lands, with a small portion being taken by the later medieval estate of Godsfield. Further, the site of the medieval village of Swarraton was not opposite Northington, but by the Grange at the south-west corner of the stream, where a narrow valley rises to the east. The lands for Swarraton were situated, then, in the small depression between the western end of Bugmore Hill to the north and the high ground of Abbotstone Down to the south. It is unlikely that New Minster originally held the "6 hides at Candover" or the 3 hides at Swarraton. The 6 hides were an addition to the foundation charter of 900/1, and the Swarraton lands were added later in the tenth century. By the time the spurious 903 charter was concocted in the early eleventh century, the 6 hides had become attached to the Northington manorial unit of Micheldever. Swarraton must have then been taken into the same unit by Domesday, because it no longer appears as a separate estate. Both manors must appear as the entry noting 6 hides of Alfsi, the 1½ hides of Aldred, and the 2 of Siward Hunter.

The bounds accompanying the grant of 6 hides at Candover (S360) do not apply to Northington, nor do they easily fit what 6 hides generally represent in land measurement. The compiler of the several original documents that went into S360 therefore incorrectly associated Northington with these bounds, presumably because in both cases, the lands lay on the Candover stream.[23] The 6 hides can be more accurately defined as those of Northington in the somewhat later 'Golden Charter' (S370). The 6-hide figure from the New Minster records, (and presumably the manor held by Alfsi in 1066), is too small an assessment for the present parish, but it may reflect the size of an original estate before assarting took place south of Burcot. The 6 hides may also refer to only one or two of the three manors into which Northington was divided in the later Middle Ages: Totford, Northington and the Grange.[24] Perhaps the best explanation is that the later medieval 6-hide manor

---

[22]   The unidentified manor of *Sudberie* was probably in the southwest part of Ellisfield parish. There is an earthwork (bury) and nearby field names of Berry Down and Lower Common.

[23]   Nicholas Brooks persuasively argues that the document cannot be an original, as Finberg held, but was a pastiche of different charters for the estates in the donation: Brooks, "The Oldest Document in the College Archives? The Micheldever Forgery," in *Winchester College Sixth-Centenary Studies*, Roger Custance, ed. (Oxford, 1982) pp. 191-196, 215.

[24]   Pipe Roll Society, *13 Henry II*: holdings of *Nove Convent*, p. 187; *Wudi Prioris, Ichen Monialum, Papenholt H'berti, Micheldever Abbatis, Totfort, Popham, Candeva, Candievra, Dummer*, p. 188; *Northington*, p. 189.

of Totford represents the early medieval 6-hide unit, and the unidentified 5-hide unit among Micheldever demesne lands at Domesday contained the remainder of the Northington lands.

It is unlikely that the bounds of S360 can refer to Northington or Swarraton because 1) neither of those places, nor Totford, is mentioned in the bounds, and 2) local medieval and post-medieval field and wood names readily identify the *Bicanhurst*, *stancistele*, and the *burn stowe*, which was possibly the source of the medieval manor and village name, *Brun Cendefer* (see Appendix B). The land units along the Candover were those of Brown Candover, Chilton Candover, and Preston Candover. The nearly 20 hide assessment for Preston must include the later parish of Bradley, which has been incorrectly identified as the *Bradleah* of Overton Hundred.[25] Lands attached to the Micheldever estate can be identified as a strip along the north side of Brown Candover parish. The 6-hide assessment of this strip seems far too high, and it is probable that this figure did not originally refer to these lands, but to the bulk of the property in Northington. When the rest of Brown Candover came into the hands of the New Minster, both parts made up the assessment of 10 hides that is recorded in S370.

The original grant by Edward to New Minster in 901 survives in S360, a composite text that includes several later additions as well as the bounds of the Micheldever estate. The strip north of Brown Candover was one of these additions, and the alteration to the text took place while the land was attached tenurially to Northington, before the acquisition of the remainder of Brown Candover, and the reuniting of that manor. Northington had an assessment of 6 hides. This figure appears in the later effort of the New Minster forgers, S370, and it is the Domesday assessment for a Micheldever holding that is probably Northington. A likely explanation is that the compiler of S360 took the hidage figure from the Northington lands and applied it to the Candover strip that was associated with Northington. The compiler may have wished to record all extant boundaries and hidage assessments, and the mis-identification of the two elements might be expected in a pastiche like S360.

The Wield boundary on the 40 hide grant at Alresford, (S242, etc.) contains several identifiable landmarks. A *mintmere* is clearly at the south-east corner of the parish, where Grundy found a field named Minchams, from *mint-hammas*.[26] From this point and the reference to *Bucgan oran* (Bugmore Hill), however, the landmarks are difficult to place. Grundy's identification of the landmarks between these two points is not convincing, and it is more likely that the whole of Wield lay outside of the Alresford grant. Wield itself drains more into the Candover valley than into the Alre, and despite tenurial associations with Alresford, it should be considered one of the Candover manors.

---

[25]   The identification is not stated in the note to Munby, *DB Hants*, chapter 2, entry 10, but the map at the rear of the text places the Candover Bradley in Overton Hundred.

[26]   The meaning is 'mint enclosures.' There is a strong likelihood that the pond and the enclosures took the secondary name from a descriptive term for the locale; see *AJ* 78 (1921), 72-73.

To sum up the information, the Candover catchment area consists of two parts: the main course of the Candover above the ridge north of the Itchen-Alre valley; and the upper reaches consisting of dry valleys north of Oxford. The latter division is a group of poor manors: Farliegh (4 hides), Nutley (5), Ellisfield (8), Herriard (5), and *Sudberie* (2½), all totalling an assessment of 24½ hides. Most of the lower portion of the catchment area consisted of the Candover villages *per se*: Preston (19 hides, 2 virgates), Chilton (10 hides), and Brown (10 hides). Preston Candover also contained Bradley parish, and Brown Candover included a strip of land that had been the subject of a separate grant. On the east side of the valley were Wield (10 hides), Swarraton (3½), and Abbotstone (10), while along the west side were the Northington lands, assessed at 6 hides. The recorded maximum hidage of the lower Candover valley was 68½ hides, 2 virgates. The assessment for the entire Candover valley totals 93 hides, 2 virgates. This number, based solely on a topographic grouping of estates, is decidedly close to an even 100 hides, repeating the findings for the Tichborne and Alre valleys. As will be demonstrated below, the hidage figures for Micheldever valley come to 7 hides over a similarily even amount, suggesting a mingling or transferral of lands and their hidage assessment, across the Micheldever/Candover watershed.

THE ITCHEN VALLEY (SOUTH SIDE)

Ovington

S826. (n.d.) Edgar to OM, confirming 60 *cassati* at Tichborne, Beauworth, and Ovington.

S1821. (1040-1042).[27] List of lands belonging to OM's Chilcomb manor: Easton 4 hides, Avington 5, Ovington 5, Tichborne 25, Kilmeston 5, etc.

DB No entry, as part of Chilcomb.

Yavington

S1284. (900) B. Denewulf to Ealdorman Ordlaf, exchange of land, including 3 hides (*manentes*) at *Ebincgtune* given by the bishop to the clergy, which Ordlaf's grandfather Earnulf, had given to the church.

DB: 2,18 (Bountisborough H.) Bishop holds. Stigand held TRE. Then 1½ hides. Now 0.

14,6 St. Mary's, Winchester holds. Stigand held. Then 1½ hides. Now 0.

Avington

S699. (961) Edgar to OM. 5 *mansae* at *Afintun*. Bounds.[28]

S1820. (ca. 1041) List of lands belonging to OM's Chilcomb manor: Avington 5 hides.

---

[27]   Finberg suggests that this was 'le hide boc de Chilcomb' from the reign of Harthacnut (1040-1042) that was listed in Winchester in 1643: *ECW* 67.

[28]   *AJ* 78 (1921), 94-99.

DB: 3,4 (Fawley Hundred) Held by the cathedral. 5 hides.

Easton
S1275. (871-77) B. Ealferth to Ealdorman Cuthred and wife, for three lives, 8 hides at *Eastune*. Bounds.[29]
S695. (961) Edgar to kinsman B. Byrthelm 7½ *mansae* at Easton. Bounds.[30]
S827. (n.d.) Edgar to OM, for Ethelwold. Confirmation of title to 64 *mansae* in ... Chilland, Eastun, Hunton, etc.
S1820. (ca. 1041) List of lands of OM's Chilcomb manor: Easton 4 hides.
DB: 2,5 (Fawley H.) Bishop holds in lordship. 6 hides. 11 plough. 2 small churches.
Geoffrey holds 3 hides, Brichtric jointly held them from Bishop. Alwin has 1 hide, 1 virgate.

Winchester Cathedral owned at least 8 hides at Easton ca. 875, when the bishop leased them out. The bounds accompanying this document are not easily identified. In 961, King Edgar granted to his relative, the Bishop of Winchester, 7½ *mansae* at Easton, presumably an additional grant of land. But when the list of lands in the Chilcomb hundredal manor was drawn up, ca. 1041, Easton was assigned only 4 hides. By 1066, it was assessed at 6 hides, but had land for 11 ploughs. It seems clear that the 'Easton' of these documents refers to differing tracts of land south of the Itchen River.

The 7½-hide grant by Edgar has boundary features that show it to have included all of Easton, as it shares a series of landmarks with the Avington charter, and elsewhere has features identifiable on the later parish boundary. Grundy suggested that the 7½ hides were far too small to represent a tract of this size, and he concluded that the estate had already been reduced by beneficial hidation. If the 7½ hides (an unusual figure) marked a 50% ·reduction (which in itself is a common reduction), the resulting 15 hides for Easton would be most appropriate for the above-average size of the parish.

The 961 Easton bounds are substantially those of the modern parish, but the ca. 875 charter of 8 hides at Easton has different landmarks in its boundary clause. This difference led Grundy to suggest that the grant in question was not concerned with Easton proper, but represented a strip of land in Avington that before nineteenth-century local government changes had been a detached part of Easton parish.[31] While other scholars have followed Grundy, a close examination of the text does not support his conclusions. A better explanation is that the 8 hides of *ca.* 875 were basically the same lands as the 7½ hides at Easton in 961. The earlier estate has been seen to represent the entire parish of Easton. The loss of ½ hide from the ninth-century assessment could be related to the absence of several

29   *AJ* 81 (1924), 88.
30   *AJ* 81 (1924), 88-92.
31   *AJ* 78 (1921), 95.

boundary points south of *smalan dun*,[32] suggesting that the boundary was slightly shortened, but it probably represents the tenth-century concern for greater accuracy, which yielded this improved figure for half of 15 hides.

The identification of the lands of S1275 with the integral Easton estate means that the 8 hides need no longer be sought in the eastern side of Avington, where a small strip contained exparochial lands of Easton, Itchen Stoke, Itchen Abbas, and Avington parishes. Rather, the strip may be better viewed as the result of later medieval disintegration of the Yavington estate that was assessed at 3 hides in DB, but was already divided into two manors, and is today represented by a farm of that name forming the eastern side of Avington parish.

There are curious aspects to the other estates, as well. Avington was considered a 5-hide manor in 961 when Edgar granted it to the OM (S1299) and in the Chilcomb land list compiled under Harthacanute (S1820). At Domesday it was valued at 5 hides. Yavington, we have noted, was at 3 hides in 1066. Ovington has no surviving grant, but appeared on the Chilcomb land list (S1820) as 5 hides, and it remained in Chilcomb manor at Domesday. Earlier, Ovington was one of the manors we have noted in a dubious confirmation by Edgar to the OM of 60 *cassati* at Tichborne, Beauworth, and Ovington (S826), and its hidage can be calculated at 5 hides then.

We have also suggested that the 8 hides of Easton were probably reduced at an early date from a higher assessment, considering the size of the manor, especially when comparing it to the 20-hide unit across the river, of the Itchen Stoke and Itchen Abbas. The combined manors of Itchen Stoke and Abbas may serve as the common denominator for manors here, for there is no suggestion that their 20 hides were artificially reduced. The neighboring manors south of the Itchen had identical geography, and their low hidage suggests that they had early on received beneficial hidation, and that their proper assessments should be double those recorded. Thus, one can propose several series of figures for the Easton to Ovington group of manors. At its very least (with an 8-hide Easton) it totals 21 hides. If the estates had undergone beneficial hidation (as seems likely), the amounts would be Easton 15, Avington 10, Yavington 6, Ovington 10. Grundy's detached strip in Avington parish may very neatly fit the description of the 4-hide parcel that the Chilcomb land list (S1820) assigned to Easton. This tract may have been only recently acquired by the cathedral, and was attached to the Chilcomb estate as a part of Easton held not by the bishop but by the cathedral.[33] Its location adjacent to the Yavington manor that was still extant in 1066 suggests that all three holdings (two Yavington manors and the strip to the west) had once formed a manorial unit assessed at 10 hides. If this were so, then the original hidage of the south side of the Itchen valley would be Easton 15, Avington 10, Yavington 10, Ovington 10; total 45 hides.

---

[32] Perhaps the detachment of the eastern lands of Eada's 'worth' (*Edeswyrth*) was the cause of the half-hide reduction.

[33] In this case, it would appear not to have been beneficially reduced, which would fit its origins as a private bequest (now lost) rather than a royal grant.

ITCHEN VALLEY (NORTH SIDE)

Itchen Stoke
No charter.
DB: 15,2 (Bountisborough H.) Romsey Abbey held TRE 8 hides, now 6.

Itchen Abbas
No charter.
DB: 44,1 (Bountisborough H.) Abbey of St. Mary's Winchester held TRE. Then
12 Now 3½, land for 3 ploughs.

Chilland
S351. (939) 'Alfred' (Athelstan) to thegn Heahfyrth. 8 *mansae* at *Worthige*. The
formula is that of Athelstan, but the witness list is a forgery. Bounds.[34]
(*Ceoligland*.)
DB: No entry.

Martyr Worthy
S283. (825) Egbert to OM, 5 *cassati* at *Worthige*. This charter was adapted from
an original grant by Egbert to a layman.[35] Bounds.[36]
S304. (854) Ethelwulf to thegn Hunsige. Exemption of all secular dues of 3 *cassati*
in *Wordi*. Part of Ethelwulf's 'Second Decimation.'[37] Bounds.[38]
S340. (868) Ethelred to thegn Hunsige, 5 *cassati* at *Worthige*. Bounds identical to
those of S383.[39]
DB: 3,13 (Barton H. ?) Always in the hands of the monastery (OM). TRE 3 hides.

Abbots Worthy
S962. (1026) Cnute to Lyfing Bishop of Credition, 5 *cassati* in *Worthy*. Bounds.[40]

DB: 6,17 (Micheldever H.) New Minster holds *Ordie*. 7 hides, but never paid tax.
Land for 3 ploughs.

Kings Worthy
No charter.
DB: 1,17 (Barton Hundred) Barton is of the king's revenue, paying a half-day's
revenue in all things. *Ordie*, an outlier, is attached. It was never assessed in hides

---

[34] *AJ* 83 (1926), 18-19.
[35] *EHR* (1933), 357.
[36] *AJ* 83 (1926), 182-185.
[37] Finberg discussed the 'Second Decimation' in detail in *ECW* 187-206.
[38] *AJ* 83 (1926), 185-187.
[39] Ibid., 182-185.
[40] Ibid., 167-169.

except for 6 hides that were held by freemen. They did not state the number of hides. Land for 25 ploughs.

Headbourne Worthy

S309. (854) K. Ethelwulf to OM, restitution of 3 *mansae* at *Worthige* originally granted by Cenwalh. The text is nearly identical to the two spurious charters of Alresford. Bounds.[41]

DB: 29,3 (Barton H.) Ralph de Mortimer holds. Chipping held TRE. 1 hide. land for 5 pl. The manor was bought out of the Church (OM) After the third heir, it will have it back with all its stock.

29,4 Ralph holds *Ordie*; Edsi held in 1066. 1 hide, 1 virgate; now 0. Land for 1 plough. It was a manor, is now placed in another.

39,3 Bernard Pancevolt holds (as one of a series of small properties once owned by Godwin). Godwin held of King Edward. 1 hide. land for 2 pl.

Littleton

No entry.

DB: No entry.

Littleton church was one of the seven parochial churches around Winchester that were held by the Cathedral, and consequently its manor has been assumed to have been included in the Chilcomb estate's seven subsidiary manors.[42] Munby placed Littleton in Falmer Hundred; it was later in Falmer's replacement, Buddlesgate Hundred.[43]

It is not possible here to discuss the many boundary clauses of the Worthy charters.[44] The general lines of the manorial boundaries show that they do not represent the total area of the combined Worthy parishes. Thus, while it is evident that the Worthies represent an ancient great estate, the process by which the later medieval land units were formed is in no way obvious.

The total hidage assessment for the manors along the north bank of the Itchen cannot be established with certainty, considering the amount of beneficial hidation and the non-hidation of the royal *feorm* at Kings Worthy. Some estimates of the total can be made, based on those surviving figures that can claim some degree of reliability. To start with, there are the Domesday 20 hides at Itchen Abbas and Itchen Stoke. The proportions of the lands of these parishes to that of the total area is very roughly 1:3, resulting in an approximate total of 60 hides.

---

[41]   Ibid, 127-130.

[42]   These seven manors are presumed to be associated with the seven churches held by Winchester Cathedral (*VCH* vol. 3, p. 316).

[43]   As illustrated in the map at the end of *DB Hants*.

[44]   The Worthy charters are discussed in detail in Eric Klingelhöfer, "Anglo-Saxon Manors of the Upper Itchen Valley: Their Origin and Evolution," *Poceedings of the Hampshire Field Club and Archaeological Society* 46 (1990), 31-39.

Individual assessments can be estimated as well. Martyr Worthy and Abbots Worthy have a 1066 total of 10 hides, but this does not include Chilland, and the Martyr Worthy assessment is much too low for its size, even without Chilland. It may be that the north part of Martyr Worthy that was later in Micheldever Hundred was not included in the early manor. The size of the manor may be misleading when hidage is presumably based upon the value of the land, not its extent. But the scale of this study, comparing hidage of more than eighty manors, makes that unlikely. This particular locality displays a high degree of geographic homogeneity. The lands are similar geologically and topographically, though there is no good indicator of the amount of woodland, and the pattern of medieval village distribution conforms to this homogeneity. Fifteen hides for the three manors of Abbots Worthy, Martyr Worthy, and Chilland is an appropriate figure. The hidage for the remaining three manors is more difficult to recover. The recorded hidage is only three for Headbourne Worthy in the questionable confirmation by Ethelwulf (S309), and the Domesday figure is 3 hides 1 virgate, with no entry for Littleton and with Kings Worthy unhidated. The three hides for Headbourne Worthy are again low for the amount of land concerned, especially as it had land for eight ploughs, a more accurate measure of land. As the area comprising Littleton, Headbourne Worthy, and Kings Worthy is slightly larger than the Abbots Worthy, Martyr Worthy, and Chilland block, an assessment of 20 hides would not be far off.

The approximation based on comparative size was 60 hides for manors on the north bank of the Itchen. This is similar to the more specific combined totals (estimates and absolutes) for the three blocks of land there: $20 + 15 + 20 = 55$ hides. The hidage assessment for the south bank of the Itchen valley topographical unit, from Easton to Ovington, came to 45 hides. These figures include estimates and corrections of reduced assessments, and the resulting total of 100 hides is a guideline for an original assessment rather than a claim to specificity.[45] Nevertheless, once again, a geographic division of the Itchen river drainage basin has yielded a grouping of Anglo-Saxon manors that give every indication of having been assessed originally a total of 100 hides.

The Test River Drainage System

THE TEST UPLAND

Ashe
No charter.
DB: 30,1 (Overton H.) Alwaker held it from Earl Harold. Then 8 hides, now 3.

---

[45] Early large blocks of land, like those in the upper Itchen topographical unit, typically have hidage assessments in multiple of ten. Using the principle of equivalency, and blocks of 10 hides only, one concludes that the hidage for the Upper Itchen valley must have been close to 100 hides.

Ashe presumably was retained as royal property until it was granted to Earl Harold, or perhaps his father Earl Godwin.

Deane
No charter.
DB: 32,2 (Chutley H.) Tovi held from K.Edward in freehold. TRE 20 hides, now 11.

Oakley
S1818. (979-1016) K. Ethelred to ... , 11 hides at *East Okley*. (Fragmentary.)
S1821. List of lands of Winchester Cathedral, includes *Aclea*, 10 hides.
The OM record of 10 hides at *Aclea* is probably the same land as the 11 hides granted out by King Ethelred at East Oakley, because all the Domesday lands at Oakley were still held by King Edward in 1066. East Oakley is a hamlet in Wootton St. Laurence.

Wooton St. Laurence
S874. (990) K. Ethelred grants to Ethelweard, minister, 15 *tributoria* at Wooton.
S1821. List of lands of Winchester Cathedral. Includes *Wudatuna*, 20 hides.
DB: 3,24 (Chutley H.) The monks hold from the bishop of Winchester (or 'the monks of the Bishop of Winchester hold') 20 hides.
23, 58 Aemer and Alfgeat held from K.Edward in freehold 5 hides.
East Oakley must have been included among the lands of Wooton, as there is no separate 10-hide piece, though it is possible that it was reduced in size or assessment and thus became the 5 hides held separately. This is unlikely, however, because there is no evidence that the lands ever left the Church.

Steventon
No charter.
DB: 69,48 (Basingstoke H.) Alfhelm held from K.Edward. Formerly 5 hides, but TRE and now 3 hides.

North Waltham
S376. (909) K. Edward confirms to Bishop Frithestan his title to Overton, etc., and 15 hides at *Wealtam*. Bounds.[46]
S827. (n.d.) K. Edgar confirms for Bishop Ethelwold to OM's title to Overton, etc., and 15 hides at North Waltham.
DB: Waltham is inclded in the 14 hides of Overton (see below).
North Waltham was one of a group of OM properties that according to Finberg were probably held by the canons dismissed at the time of the Church reforms of 964, but had no documentary support.[47] A forgery was made to date its granting to 909, with a more regular confirmation apparently unfulfilled at the time of

---

[46]   *AJ* 84 (1927), 172-177.
[47]   *ECW* 237.

Edgar's death. It is unlikely that Edward granted the property to the Old Minster at all, though he might have confirmed a title to it for a price, and a fairly large grant like this probably did come from royal hands.

Dummer
No charter.
DB: 23,31 (Bermondspitt H.) Alric held from K.E. 5 hides.
69,7 Auti held from K.E. 5 hides.

Kempshott
No charter.
DB: (Basingstoke H.) Aldred helf TRE. TRE and now 2 hides.

In the Test catchment area beyond the present source of the river are two now-dry valleys, leading north-east and south-east. Ashe is at the base of this group, and along the south-east valley are the villages of Steventon, North Waltham, and in its upper reaches Dummer and Kempshott. The north-eastern valley contains Deane, Oakley, and Wooton St. Laurence. These parishes at the far end of the drainage system formed a topographical unit dependent upon the upper valley catchment area. It is similar to that above the Candover, and place-name evidence shows both areas to have been heavily wooded (see Appendix B).

The hidage figures for the Test upland group are more readily available than for most groups of manors in this study. The eastern end of the area had Dummer (10) and the little manor of Kempshott (2). Both may have been originally upland settlements of Waltham (15) and Steventon (5), further down the valley. East of this point were Oakley (13 hides, 1 virgate), Deane (20), and Ashe (8). The two manors of Wooton St. Laurence add 20 and 5 hides to the group. The total hidage assessment for the Test Headwaters and the dry valleys beyond comes to over 98 hides.

THE UPPER TEST VALLEY

Whitchurch
S378. (909) K. Edward to OM, confirmation of 50 hides at *Hwitancyrice*. A composite, amended text.[48] Bounds.[49]
S377. (909?) K.Edward confirms lands of the Bishop: Overton, Tadley, Waltham, and 5 hides at Bradley.[50]

---

[48]   Ibid, 37.
[49]   *AJ* 84 (1927), 295-299.
[50]   The Bradley of the Overton Charter S377 was correctly identified by Grundy as Bradley Wood in northern Whitchurch parish: Ibid., 299-300. It is not the Bradley of the Candover valley.

DB: 3,5 (Evingar H.) In the OM monks' supplies. TRE 50 hides. Then 38, now 33 hides. Land for 33 ploughs. Includes manors of Freefolk (9 hides TRE now 4), and Whitnal (7 hides TRE, now 7), as well as 1 hide in the village and 1 hide held by the priest.

Freefolk
No charter.
DB: 3,5 (Evingar H.) Freefolk was included in Whitchurch. Ednoth held it from the Bishop, 9 hides TRE, now 4.

Laverstoke
No charter.
DB: 6,12 (Overton H.) NM holds the manor. Wulfeva Beteslau held it from the abbey until her death. After her death K. William gave it back to the church for the sake of his soul and his wife's. TRE 10 hides, now 6 hides, ½ virgate. Land for 6 ploughs.

Overton
S377. (909) K. Edward to B. Frithestan, confirmation of his title to 20 *mansae* at Overton, etc., 5 at Bradley. Bounds.[51]
S824. (n.d.) K. Edgar confirms to OM 20 *mansae* at Overton, etc., 5 at Bradley.
S1821. List of lands of Winchester Cathedral. Includes Overton 40 hides.
DB: 2,10 (Overton H.) Bishop holds Overton and always had. TRE 41 hides.

Polhampton
S465. (940) K. Edmund grants to the nun Aetheldryth 5 *mansae* at Polhampton. Bounds.[52]
S613. (956) K. Eadwig grants to thegn Beornric 5 *cassati* at Polhampton. Bounds.[53]
S970. (1033) K. Canute grants to Earl Godwin 10 *mansae* at Polhampton. Bounds.[54]
S1821, (11th century) List of lands of Winchester Cathedral. Includes the two Polhamptons, 10 hides.
DB: 3,10 (Overton H.) Ralph holds from Bishop. TRE for supply of monks. Then 5 hides, now 3½.
31,1 William Bertram holds from King, Tosti held TRE. Then 3½ hides.

The estates of the upper Test valley had a patchwork appearance by the late Saxon period. Bradley, a hamlet in Overton, was attached to Whitchurch. So were the adjacent small manors of Whitnal and Freefolk, the latter of which became a

51 Ibid., 261, 262.
52 Ibid., 177-179.
53 Ibid., 179, 180.
54 Ibid., 180-182.

village in its own right. While Overton was a major estate center and the surrounding places served as subsidiary centers, Laverstoke did not appear in the documents until Domesday Book. Perhaps it was a very recent acquisition by the New Minster, or one for which the abbey had no acceptable proofs of ownership. The boundaries of the Overton and Polhampton charters have been examined carefully by Grundy, and the details need not be repeated here. The extent of the lands from the combined charters equals the present Overton parish, a north-south band from the 'Portway' Roman road linking Old Sarum and Silchester at the north, down into the Test Valley, and up again to the barrow group called the Popham Beacons on the high ridge separating the Test and Micheldever valleys. The Overton charter (S377) covers the western half of this area, with the hamlet of Southington (*Suthamtun*) downstream from Overton.

The Polhamton estate formed the eastern half of Overton parish. The smaller estate of the two Polhamptons is probably that of Quidhampton, a little hamlet between the now-deserted Polhampton and Overton.[55] Its extent consisted of an extremely narrow strip extending the full distance across the Test drainage basin. It was Grundy's contention that the two grants by Kings Edmund and Eadwig (S465 and S613) referred to the same tract of land.[56] If so, then a small estate around Polhampton was granted out from the royal lands twice in the tenth century. At some point (the death of the thegn Beornric?) the land became the property of the Old Minster, which retained both grants. As we have noted earlier with the Tichborne charters, the two documents for Polhampton were mistakenly tallied up as two properties, together making 10 hides. Another estate there was granted to Earl (*Dux*) Godwin, and the Tostig who held this other manor in 1066 was probably his son; from the confiscation of his lands it came to King William in 1086. This Polhampton also seems to have received a beneficial hidation of $2/3$ at some point, having been reduced from 10 hides to 3½. The other manor, probably that of Quidhampton, was reduced as well, from 5 hides to 3½. In the Itchen valley, there was a probable hidage reduction of ½, while here in the Test, it seems to have been $2/3$.

The boundaries of the manors of the upper Test valley are generally well defined, with a number of Anglo-Saxon charters available to recreate the early medieval manorial divisions. At its end downstream, near the junction of the Test and Hurstbourne valleys, was the manor of Whitchurch, which with its subsidiary settlements of Whitnal and Freefolk was assessed at 50 hides. Bradley hamlet (5 hides), north of Whitchurch, was manorially associated with Overton (20) further upstream near Laverstoke (10). Beyond Overton were Polhampton and Quidhampton (15). Here is the present source of the River Test and the upper end of the main course of the valley. These manors form a coherent topographical group, and the

---

[55]   There appears to be a minor error in the placement of Polhampton on the map in *DB Hants*. It is represented at the extreme north of the present parish, but that is the site of the post-medieval Polhampton Lodge, not the shrunken hamlet of Polhampton Farm: O.S. 1" map sheet 168 (1963 ed.).

[56]   *AJ* 84 (1927), 172-173.

sum of the hidage assessments here at 100 hides, plus the 99 hides up the valley, complies with the pattern we have traced through the topographic units of middle Hampshire. The resulting unit is equivalent to what was termed a "double hundred."

THE MIDDLE TEST VALLEY

Tufton

No charter.

DB: 16,2 (Welford H.) Wherwell abbey holds *Tochiton*. It always held it. TRE 7 hides, now 3½ hides.

Tufton may have been in the possession of Queen Aelfthryth, and given by her to Wherwell Abbey upon its foundation (for the origin of the name, see Appendix B). Tufton or Toking Way continued until recently as the name of a track leading north-west from Micheldever village through Hunton and Cranbourne.[57]

Middleton (Longparish)

S417 (932) Athelstan grant of land at Meon, dated from *Middeltun*.

S727 (964) Edgar grants to himself 40 *cassati* at Steeple Ashton, Wiltshire with a postscript dated 968 giving the bounds of an unidentified *Mideltun*.

DB: 16,5 (Welford H.) Wherwell abbey holds, TRE 20 hides, now 10.

The surviving evidence reveals that Middleton was a royal estate, possibly the site of Athelstan's signing. It was then made bookland by Edgar, who probably passed it along to his wife Aelfthryth, the founder of Wherwell Abbey. The extent of Middleton probably coincided with the present parish of Longparish, including the villages of Forton, Middleton, Longparish, and Aston, plus lands on the east side of the Test extending to Tidbury prehistoric camp. Here, the northern boundary of Drayton was referred to as *middel haema mearce*.

Bransbury.

S1016. (1046) K. Edward to OM grants 3 *mansae* and 4 hides, etc., in *Brandesburi* and *Forde*.

DB: 3, 15 (Barton H.) Richard Clerk claims it from the Bishop. TRE Bishop Alfsi held it of (Archbishop), Stigand. For the monks' supplies. 4 hides then and now.

The Bransbury charter of 1046 either was a spurious compilation of entries from Domesday Book for Bransbury and Forton (it lists 4 hides, 7 villani, 5 bordarii, with 1 mill worth 15s.), or was taken from an earlier inventory of the mid-eleventh century. Forde (Forton across the Test) would have been an attached hamlet of 3 *mansae*. As the first entry for Bransbury is mid-eleventh century, and the name is probably of Scandinavian origin (see Appendix B), the Anglo-Saxon

---

[57]   It still appeared on the 1945 1" O.S. map.

rather than Danish name for the place might well have been based upon the Leofwine whose lands were west of Drayton in 1019 (see below).

Drayton

S370. (903, sp.) K. Edward grants to New Minster list of lands, including 4 hides at *Draiton juxta Niwetone.*
S1420 (995-1006) Ab. Aelfsige of NM grants for life to Wulfmar 1 hide at *Bertune* and 1 at *Dregtun.*
S956. (1019) K. Canute to NM restoration of 5 hides at Drayton. Bounds.[58]
DB: 6,16 (Micheldever H.) Listed among the lands of Micheldever.

The bounds suggest that the lands of Drayton occupied much of the triangular tract formed by the Tidbury Ring promontory, the Dever stream, and the Test.

Barton Stacey

S1420. (995-1006) A. Aelfsige of NM to Wulfmaer for life 1 hide at *Bertune* and 2 at *Dregtune.*
S1016. (1046) K. Edward to OM granting 3 *mansae* and 4 hides, etc., in *Brandesburi* and *Forde*, and 5 virgates in *Hertone Staci.*
DB: 1,17 (Barton H.) held by K. Edward for a half-day's revenue.
29,2 Chipping held from K.E. jointly 1 hide.
47,1 Edsi the sheriff held ½ hide from K.E.

New Minster held the manor at Barton ca. 1000 when it leased 1 hide there to Wulfmaer. Edward the Confessor may have made the grant of an additional 5 virgates, but the document is dubious (see above, Bransbury). If it represented a separate holding in the eleventh century as seems likely, then why is there no reference to it in Domesday Book? Two pieces of land in Barton were held directly from King Edward. They seem to have been 'court' positions, granted to a royal thegn, Chipping, and to Edsi the Sheriff. Perhaps the New Minster lost control of the one hide of land they had leased out, or new arrangements were made to accommodate Canute's conquest, or William's, or one of the political upheavals between the two. Is it a coincidence that the one hide ca. 1000 and the 5 virgates of 1046 equal the 1½ hides of tenant lands in 1066/1086? Little Somborne was held from the king, and King's Somborne was still part of the royal demesne. It probably included Ashley, Sparsholt, Compton, Brook, and Farley Chamberlaine, woodland settlements on the east and south flanks of the little valley.

---

[58]   This charter was not covered by Grundy in *AJ*. The bounds appear in *Liber de Hyda*, p. 325.

Newton Stacy

No information appears for this village and manor in the pre-Conquest documents, beyond the reference to *Draiton juxta Niwetone* (S370). This Micheldever grant is spurious, and probably dates to the end of the eleventh century.

Chilbolton

S376: (909, sp.) K. Edward confirms to O.M. Chilcomb with Nursing and Chilbolton.
S427: (934) K. Athelstan gives to OM lands including 10 hides at Chilbolton.
S1820: (ca.1041) Lands of the OM manor of Chilcomb. *Ceolbundingtune* 20 hides.
DB: 3,3 (Buddlesgate H.) Always held by OM. TRE 10 hides, now 5.

The contradictory assessments for the Chilbolton lands can be explained two ways. The estate may have been always valued at 10 hides, and the compiler of the list of lands associated with the Chilcomb estate made a not uncommon error in combining two documents referring to the same piece of land. Alternatively, the spurious Edward grant may have been an attempt to substantiate already held property, in addition to that given by Athelstan. All the other pre-Conquest documents would then have a certain substance to them, and the Domesday figure would represent another instance of unrecorded beneficial hidation, as so often happened, on Cathedral property. The larger-than-usual size of Chilbolton parish may support the second explanation, but it is hardly definitive proof.

Leckford

S526: (947) Eadred to priest Eadulf, 10 *mans.* in *Leghford*. S1419: (947-955) Bequest by Eadwulf of 5 *stowan* at *Leahtford* to NM where he is to be buried, and other 5 to Nunnaminster. Bounds.[59]
DB: 6,15 (Somborne H.) NM holds. 5 hides.
14,3 St. Mary's (Nunnaminster) holds. 5 hides.

Leckford appears to have been royal land until granted to Eadulf in 947, whose death ca. 955 turned the lands over to NM and Nunnaminster of Winchester. The descent is thus a simple instance of a tenth-century 10-hide manor split into two 5-hide estates in the eleventh century. The later document (S1419) also illustrates the vernacular use of the word *stow* in its general sense of 'inhabited place,' rather than 'religious place,' and here having a more finite use as farmstead, or hide. The bounds give no indication that they represent anything but the entire 10 hides of Leckford, but internal evidence suggests they refer only to Leckford Abbas, the manor held by the New Minster.[60] First is the unusual mention of the authority for the bounds, a reference to truthful old men. This does not sound like a royal grant. It seems more like a later attempt to fill in details that were absent in the original document. Secondly, the bounds of the lands in question appear to start at

---

[59]   *AJ* 83 (1926), 172-174.
[60]   *ECW*, 43.

Leckford itself and run eastward via a ditch, leaving the entire northern half of the parish outside of the estate. The northern part of Leckford no doubt formed the 5-hide manor of Leckford Abbas.

A reconstruction of the ancient hidage assessment for the manors of the middle Test valley group is frustrated because one of the manors, Barton, was never hidated, except for two small parcels apparently held under 'service' tenure. Bransbury originally was a 4 hide portion of the larger Drayton manor, which when reduced had 5 hides for itself. Leckford measured 10 hides, Tufton 7 hides, and Chilbolton probably 10. Middleton manor spanned the valley with 20 hides. The lands on the west side of the Test are not recorded separately here, as their boundaries are not contiguous to Micheldever Hundred or its outlying manors. These western estates were Wherwell (22h), Fullerton (5), and Longstock (4). The total hidage recorded for the manors of the middle Test comes to 87 hides without Barton holdings. This would permit 13 hides for Barton to bring it to the expected 100-hide total. This figure is appropriate for a manor larger than Leckford and smaller than Middleton, and without the fertile meadowland along the Test that Wherwell and Bransbury enjoyed.

THE SOMBORNE VALLEY

Crawley

S381: (ca. 909) K. Edward confirms to B. Frithestan 20 *manentes* at *Crawanlea*. (and 8 at Hunton). Bounds.[61]

S1821: List of lands of Winchester Cathedral. *Crawlea* 28 hides.

DB: 2,8 (Buddlesgate H.) Bishop holds the lordship. TRE and now 6½ hides, land for 14 ploughs. Hugh holds 3 hides of the manor. Alwin Still held TRE from the bishop.

The sub-tenantry of Hugh is no doubt the small estate at Hunton that is otherwise unrecorded in Domesday Book. Hunton, it seems, had received beneficial hidation, a reduction from 8 to 3 hides, or approximately a ⅔ reduction. Crawley itself may have undergone the same reduction in assessment. If the Hunton 3 hides were not included in the Domesday manorial figure, then Crawley decreased from 20 to 6½ hides, as close to a ⅔ reduction as possible for the Anglo-Saxon hidage assessment. On the other hand, the Domesday ploughland available came to 14 ploughs, which may suggest a ½ reduction, similar to that which may have taken place in the Upper Test valley.

---

[61] *AJ* 81 (1924), 42-46.

Somborne

S381. (See Crawley) Among the landmarks of the Crawley bounds is (to) *Swinburnan.*[62]

DB: 39,2 (Somborne H.) Godric held from K. Edward. 2 hides TRE, now 1 virgate.

1,47 In the King's lordship. Not apportioned into hides. Land for 10 ploughs.

45,8-9 Ednoth 1½ hide from K. Edward. Land for 1 plough. Maynard 1 hide from K. Edward. Land for 1½ ploughs.

The holding of Godric was Little Somborne, while the other lands were Kings Somborne itself and the dependent hamlets of Up Somborne and Compton, but they are not divisible into their separate components.

The topographic unit of the Somborne valley crosses the Test to take in a far less extensive, complementary basin to the west. The post-medieval hundred of Somborne included all the Somborne villages, as well as Ashley and even Farley just beyond the slope of the watershed divide to the south, but not Crawley or that part of Sparsholt that drained westward.[63] Along the east bank of the Test it included the hamlet of Brook south of Kings Somborne, and those of Stockbridge and Leckford to the north. On the west side of the river, most of Houghton parish was included in the hundred, as were Longstock and Fullerton parishes. This hundredal jursidiction is the same as that of the Domesday Book listing of manors in Somborne Hundred, with outlying lands that are not pertinent to the discussion here. The hundredal division may indeed mark the line of ancient boundaries, but it does not coincide with the topographic unit of the Somborne basin. To the list of village lands within the hundred should be added Crawley and Sparsholt, and probably Bossington just west of the junction of Somborne and the Test. On the other hand, Fullerton is too far north of the drainage basin and the high ground surrounding it. So too is Leckford and all but the south end of Longstock parish. It may be no coincidence that in south Longstock parish, the hundred boundary met two others at the base of the imposing prehistoric hillfort, Danebury, and the boundary briefly ran in an east-west direction, which, if continued across the Test, would arrive at Atners Tower, earlier known as Midlas Hill, and the site of the *Aettenho* ('Giant's Promentory') on the boundary between White Somborne or Stockbridge, and Leckford to the north (see above).

The hidage totals for these manors present some complicated figures. Crawley was granted at 20 hides, though there is no mention of Sparsholt, nor of Ashley. There is no record for Up Somborne either, but Little Somborne was valued at 2 hides TRE, and Kings Somborne had two small estates at 2½ hides. There was land for 2 ploughs at the two Kings Somborne estates. The main manor of Kings Somborne had no hidage assessment as it was a royal demesne holding, but there was land for 10 ploughs. The conclusion to be drawn is that if an

---

[62]   Ibid.

[63]   The hundred boundary is depicted on Isaac Taylor's 1759 map of Hampshire (H.R.O. 34 M 62/3).

assessment had been made, it would have been at or close to 10 hides, and all the lands totalled at least 14½ hides.

The lands at the south part of the Somborne valley appear in the Domesday Book as Compton with 4½ hides and Farley with holdings of ½ hide and another of 5 hides. The properties on the south side of Somborne thus total an even 10 hides. An extensive Somborne estate assessed at 14 hides appeared in Domesday as that held by Toli the Dane TRE. Munby identified it as the later medieval manor of Stockbridge north of Kings Somborne, which was also known as White Somborne.[64] The hidage figure is too high for the small size of this manor, and an alternative identification may be the missing Ashley or even Sparsholt. At any rate, the recorded hidage (and that based on the ploughland at Kings Somborne) of the Somborne basin east of the Test River totals 58 hides, and there is a strong case that some of the lands went unrecorded.

On the far side of the river, Houghton parish covers most of the length of the area concerned. It contained three estates assessed at 24, 5, and 5 hides TRE. It is likely that one of the smaller estates was later included in Longstock. The argument for this is the course of the hundred boundary and the remarkably low hidage assessment of Longstock at 4 hides. Topographically, the south end of Longstock parish is an extension of Houghton, containing the upper end of a valley that starts at the hamlet of North Houghton. Although the topography begins to change at this point, the Bossington parish boundary is for most of its length a continuation of Houghton's, and it runs down to the Test to meet the south boundary of Compton tithing. It was assessed 2 hides, 1 virgate TRE, later nothing. The total hidage from the west side of the river thus comes to 36 hides, 1 virgate, assuming that Houghton originally incorporated the larger territory that its high assessment suggests.

The resulting total recorded hidage for the entire Somborne catchment area comes to just under 95 hides, a figure reasonably close to the even 100 hides found elsewhere in this study. The remaining hidage is most probably to be accounted for among the poorly recorded lands in the southeast side of the Somborne valley.

THE MICHELDEVER VALLEY

The land draining into the Micheldever stream, locally called the Dever, beyond the side valleys flanking the Test, forms a topographic unit incorporating manors from Bullington east to Woodmancote. All the manors are in the form of rectangular blocks of land, leading up the valley slope from meadows along the Dever to woods and grazing land on the high ridges forming the watershed divisions between valley catchment areas. Each manor has a roughly equal share of the available resources, resulting in fairly equivalent amounts of pasture, arable land, meadow and woodland among the manors.

---

[64]   *DB Hants*, notes for chapter 29, entry 3 (n.).

Bullington

S904: (1002) K. Ethelred to Wherwell Abbey, grant of several manors, with a postscript dated 1008, noting the king's further grant of 10 *mansae* at *Bulandon*. DB: 16,6 (Welford H.) Wherwrell Abbey holds 10 hides.

One may assume that Bullington was royal land until 1008.

Cranbourne

S360: (900/1) K. Edward founds New Minster.

Cranbourne was given to the New Minster as an estate separate from Micheldever. It was no doubt from a later grant, as the charter is a composite of several documents.[65] Analysis of the bounds shows that the estate held by the NM in the tenth century was the one in Hampshire, not the one in Wiltshire, as Edward Edwards believed.[66] Furthermore, it was not the same as the present parish of Wonston north of the Dever, as was claimed by Grundy, but was rather Cranbourne manor without the Norton lands to the northwest.[67] In the Domesday Book, Cranbourne has no entry of its own, but appears among the Micheldever estates held by Hugh de Port, and Norton was held quite separately from King Edward (see below).

Norton

No charters.

DB: 69,2 (Barton H.) Odo holds Norton, Fulk held from K. Edward. 5 hides TRE, now 2 hides 3 virgates.

This is a typical holding of a king's thegn. The name *Fulchi*, however, may not be English, but the French 'Fulk,' perhaps a Norman holding under King Edward.[68] In size, Norton is a small manor, whose 5 hides are proportional in area to the 10 hides of Bullington and the 8 of Cranbourne. It seems to have always been held by the Crown, and thus had no charter.

Sutton Scotney

S1507: (ca. 890) King Alfred's will bequeaths to Edward lands at Hurstbourne, and *aet Suttune*, and at Leatherhead, etc.

DB: 69,1 (Barton H.) Odo holds Sutton from king. Alfward held from Earl Godwin. 5 hides TRE, now 2 hides 1 virgate.

---

[65] *AJ* 84 (1927), 305-308.

[66] *Liber de Hyde*, p. 88. But Edwards's index (p. 381) has *Cramburne* in Hampshire.

[67] As evident from his comments on the charter bounds in *AJ* 84 (1927), 306, 307.

[68] Yet no such name appears a century later in nearby Winchester, in the Winton Domesday entries for 1110 or 1148: Olof von Feilitzen, "The Personal Names and Bynames of the Winton Domesday," in *Winchester in the Early Middle Ages, Winchester Studies Vol. I*, ed. M. Biddle (Oxford, 1976), pp. 143-230.

28,7 Robert Fitzgerald holds now, Tovi held from Earl Godwin. 5 hides TRE, 2½ hides now.

The two Sutton entries in the Domesday Book are identical, with the same hidage figures, church, mill, and valuation, although the tenant listings are different. Moreover, these same figures are those given for the manor of Norton. This represents an error in copying the hundred or county returns. But which Sutton is correct, the Odo/Alfward or Robert/Tovi? The answer is not of immediate concern to this survey because a likely explanation for the duplication is that *both* entries are for Sutton, though only one has the correct details. Sutton Scotney is a faily large parish, and 10 hides would be appropriate for its size. No record exists of Earl Godwin's acquisition of the estate. It would seem to be a recent grant by the Crown, which probably held the property as the *Suttun* bequeathed by King Alfred.

The ten hides that Edward gave to the New Minster in 904 (S374) should not be identified with the 10 hides of Sutton in 1066. Grundy tried to make the boundary points of that charter fit the landmarks of Sutton Scotney parish, but very few of the points can possibly correspond.[69] Sutton was therefore not granted to the New Minster, which is what one would have expected from Earl Godwin's ownership before the Conquest. It is unlikely that the new Minster turned the land over to him without any record of the event, even if the abbot at the time was Godwin's relative.

Wonston

S374: (904) K. Edward to OM refectory, 10 *mansae* at Micheldever. Bounds.[70]
S1821: List of lands of Winchester Cathedral. Includes *Myceldefer* 10 hides.
S381: (909) Hunton charter bounds include *foran gean thas abbodes byrig*.
DB: 2,14 (Barton H.) Held by OM 10 hides TRE, 7 hides now.

Grundy believed the charter to pertain to Sutton Scotney (see above). Rune Forsberg correctly identified it as the manor of Wonston,[71] and it is clearly the same as the 10 hides at 'Micheldever' held by the OM. The abbot having the 'bury' at Wonston in 909 was the religious head of the Old Minster, a figure who after the tenth-century reforms of the Cathedral monastery would have been referred to as a prior.

Stoke Charity

S1821: List of lands of Winchester Cathedral. Includes 50 hides at Waltham and Micheldever.
DB: 2,14. (?H) The bishop holds *Stoches* in lordship. TRE 10 hides, now 7, and Geoffrey holds 4 hides from the bishop (totalling 11 hides in 1086).

---

[69]   *AJ* 84 (1927), 308-310.
[70]   Ibid.
[71]   Rune Forberg, *A Contribution to a Dictionary of Old English Place-Names* (Uppsala, 1950), p. 202.

Munby contends that the Domesday Book reference is to Stoke by Hurstbourne, but an equal case can be made for Stoke Charity.[72] The 12 hides at Micheldever held by the Old Minster (50 less 38 of North Waltham) are no doubt the 11 hides recorded in Domesday Book (10 hides TRE) at *Stockes*, in what appears to be a slight case of beneficial hidation. The reference is not surprising, as the manor west of Stoke, Wonston, was also simply referred to as 'Micheldever' in 904 (S374). With the 'Wonston' Micheldever to the west and the 'true' Micheldever to the east, the Stoke hidage should also be expected to bear that name. The division in 1086 of the estate into the bishop's 7 hides and Geoffrey's 4 hides might be the origin of the later manors of Stoke Charity by the Dever stream, and further up the slope, the smaller holding called 'Old Stoke' (see Appendix B).

Hunton

S381: (c.909) K. Edward to B. Frithestan, confirming his title to 20 *manentes* at Crawley and 8 at *Hundatune*. A fabrication, possibly based on authentic material. Bounds.[73]

S1821: List of lands of Winchester Cathedral. Includes Crawley 28 hides.

DB: No reference to Hunton, but it was one of the two estates entered under Crawley (see above). One answered for 6½ hides TRE, but had land for 11 ploughs, and the other was valued at 3 hides and had land for 2 ploughs. Both were held by the bishop.

As noted for Somborne, some episcopal and cathedral lands appear to have undergone a beneficial hidation reduction. The Crawley 6½ hides and the Hunton 3 hides add up to 9½ hides, which might have been ⅓ (at 10) of the original 28 hides (at 30). We have also seen that the ploughland for Crawley suggests a ½ reduction, but Hunton's 3 hides are still not far off one half of 8. Examination of the bounds shows the Saxon estate to be the same as the later parish.[74]

The Micheldever Estate (Micheldever, Stratton, Popham, etc.)

S360: (901) K. Edward grants to NM 100 *cassati* at *Miceldefer*. Bounds include the manors of the upper Dever valley.[75]

S370: (903, sp.) The 'Golden Charter' by which K. Edward repeats the foundation charter, with embellishments and additions. No boundary survey. The endowments include 100 *cassati* at Micheldever, with its hundred and both churches, 9 hides at *Strattone*, 4½ hides at *Burcote*, 8½ hides at *Popham*, 10 hides at *Woodmancote*, etc.

---

[72]   See *DB Hants*, note 14 (*Stockes*) for chapter 2 (n.).
[73]   *AJ* 83 (1926), 147-149.
[74]   The boundary clause is analysised in "Micheldever," pp. 616-619.
[75]   *AJ* 83 (1926), 232-236.

DB: 6,13 (Mansborough H.) Candover TRE 20 hides. Now 13 hides 2½ virgates, plus 6 hides 2½ virgates of Woodmancote.

6,16 (Micheldever H.) Micheldever TRE 106 hides. Now 83 hides ½ virgate plus 22½ hides 1 virgate held by Hugh de Port. TRE 4 free men held it as 4 manors: Cranbourne, Drayton, Stratton, Popham.

Analysis of the boundary clause reveals that the 900/1 grant by Edward (S360) included north of the Dever: the land of Weston, Northbrook, East and West Stratton, Popham, and perhaps some of Woodmancott; on the Candover: Totford, Swarraton, Northington, and the Grange; and south of the Dever: Burcot, and questionably Papenholt and the south half of Southbrook tithing.[76] Most of these lands are in the Micheldever valley, and from them we can arrive at an approximate total hidage assessment for the catchment. The computations are complicated because infeudation of the Micheldever estate after the Conquest reduced the manor from 106 hides TRE to 83 hides 1 virgate in 1086. It seems more than coincidental that the hidage was reduced by just under 23 hides and that the holding of Hugh de Port was assessed at 22½ hides 1 virgate.[77] The assessment of Micheldever thus appears to have been reduced only by the lands held by Hugh de Port.

The Domesday Book entry does not specify the hidage of the individual manors comprising the Micheldever estate. Cranbourne, Drayton, Stratton, and Popham were held by Hugh de Port; Woodmancott and Brown Candover were associated with Micheldever, and measured 20 hides. The spurious 'Golden Charter' (S370) purporting to date from 903 does list the hidage of some of the Micheldever manors, and the document is probably not far removed in date from the Domesday survey. In the Golden Charter, Micheldever was considered 100 hides, to which other manors were added: Stratton 9 hides, Burcot 4½, Woodmancote 10, Candover 10, Cranbourne 8, Drayton 4, Swarraton 3 hides 1½ virgates, and Northington 6. The manors later held by Hugh de Port therefore totalled 29½ hides before the Domesday survey.

Other tenanted manors were recorded in Domesday Book: 3 men held TRE 3 holdings, of 7 hides, 5 hides of demesne, and 4½ hides of demesne. Other minor tenants TRE were Alsi with 6 hides, Aldred from his wife's dowery 1½ hides, and Siward Waleran 2 hides. The totals for these groups are 16½ hides and 9½ hides, combined to make 26 hides, to which another hide of Alsi could be added.

We can justifiably suggest some identifications. Alsi held 6 hides at Northington, later identified as Totford. Aldred and Siward held Swarraton, and the 4½ hides held separately was Burcot. The 7-hide and 5-hide lands are harder to identify; these units are not previously recorded. The 7-hide unit, however, must have been Papenholt, later Papenholt Herberti, which was held by 3 men TRE and by Herbert the Chamberlain in 1086. The remaining 5 hides of demesne land would

---

[76] See "Micheldever," pp. 583-595. Some of the boundary points have since been reinterpreted.

[77] A copyist error certainly occured here, because 83½ hides less 1 virgate, when added to Hugh de Port's 22½ hides 1 virgate, matches the pre-Conquest total of 106 hides.

then be the land in south Micheldever that was excluded from the original grant, or perhaps lands to the south-east in the present Northington parish.

The hidage figures for the eastern estates of the Micheldever manor within its drainage basin yield: Stratton 9, Burcot 4½ hides, Popham 8½, Papenholt 7, plus 5 and 1 hide 'held elsewhere,' totalling 35 hides.[78] The extent of the unspecified Micheldever lands can be gauged by subtracting the hidage of the listed estates from the Domesday Book total. Along with the upper Micheldever group of manors, the Domesday Book entry also included: Swarraton 3 hides 1½ virgates, and Totford 6 hides, as well as Cranbourne 8, and Drayton 4, all totalling 21 hides and 1½ virgates. Combining these manors beyond the upper Dever valley with those within it yields 21 hides and 1½ virgates plus 35 hides, resulting in 56 hides 1½ virgates. It is this figure that must be subtracted from the Domesday Book total to give the hidage for Micheldever manor alone. The 1066 figure of 106 hides should be used in preference to the 1086 amount of 83 hides and ½ virgates (probably an error for 83½ hides, less 1 virgate), which is likely a reduction of the total by the extent of the lands held by Hugh de Port with immunity. The result of the subtraction is the remarkably even figure of 50 hides (give or take a single virgate). Thus, the 'core' manor of Micheldever was a block of 50 hides, comprising its tithings of Northbrook, Southbrook, Weston, and possibly West Stratton, but without the lands at the east end of the valley.

With the assessments of the early medieval manors thus established, we can reconstruct the composite hidage figures for the upper Dever valley. Micheldever we have shown was 50 hides, while the other estates in the valley came to 35 hides. To the east, the lands of Woodmancott were more in the Micheldever catchment area than in that of the Candover, even though it was early on attached to the Candover estate (see above). Consequently, its 10 hides are assigned to the Micheldever gouping. The upper Dever, then, contained manors assessed at 95 hides.

The manors of the lower Dever valley supply the remaining assessments for the topographic unit. following the descent of the stream, we have seen these manors to have been Hunton (8), Stoke Charity (12), Wonston (10), Sutton (10), Norton (5), Cranbourne (8), and Bullington (10). The manors of the lower Dever valley have a well recorded and fairly simple assessments, and their total comes to 63 hides.

The hidage of the entire Micheldever valley is the sum of the 63 hides of the lower Dever and the 95 hides of the upper Dever. They total 158 hides, which is close to the hundred or half-hundred we have found throughout this study. Indeed, the complicated and ill-defined boundary between the Micheldever estates and the ones along the Candover probably accounts for the slight irregularity. The figures arrived at for Micheldever and Candover valleys are 158 and 93,

[78]   There is nothing to warrant an assumption that the unidentified lands associated with Micheldever were distant parcels. Micheldever had no known holdings outside the Micheldever and Candover valleys.

respectively, which suggests that 7 or 8 hides assessed in Micheldever were originally part of the Candover group, most probably lands at Northington or Woodmancote that spanned the divide between the two drainage basins.

Appendix B

Place-Names of Middle Hampshire

Historical evidence is not confined to the written or buried record; there is also the spoken record. A thousand-year-old name is as much a part of the subject matter of history as an enrolled charter or archaeological remains. In the absence of documentary sources, the data gained from a careful evaluation of toponymic forms and their evolution are particularly valuable. Toponymic analysis is based upon a simple premise: the names chosen for places, rivers, settlements, etc., were limited to words available or conventional at the time of naming. As this core of words changed with time, it also changed with the language, and both changes reveal certain traits or beliefs held by the people giving or retaining place-names. For instance, 'Kingston' indicates the existence of kingship, and 'Walton' shows surviving communities of Britons (Welsh) among the Anglo-Saxons. The distribution of these and similar terms reveal early English social and tenurial patterns that might otherwise be invisible to the documentary researcher.

The specific chronology of English toponymic usage was established by the etymological work of Eilert Ekwall, whose monograph, *English Place-Names in '-ing'* (1923), refined the earlier observation by Kemble that such names referred to places occupied by the earliest emigrants from Germany.[1] Furthermore, Sir Frank Stenton's series of papers on "The Historical Bearing of Place-Name Studies" had as its foundation Ekwall's seminal work.[2] The volumes of county toponyms published by the English Place-Name Society and Ekwall's *Oxford Dictionary of English Place-Names* represent a more advanced stage of research.[3] This enterprise came to maturity with the appearance of works by Kenneth Cameron and P.H. Reaney at the beginning of the 1960s, in which the conclusions of that generation of philologists were fully presented.[4] They established a chronology based upon those place-names assumed to be earliest:

> 1 those with *ingas* and *ingaham* added to a personal name, which were taken to represent the first and second stages of settlement by Anglo-Saxon war bands;
>
> 2 the names of pagan sites;

[1]   Eilert Ekwall, *English Place-Names in '-ing'* (Lund, 1923).

[2]   Stenton's series of papers on "The Historical Bearing of Place-Name Studies," appeared in *Transactions of the Royal Historical Society*, 4th ser., 21-25 (1939-1943).

[3]   Eilert Ekwall, *The Concise Oxford Dictionary of English Place-Names* 4th ed. (London, 1960). It does not contain any of the revised toponymic chronology, and should be used with caution.

[4]   Kenneth Cameron, *English Place-Names* (London, 1961); and P.H. Reaney, *The Origins of English Place-Names* (London, 1960). It must be noted that both scholars have since given their support to the reinterpretation of toponymic chronology.

3 those words or personal names that were considered to be archaic in Old
English usage;

4 names that referred to a type of habitation as opposed to topograph-
ically-related names, which were assumed to have a later origin.[5]

They recognized that names ending in *tun* and *thorp* came somewhat later than the
others, and a schematic sequence was set out: *ingas, ingaham, ham, hamtun, tun,
thorp*, with pagan names at the early end and Christian names at the later. This
relative chronology was used to date the spread of Anglo-Saxon settlers. For Stenton
and others it served as a guide for reconstructing the development of early English
society from an original occupation by troops of land-takers, as evidenced by their
pagan burials, to the complex arrangement of manors, villages, and outlying
dependencies that appear on the late Saxon charters and in the Norman Domesday
survey.[6]

These views, however, have been abandoned by place-name scholars,
following the publication since 1966 of a number of papers by a new generation of
philologists: J. McN. Dodgson, Margaret Gelling, Barrie Cox, and Margaret
Faull.[7] The revised toponymic chronology is not yet a new paradigm, but rather
a qualification of many points of the older view. Both the *ingas* names and those
bearing a personal name are now judged just as likely, if not more so, to be based
on the name of a late owner of the manor, than on the name of an earlier warrior
chief. Similarly, the pagan worship sites most probably received their names when
such worship was the exception, and not in the early centuries of Anglo-Saxon
settlement. The earliest types of toponyms are now thought to be those with *ham*
suffix (particularly Wickham, which may refer to sub-Roman occupation), and
certain of those with a topographic element. Consequently, the pattern of conquest,
settlement, and rural development based on the older chronology is now seriously
in question. A new interpretation has not yet been formulated, but Margaret Gelling

---

[5]   The synopsis of the earlier paradigm is based on Margaret Gelling, *Signposts to the
Past: Place-Names and the History of England* (London, 1978), pp. 106-107.

[6]   *ASE* 18, *passim*.

[7]   Seminal works by these philologists include: J. McN. Dodgson, "The Significance
of the Distribution of the English place names in *-ingas, -inga-* in South-east England,"
Medieval Archaeology 10 (1966), 1-29, and "Place-Names from *ham*, Distinguished from
hamm Names, in Relation to the Settlement of Kent, Surrey and Sussex," *Anglo-Saxon
England* 2 (1973), 1-50; Barry Cox, "The Significance of the Distribution of English
Place-Names in *-ham* in the Midlands and East Anglia," *Journal of the English Place-Name
Society* 3 (1972-3), 15-73; M.L. Faull, "The Semantic Development of Old English *Wealh*,"
Leeds Studies in English new ser. 8 (1975), 20-44; Margaret Gelling, "Place-Names and
Anglo-Saxon Heathenism," *University of Birmingham Historical Journal* 8 (1961), 7-25, and
"English Place-Names Derived from the Compound *Wickham*," *Medieval Archaeology* 11
(1967), 87-104.

and Gillian Fellows-Jensen have stressed the close connection between place-names and settlement history.[8]

Gelling herself has found a particularly noteworthy pattern in some areas where topographical settlement-names were "regularly used for the main settlement in large conglomerate estates, within which there may be a number of less important settlements with habitative names."[9]

The following survey treats first the place-names of the Micheldever valley and the Candover valley, then the parish and settlement names of the adjacent area of Hampshire, and finally Hundred names of that region. The toponymic survey follows the procedures of the English Place-Names Society, which avoids tedious detail and repetition by giving secondary references only when the toponym has a dubious or controversial identification.[10] Otherwise, A.H. Smith's *English Place-Name Elements* may be considered the authority upon which most identifications have been made.[11]

All the major Hampshire place-names have undergone some previous examination. Much of the material for middle Hampshire was compiled by this writer and P.J. Fasham in 1973-74 for the M3 Archaeological Rescue Committee, which studied portions of the Micheldever and Itchen valleys as part of a wider archaeological program.[12] This in turn drew from the 1961 unpublished manuscript study of the place-names of Hampshire by G.E. Gover.[13] To these sources, commentary has been added from G.B. Grundy's brief study of the same, Eilert Ekwall's *Oxford Dictionary of English Place-Names*, and Margaret Gelling's recent syntheses, *Signposts to the Past: Place-Names and the History of England* and *Place-Names in the Landscape*.[14]

This survey does not claim to be an authoritative etymological analysis of the toponymic record of middle Hampshire. Rather, it is a presentation of the best available commentary on the identification and origin of certain names given to settlements and landscape features during the early medieval period. While fully aware of the warning that "historians and archaeologists are embarrassingly

[8]   In Gelling, *Signposts*, pp. 191-214; and Gillian Fellows-Jensen, "Place-Names and Settlement History: A Review," *Northern History* 13 (1979), 1-26.

[9]   Gelling, *Signposts*, p. 123.

[10]   A publication in its county series illustrates both the procedures of the Society's philological studies, as well as recent conclusions about toponymic development: Margaret Gelling, *The Place-Names of Berkshire*, English Place-Names Society, vols. 49-51 (Cambridge, 1974-1976).

[11]   A.H. Smith, *English Place-Name Elements*, English Place-Name Society, vols. 25, 26 (Cambridge, 1956).

[12]   The toponymic survey is deposited with the files of the M3 Archaeological Rescue Committee at the Wessex Archaeological Trust, Salisbury.

[13]   G.E. Gover's typescript "Place-Names of Hampshire," was not published by the English Place-Name Society. Copies are on deposit at the Society's headquarters and at the Hampshire Record Office, Winchester.

[14]   *ODEPN*; and Gelling, *Signposts* (see note 5) and *Place-Names in the Landscape* (London, 1984).

disaster-prone when discussing place-names,"[15] avoiding the all-too-apparent difficulties would exclude the body of information that this source offers.

TOPONYMS

These comprise only those likely to be of early medieval date, and are arranged by parishes and tithing (see figure B.1). The earliest recorded name is followed by the date given on the document, and in some cases, the date of the surviving version is given to doubtful or spurious documents to distinguish them from original ones. Abbreviations for the sources presented here are taken from *ODEPN*, and Gover's unpublished study. In addition, the following are used: Hyde: *Liber Vitae de Hyde*; Hyda: *Liber Monasterii de Hyda*; FF: Feet of Fines; Fees: Book of Fees; FA: Feudal Aids; Ass: Assize Roll; TA: Tithe Award, DB: Domesday Book; S: Sawyer's *Anglo-Saxon Charters*, Harl.: B.L. *Harl.* 1761; Cl.: Close Roll; Pat: Patent Roll; Ch: Charter Roll; P: Pipe Roll; Oxford: *Facsimiles of Early Charters of Oxford*; Ipm: *Inquisitiones postmortum*; Winch Cath: Winchester Cathedral Archives; Cas.: Winchester Castle muniments; Tax: *Taxatio ecclesiastica*; ASC: Anglo-Saxon Chronicle; Sel: *Charters ... relating to Selbourne*; Min Acc: Ministers Accounts; Winch. Coll.: Muniments of Winchester College.

The Micheldever Valley (from West to East)

BARTON STACEY: *Bertune* (ca. 1000, Hyde), *beretun* 'corn, barley farm,' later with the meaning of demesne farm. Stacey is a manorial, family name.
Bransbury: *Brandesburi* (1046, S1016), 'Brand's burg, fortified site.' Brand is probably a Scandinavian name.
Drayton (tithing): *Draegtune* (ca. 1000, Hyde) 'portage' is the probable meaning for this *tun* where the Test divides into several channels.
Newton Stacey (tithing): *Niuuetone* (903, S.370), 'new farm.'

BULLINGTON: *Bulandon* (1002, S904), the *dun* 'down,' 'hill' of *Bula*, or more likely *bula* 'bull.'
Tidbury Ring: *Tudanbury* (1019, Hyda), the fortified place of *Tuda*, a name without other examples, though there are several instances of *Tudda*. An alternative might be *tydd* 'brushwood,' 'shrub,' or the related *todd* 'bushy mass,' 'fox.'

WONSTON: *Wynsiges tun* (900, S360), Wynsige's farm.
Sutton Scotney: (tithing), *sudtune* (1086, DB0, 'south farm.'
Sutton Down Farm: probably originally *sud dun* 'south hill pasture.'
Norton Manor (tithing): *Nortune* (1086, DB) 'north farm.'

[15]   Gelling, *Signposts*, p. 11.

Cranbourne Grange: (tithing) *Cranburnan* (900, S360), *craneburna* (1174, P), 'stream frequented by herons' (cranes). The medieval moated site is situated along the course of the Cranbourne stream.

STOKE CHARITY: *Stoches* (1086, DB), *Eledesstoke* (1256, Ass), Charity is a family name (De la Charite). Gover notes Ekwall's suggested identification with an *aelede stoc* 'burnt stake,' which was later confused with *eald* 'old,' giving Old Stoke, a present farm name.

HUNTON: *Hundatun* (909, S376), *tun* 'farm' where dogs (hounds) were kept.

MICHELDEVER: *Micendefer* (862, S335), *Miceldefer* (900, S360), from the river name, see below. Referred to as *M. Abbatis* (1167, P) as owned by Hyde Abbey.
Weston Colley (tithing): *Westone* (1280, Ass), 'west farm or hamlet.' Gover believes that Colley was not a manorial name, but was related to the field name *colhaywarde* (1541, Min Acc), perhaps a place containing *(ge)haeg* 'enclosure' and *cole* 'a hollow.' Weston is on the stream, and *col* 'cool,' while common in stream names, could be attached to a piece of bottom land. But such secondary names are nearly always manorial in Hampshire and should be assumed so unless hard evidence exists to the contrary.
Northbrook (tithing): *Northbrok* (1256, Ass), '(settlement on) the northern stream.'
Southbrook (tithing): *Suthbrok* (t. Hy. III, Harl), 'the southern stream.'
Norsebury Ring: *to naesan byrig* (900, S360), 'defended camp' on a *naess* 'projecting piece of high ground,' related to *nasu* 'nose,' and it was called Nosebury (t. Ed. I, Harl).
Godwinesdowne (t. Hy. III, Harl), now Warren Farm, *Warren voc' Goodwynnnes downe* (1540, Harl), 'Godwin's hill pasture.'
Papenholt (1253, Cl), now Micheldever Wood, *an papan holt* (900, S360), probably from the personal name *Papa* and *holt* 'wood,' hence 'Pap's wood,' but it may also refer to Latin *papa* 'priest, pope, bishop,' (perhaps also to 'abbot,' but it had the name before it came to the New Minster). Nearby was *Papenacre* (t. Hy. III, Harl). The name was lost in the late Middle Ages, perhaps upon the Dissolution of the abbey estates.
Bazeley Copse: *Babbeslegh* (1280, Ass), the first element is possibly the personal name *Babba*, and *leah* is the second element, giving 'the grove or clearing of Babba.'

EAST AND WEST STRATTON: *Strattone* (903, S370), *tun* 'homestead, hamlet' on a *straet* 'Roman road, made road.' East and West Stratton appear in the early fourteenth century (1316, F.A., and 1308, Winch. Cath., respectively). It is a fairly late division, and seems likely to have been connected to manorial rearrangements. This might be the reason for the apparent disappearance of a place in the East Field of Micheldever, recorded as *Eastone* (1225), *Stone* (1233), and by a Robert de Astone (*ca.* 1250). This 'Estone' may have been the mirror of the 'Westone' (Colley) that served as a dependent *tun* beyond Micheldever's West Field.

Burcot's Farm: *Burcote* (903, S370), *burgcote* (1236, Ass). Gover suggests ''cottages by or relating to a *burh*' (dwelling), but at the present day there are no earthworks in the neighbourhood.' Timber buildings need not leave any surface trace.

POPHAM: *Popham* (903, S370, *ca.* 1140, both 14th-cent. copies), *Popeham* (1086, DB, 1176, P); *Poppham* (1212, Fees); *Poppeham* (1311, Ass). Gover and Ekwall find this etymology difficult, suggesting an origin in *pop*, a possible short form of *poppel* 'pebble.' Smith cites *popig* 'poppy,' and the fact that 'Popham' appears in only late copies of charters, suggests that the 11th- and 12th- century references to 'Popeham' might be more correct. It may be, however, that pebbles refer not to flint nodules in the chalk, but to the gravel surfacing of the Roman road that passes beneath the village.

WOODMANCOTT: *Wodemancote* (903, S370), 'cottag(es) of the woodmen.'

The Candover Valley (from South to North)

ABBOTSTONE: *Abbodestan* (c.1000, S.1821), 'farm belonging to the abbot.' The manor is one of those owned by Winchester Cathedral Priory in the late Saxon period, but by Domesday had been transferred to the bishop.
Finchley Wood: *Finchesly* (1263), 'wood frequented by finches,' or a personal name.
Rypling (lost tything): *Rippling* (1236, Ass). Gover believes it is derived from *rippel* 'strip of woodland' or a personal name with *-ing*, rather than a folk-name *rippelingas*. But Smith proposes a *rip(p)* 'edge, border,' which would make Rypling have the genitival sense of 'the place along the edge,' perhaps the ridge here. Could it be the same as Godfield?

SWARRATON: *swerwetone* (903, S370), *Serveton* (ca.1150, 1341 Pat), *Sarweton* (1242, Fees). Ekwall tentatively suggests a compound *swaer-waed-tun* 'farm by the heavy wading-place of ford,' presumably one with a heavy or sticky bottom.
Godfield (tithing): *Godefeld* (1208, Ch), 'God's field' or perhaps the personal name *Goda*. A detached part of Itchen Stoke parish, which was granted to the Knights Hospitaler in the late twelfth century, and is now in Old Alresford parish.

NORTHINGTON: *Northametone* (903, S370), *Norhameton* (1167, P), from *North-haema-tun*, '*tun* of the dwellers to the north.' Ekwall and Gover believe that this direction referred to Winchester, but that town is too far away to logically affect this place-name. Local relationships would point to Abbotstone, just downstream.
Totford (tithing): *Totefort* (1167, P), 'Totta's ford.'

BROWN CANDOVER: *Cendefer* (ca.880, S1507), from the river name (see below). The epithet appears (1256, Ass) before the earliest known date of landholding by the Brune family. Perhaps it is from *brun* 'the brown one,' as a personal name or an alternate stream name.

Brick Kiln Copse: *tigel hangran* (900, S360), 'hanging wood where tiles were made, or found,' seems to be the Old English description of the same location.

Bugmore Hill: *bucgan oran* (ca.830, S242, S284), *bugenore* (1245, C), 'slope or bank of Bucge (woman) or Bucga (man).

CHILTON CANDOVER: *Childe Candever* (XIII, Harl), simply *Chilton* (1291, tax; 1316, FA). *Cilda tun*, 'tun (farm) of the child or prince' most likely refers to ownership of this manor by a noble youth. Smith notes the father of Earl Godwin was *Wulfnoth Cild*, and *Edgar Cild* was the grandson of Edmund Ironside.

Becket's Down: *on bican hyrste* (900, S360), 'Bica's wood, or wooded slope.'

Stanchester: the field name is identical to *than stan cistele* (900, S360), a not uncommon reference to a villa site, as here, meaning 'a heap of stones.' *Ceastel*, *cestil* was sometimes later confused with *ceaster* 'chester, old fort.'

PRESTON CANDOVER: *Preste candevere* (1262, FF), *preoste*, 'Candover of the priests.' The use of the plural form suggests that it was for the use of a community of priests, rather than a local incumbant. An alternative origin is *preosta tun* 'farmstead of the priests,' a similar formation to Chilton.

Moundsmere Manor: *Mundesmere* (1249, Winch. Coll; 1320 Ch), the element might be a strong form of the personal name *Munda*, but *mund* 'security, protection' may be here in a concrete sense; the second element is *mere* 'pool.'

Stevenbury (now Preston House) *Candidra Stephani* (1167, P), *Steven bur* (1328, Ch), 'Steven's manor.' Gover considers this the only Hampshire example of a name type that is common elsewhere. Probably later medieval.

BRADLEY: *Bradan leage* (909, S377; 1086, DB), 'wide *leah*' wood or clearing in wood. There is some confusion over the identification of the place-name in this spurious charter, Grundy had definitely placed it at this location.

WIELD: *Walde* (1086, DB), *weald* 'wood.'

The Candover Uplands (in Bermondspitt Hundred)

NUTLEY: *Noclei* (1086, DB), *Nutlie* (1212, Fees), 'clearing or wood, where nuts grew.'

Axford: probably from *Aesca-ford*, 'ford by the ash trees.' It was the historical source of the Candover stream.

Gobley Hole: perhaps from *geap* 'steep,' meaning 'hollow place in the steep-sided wood or glade.' It is less likely from *gop*, 'slave, servant.'

DUMMER: *Dummere* (1086, DB), *Dunmere* (1196, P). 'mere or lake by down or hill.' There is no lake there now. Only the eastern part of the parish drains into the Candover; the rest drains westward into the upper Test.
Tidley Hill: '*Tida*'s wood or clearing,' it lies at the point of divide, and also just beyond the upper drainage of the Micheldever valley.

FARLEIGH WALLOP: *Ferlege* (1086, DB), *Farnly* (1337, Dh), *fearn-leah* 'fern-covered glade, clearing.' Farleigh was held by the Wallop family in the late 14th century.

ELLISFIELD: *Esewelle* (1086, DB), *Elsefield* (1167, P). The first element may be the personal name *Aelfsige* or a short form of it. The base would then be *Ielfsiges* or *Ielfsan feld*, but it is more likely from *elle(r)n* 'elder tree.' Gelling believes that *feld* was used only for open country on the edges of woodland, and the name might then mean 'open country by the elder trees.'

HERRIARD: *Henerd* (1086, DB), *Herierda* (1162, Oxf), *Heriet* (1167, P). The second element is *geard* 'enclosure.' The first may be *hearg* 'heathen place of worship,' but the Domesday form could be related to the Hen Wood at the top of a hill at the north of the parish, a good place for a shrine, which if not from *henn* 'wild bird,' might be from *hine* 'household, community,' perhaps a reference to a community of worshippers. Dr. Gelling, however, considers a more convincing origin to be *here-geard*, 'army enclosure.'[16]

The Somborne Valley

SOMBORNE: *Sumburne* (1086, DB), *Sunburna* (1159, P);
Kyngessumburne (1256, Ass) 'King's Somborne;' *Parva Sunburn* (1242, F) 'Little Somborne;' *Upsonburna* (1167, P) 'Upper Somborne.' All are hamlets named from the stream, *Swinburna* (see below).
Compton: probably from *cumb-tun* 'farmstead in a narrow valley.'

ASHLEY: *Asselegh* (1275, Ipm), *aesc-leah* 'ash wood' or 'clearing by the ash trees.'

CRAWLEY: *Craweleainga mearc* (909, S376), *Crawanlea* (ca. 960, S827), *Crawelie* (1086, DB), 'Crow's wood,' probably from the bird rather than a personal name.

---

[16] Personal communication, 1986. The northernmost part of the Hampshire Downs would be strategic position for an army post; it could guard the ancient route (see Lunway, below) from Totford via Bradley toward the *Weargburn* (Warnborough) valley and the Thames.

SPARSHOLT: *Speoresholt* (900, S359) 'wood where shafts for spears were obtained.' Sparsholt also drains into the Itchen, and is associated with Winchester because of its proximity.

Lainston: *Lewyneston* (1280, Ass), 'Leofwine's farmstead.'

The Middle Test Valley

HOUGHTON: *Hohtuninga mearce* (982, S840), *hoh-tun* 'farmstead on the spur of a hill.'

LECKFORD: *Legh, Leaht-, Legford* (947, S526); *lech-, lecford* (1086, DB). The first element may be an unrecorded *leaht*, related to *lecan* 'to water, irrigate,' and the place was a 'ford at the irrigation channels.'

LONGSTOCK: *Stoches* (1086, DB), *aet stocc* 'trunk of tree,' perhaps in the sense of 'footbridges.'

FULLERTON: *Fugelerestune* (1086, DB), from *fuglere* 'bird-catcher,' giving 'the *tun* of the bird-catchers.'

WHERWELL: *Hwerwyl* (955, S1515), *hwer* 'kettle, cauldron,' therefore 'cauldron springs' where the water issued forth bubbling.

CHILBOLTON: *Ceolboldingtun* (909, S376). 'the farmstead of Ceolbeald's people,' or more likely the more direct genitival sense 'Ceolbeald's farm.'

FORTON: *Forde* (1046, S1016), *Forton* (1312, Ipm), 'the farmstead by a ford.' Middleton (supplanted by the more recent Longparish): *Middeltune* (1086, DB), 'the middle farmstead' between Forton and Aston.

The Upper Test Valley

TUFTON: *Tochinton* (1086, DB), *Tokinton* (1198/1260, Ch), Tokington (c. 1270, Ep), 'Toca's or Tucca's farmstead.' The *Tuccingweg* (see below) presumably lead to this site.

WHITCHURCH: *Hwitan Cyrice* (909, S378), 'white church,' but Ekwall notes that it very likely meant 'stone church,' as Bede wrote that *Hwitan Aerne* 'white house' was so called because it was made of stone.

FREEFOLK: *Frigefolc* (1086, DB), *Frivolk* (1215, Ipm), perhaps 'free people' referring to a group of freeholders. But it is more likely 'Frig's people,' referring to Woden's wife. Two other Hampshire places were originally *Freohyll*, 'the hill of the goddess Frig.'

LAVERSTOKE: *Lavrochestoche* (1086, DB), '*Stoc* or enclosure, outlying farm, frequented by larks.'
Southington: *Suthampton* (1346, FA), *Suthyngton* (1412, FA). Perhaps *Suth-haema-tun*, 'the farmstead of the people to the south.' The hamlet lies south of the stream, while Overton's original site seems to have north of it.

OVERTON: *Uferantun* (909, S378), from *ufera tun* 'upper farmstead.'
Quidhampton: *Quidhampton* (1316, FA), first element is probably *cwead* 'dirt, dung,' hence 'muddy spot.'
Poolhampton: *Aet Polhaematune* (940, S465). The first element must be *pol* 'pool or stream.' The site is at the present source of the Test.

ASHE: *Esse* (1086, DB), from *aesc*, 'ash,' perhaps the dative plural *aescum*.

STEVENTON: *Stivetune* (1086, DB), first element is probably *styfic* 'stump' or less likely a personal name *Stif*. Thus *tun* where there are stumps, rather than Stif's *tun*.

NORTH WALTHAM: *Wealtham* (909, S377), *weald-ham* 'the *ham* at the wood.' *Northe Waltham* (1289, Ep), in relation to Bishop's Waltham, in southern Hampshire.

DEANE: *Dene* (1086, DB), *denu* 'valley.'

DUMMER: partly drains into the upper Candover hills, and is identified above.

The Upper Itchen Valley (from West to East)

LITTLETON: *Litleton* (1171, Winch. Cath.), 'small farm.'

HEADBOURNE WORTHY: *Aet Worthige* (854, S311), *aet Worthigsaetena mearc, andlang Worthihaema mearc* (904, S374), *to hide burninga gemaere* (909, S376), *Hideburne Worthy, Wordy Comitis, Wordy Mortimer alias Hydeburne Mortimer* (1236, etc.). One of the estates of Worthy, from *worthig* 'an enclosure.' Roger Mortimer held the manor at Domesday.

KING'S WORTHY: *Ordie* (1086, DB), *Chinges Ordie* (1155, P). The royal manor of Worthy.

ABBOT'S WORTHY: *with easton Worthige* (909, S376), *Wordie* (1086, DB). The estate at Worthy granted to New Minster in 909.

MARTYR WORTHY: *aet Worthige* (825, S273), *to Worthig forda* (*ib.*), the manor at Worthy held by the family of Henry le Martre (1201, Cur).

Chilland (tithing): *ceoligland* (XI, S827), the first element also occurs in the bounds of Martyr Worthy as *cyoling mor* (939, S351). *Ceolig* might mean 'ship (keel-shaped) island,' with reference to a piece of land in the Itchen. *Ceoling mor* might then be elliptical for *ceoliging mor* 'moor or marsh of the people of ship island.' Alternatively, it may derive from the personal name *Ceol*.

Churn Hill: *to cyrringe* (939, S984), from *cyrring*, 'turning, bend.'

Rutherly Copse: *Rutherly Coppice* (1695, Cas), and the boundary mark *be westan witherslea* (854, S304), *Hrither lea* 'cattle clearing.'

Shroner Wood: *Boscus de Shrewenore* (1272, Ass), 'slope or bank inhabited by shrewmice.'

Pyles Fm.: *Pyles* (1695, Cas), Smith gives *pyll* 'a pool in a river,' though it might be a family name here.

ITCHEN ABBAS: *Icene* (1086, DB), *Ichene Monalium* (1167, P), named from the river (see below). The manor was held by the Abbey of St. Mary, Winchester.

ITCHEN STOKE: *Stoche* (1086, DB), *Ichenestok* (1291, Tax), from *stoc*, 'outlying dairy farm.' Gover believes that it was attached to Itchen Abbas, and so took its name.

EASTON: *to Igsaetmearce and Eastuninga* (825, S273), *Eastun* (ca. 875, S1275), *to Eastune* (960, S695), Gover and Ekwall consider the 'east tun' to be in relation to Winchester. The earlier reference concerns 'the boundary of the Igsaet and of the people of Easton.' This charter also refers to the place *Igtunae* 'farm in the well-watered land,' which was probably the home of the *Igsaet*, with *saet* added as usual to the first element. It is quite possible that the *ig* is the same spot as *ceolig* of Chilland (see above).

AVINGTON: *Afintun* (961, S699), 'Afa's farm.'
Lovington: 'Leofa's farm.'
Yavington: 'Eabba's farm.'

OVINGTON: *aet ufinctune* (ca. 960, S826), 'Ufa's farm.'

The Tichborne Valley

TICHBORNE: *be Ticceburnan* (909, S385), named from the stream 'kid stream' (see below)

Sevington Fm.: *Sevenhampton*, ca. 1200, reference to *Suvenhem hull* 'hill of the people of Sevenham.' A boundary mark *syfan wyllan* (938, S444) suggests that Sevenhampton may be elliptical for 'Seven-well-hampton.'

CHERITON: *Cherinton* (1167, P), from *cyric-tun* 'farm with, or more likely belonging to, a church.'

HINTON AMPNER: *Heanton* (1045, S1185), *Hea-tun*, dat. *Hean-tune*. 'farmsead situated on high ground.' This is 'the almoner's Hinton,' referring to the almoner of St. Swithun's Priory, Winchester.

BRAMDEAN: *to Bromdaene* (932, S882), 'valley where broom grew.'

KILMESTON: *Cenelmestun* (961, S693), *Cylmestuna* (XII, S1820), 'Cynehelm's farmstead.'

BEAUWORTH: *Beowyrth* (938, S444), 'Bee farm,' but perhaps a shortened personal name *Beo*.

The Tichborne Valley Upland

WEST TISTED: *Ticces stede* (932, S417), *westistude* (1234-6, Sel), 'place where kids were kept.' Related to Tichborne?

PRIVET: *aet Pryfetes flodan* (755, ASC), *Pruvet* (ca. 1245, Sel), 'Privet Copse,' the stream was undoubtedly the now dry head of the Tichborne, but the place is more closely associated with the nearby Meon valley.

The Alre Valley
(also known as the Itchen or the Denewater)

ALRESFORD: *Alresford* (701, S242), from *alor* 'alder ford' in the gen. sing. *alres*.

BISHOP SUTTUN: *sudtone*, (1086, DB), *Suttona episcopi* (1167, P), 'southern *tun*,' belonging to the Bishop of Winchester.
Gundleton: probably 'Gunnhild's *tun*,' a Scandinavian woman's name. This site may not have been a tithing, but it has a noteworthy place-name. Could it be from Canute's daughter?

ROPLEY: *Ropeleia* (1198, FF), Ekwall proposes a personal name *Roppa*, giving 'Roppa's wood or clearing.'

BIGHTON: *Bicingtun* (959, S660), probably the direct genitival form, giving 'Bicca's *tun*.'

Drayton: *Dregtun* (959, S589), 'tun where there was portage across the stream,' a lost settlement, known from charter boundary marks only.

MEDSTEAD: *Medestede* (ca.1235, Sel), 'place in a meadow.'

THE HUNDRED NAMES OF THE MICHELDEVER REGION
(see Figure B.1)

The hundred-names of Hampshire have been discussed in O.S. Anderson's *English Hundred-Names: The South-West Counties*, in G.E. Gover's manuscript study of Hampshire place-names, and in *ODEPN*.[17] The procedures of reference used above for the place-names are also used for the names of hundreds. Identifications and interpretations made by these scholars are not noted individually, except where there are conflicting opinions.

The difficulty in studying hundred-names stems from the basic dichotomy of the hundred as a late Saxon and Norman institution. The hundred had two different types of name; what was named was either the meeting place where the moot gathered, or the manor to which the hundred court was attached. This confusion in designation is apparent in Domesday Book, which uses both types of names indiscriminately, no doubt following local usage, but in only rare cases was the alternative name of a hundred recorded. One might assume that the entity was referred to first as 'the hundred meeting at such and such a place,' and only later as 'the hundred pertaining to such and such manor.' But while logical, and supported by the opinions of O.S. Anderson, it may not be true, or at least not universally true, because some hundreds by their large size and regular outlines seem ancient, but have only the names of their manors, whilst some small and artificial hundreds bear the name of their meeting places.

BUDDLESGATE: *Bytlegete*, DB, *gebytle* 'buildings, dwelling' and *geat* 'gate.' The gate by the buildings' must have been the meeting place, but the site is unknown.

BERMONDSPIT: *Bermesplet*, DB, Anderson notes a depression in the ground close to Bermondspit House, east of Axford. This is perhaps the 'pit,' where *bremel* (bramble) was common. The name was later associated with the personal name *Beornmund*.

BOUNTISBOROUGH: *Mantesberg*, DB, this is an error, probably arising from confusion with Mainsborough. Other forms indicate 'Bunt's barrow.'

---

[17]   See notes 3 and 13. O.S. Anderson, *The English Hundred-Names: The South-Western Counties*, Acta Universitatis Lundensis (Nova Series) Band 35 (Lund, 1939).

BARTON STACEY: *Bertun*, DB, appurtenant to the manor of that name.

CHUTELEY: *Cillei* DB, *Chetelega* 1168, probably from *cietel* 'valley' and *leah* 'wood,' galde.' It must be associated with the *cyteling graf*, a landmark surviving in field names south of Marydown Park, west of Wooton, and close to the later meeting place of the hundred—under a hedge at Malshanger.

EVINGAR: *Evingare* DB, *efen* 'even' and *gara* 'triangular piece of land, gore.' The meeting place was probably *Evangales*, a field name one mile NW of Whitchurch.

FAWLEY: *Falelie* DB, 'fallow *lea*, glade,' from Fawley Down three miles SE of Winchester, a well-marked spur of a ridge of high ground. The Domesday hundred *Falemere*, comprising the extensive Chilcomb estate of Winchester Cathedral Priory, was later divided between Fawley and Buddlesgate hundreds.

MAINSBOROUGH: *Manesbergie* DB, perhaps from a personal name from *maegen* 'strength, force,' as in Maegenfrith (Manfred), and *beorg* 'barrow,' hence 'Maegen's barrow.'

MICHELDEVER: *Miceldefer* DB, named from the manor and stream (see below).

KING'S SOMBORNE: *Somburne* DB, from the royal manor of that name.

BISHOP'S SUTTON: *Sutton* 1236, from the manor held by the bishop of Winchester. The original hundred name was ASHLEY: *Esselei*, DB, *aesc-leah* 'ash wood,' but the place name is lost.

THORNGATE: *Tornegate* 1158, the 'thorngate' was probably a natural feature, a gap in the hills. The place is lost, though the later court leets were held at Buckholt Hill. Perhaps the 'gate' refers to the passage of the Roman road here. The early Norman name, however, was:

BROUGHTON: *Brocton, Breston* DB, from the manor by that name.

WHERWELL: *Werwell* 1158, from the manor of Wherwell, but in 1086 it was:

WELFORD: 'ford on a stream' or 'ford by a spring,' which is likely to have been the meeting place for the hundred.

Of the fourteen hundreds (including Falmer) in 1086, nine appear to bear the name of a hundred meeting-place (moot). Of the five 'manorial' names, one has an alternate 'moot' name (Broughton-Thorngate). Later four of the 'moot' names were replaced by 'manorial' ones. Thus, the middle Hampshire evidence supports the hypothesis that the earliest hundred names were those of meeting places, and the later ones had manorial names, which is what Anderson convolutedly proposed:

"the association of hundreds with later manors whose name they bear was not the more primitive arrangement."[18]

STREAM NAMES OF MIDDLE HAMPSHIRE

Based largely upon Ekwall's *English River Names*[19] (see Figure B.2).

The Itchen Drainage System

ITCHEN: *Icene* or *Ycene*, probably a Celtic word with the sense of 'powerful,' perhaps the name of a god.

HEADBOURNE: the little tributary of the Itchen at Worthy, *into hydiburnam* (854, S311). The first element has been thought to come from *hida* (household), though not directly connected to the later medieval Hyde Abbey. A more appropriate origin, however, would be *hyth*, 'landing place'; the stream at the landing place for the royal manor of Worthy.

TICHBORNE: From *ticca*, 'kid,' or a personal name *Tica* or *Ticcea*.

ALRE: a back formation from Alreford (see above). Gover suggests that the earlier name was *Denewater* 1447, *Denwater* 1453. Ropley Dean is the present name of a hamlet in the valley (dean) bottom between Ropley and Bishop's Sutton. It may be that the southern branch of the stream was the Denewater, and the northern, more direct branch was the course referred to as 'Itchen' in the Anglo-Saxon period.

CANDOVER: *Cendefer* 701 (XII), c.830 (XII), *Kendefer* 900, Ekwall thinks that the change from Cen- to later Can- may have been French influence, or from the nearby Andover. Its origin is similar to the Old Welsh *cein* 'beautiful' and British *dubro* 'water,' giving 'beautiful stream.'

The Test Drainage System

TEST: *Terste*, pre-English, probably *Trest*, related to Welsh *tres* 'toil,' in the sense of 'strong.'

SOMBORNE: *Swinburna* 909, 'stream of the wild boar.'

---

18   Anderson, *Hundred-Names*, p. 210.
19   Eilert Ekwall, *English River Names* (Oxford, 1928).

ANTON: the present name of the Andover, *Andeferas*, 955 (XIV). The old river name was *Andefer*, cf. *Cendefer*. The first element is probably identical to that in *onny*, a derivative of a British word for ash trees.

MICHELDEVER: *Myceldefer* 900, possibly a hybrid formation of *micel* 'great' and the British *dubro* 'water,' which assumes a 'Little' Dever nearby. But the earliest reference (862) is given as *Mycendefer*, in two different forms, which Ekwall believes to be trustworthy. The British *micn* (later Welsh *mign*) 'bog, quagmire' would be a better description of this minor rivulet with often wide, marshy edges.

HURSTBOURNE: *Hysseburna*, according to Ekwall, from *hys(s)e* not in the sense of 'young man,' but in the sense of 'tendril, vine-shoot.' Hence 'winding stream.'

CRANBOURNE: *Cranburnan* 900, 'stream of the herons (cranes).'

Pre-Conquest names for the streams of north-central Hampshire were thus *Icene, Ticcesburne, Cendefer, Denewater, Terste, Swynburn, Micendefer, Andefer, Cranburn* and *Hysseburn*. Of the ten names, only five are English, and they are minor streams only. Ekwall noted this pattern for Hampshire, and suggested that the larger the stream, the more likely it would be known by a wider group, and the more likely it would be retained.

Names of Roads and Earthworks

Based largely upon G.E. Gover's 'Place-Names of Hampshire' (see note 13).

THE HARROWAY: from Overton to Andover this was earlier *herepath* 'army way,' and must have mutated to a *here-weg*.

ICKLAND ROAD: The Roman road from Winchester to Cirencester is called that in 1795 (TA), probably a medieval influence from the well-known Icknield Way. The Cirencester road was earlier referred to as *straet*.

PORTWAY: The Roman road from Sarum to Silchester, a medieval term, earlier referred to as *ealdan straet*.

TUCKING WAY: *on tuccinge weg* 900, *Tockingweie* ca. 1250, apparently the old name for the Winchester to Newbury road which runs through Whitchurch. The first element is no doubt the same as that in Tufton (Tockington). The road then led to or through 'the people dependent on *Tucca*.'

LUNWAY: *lunways* 1649, a field name along the present road along the south edge of Micheldever parish. *Lun* is probably a Celtic name, seen as an element in British river names, though it could refer to the cross-country route to London, bypassing Winchester and heading in the general direction of Farnham and Guildford.

ANDYKE: at Barton Stacey, *auntediche* XIII, similar to the boundary mark *to aenta dic* 1026, at King's Worthy. The meaning is 'giant ditch.'

DEVIL'S DYKE: at Hunton, Cranbourne, it is the location of *innan greatan dic* 900, 'big ditch.'

ANALYSIS OF TOPONYMS
(See Figure B.3).

The survey examined the topographical units of middle Hampshire (excluding the highly complex Winchester section of the Itchen valley): the Micheldever and Candever valleys, the upper Candover watershed, as well as the valleys of the Somborne, Middle Test, Upper Test, the Upper Itchen, Tichborne, and Alre (Denewater). These combined areas contain 69 parishes and tithings, and 85 place-names of medieval settlements. The toponymic elements that formed these selected place-names of middle Hampshire divide into several significant categories: topographical, biological, social, and personal names, with sub-categories for each. The number of place-names here that contain each element is given after its translation.

Topographical Elements

Physical: *Dun* 'down, hill' (2); *eg* 'island, watered land' (1); *denu* (deane, narrow valley' (2); *cumb* 'combe, short, broad valley' (1); *hoh* 'hill-spur' (1).

In every case, topographical elements seem appropriate to the physical location of the place-names. None appears to have been transferred from other sites, as might have happened with a change of land ownership or a population movement. Margaret Gelling's opinion that topographic names may be among the oldest surviving place-names is based upon her extensive toponymic studies of Oxfordshire and Berkshire in the English Place-Names Society series, as well as her re-examination of Essex.[20] The Berkshire Volume is particularly relevant to the study of Hampshire names, because the border between the two counties is clearly artificial, created in the eighth or ninth century (perhaps by Offa), well after most of the place-names for both counties had been established.[21]

Communication: *straet* 'made road' (1); *ford* (4); *draeg* 'portage site' (2).

These elements are few, but when used as the second element in a place-name, they may suggest an early date. When 'ford' is used as a second

---

[20]   Gelling, *Signposts*, pp. 118-129.
[21]   Gelling, *Berkshire*, pp. 838-842.

element, it might be especially early. Otherwise, these elements usually appear as the first, or adjectival, elements, and often with the later habitative element *tun*.

Water-related: *mere* 'pond' (3); *wyll* 'spring' (2); *pol* 'pool' (1); *burna* 'stream' (4); *dubro* British 'stream word' (3); *cwaeth* 'mud' (1).

The water-related names form a somewhat larger group than the elements associated with physical relief and communication. Most stream names have been taken by a settlement along their banks. North Hampshire and the adjacent parts of Wiltshire and Berkshire have particularly large numbers of 'bourne' names, as well as British stream names, Itchen and Test being noteworthy examples. In fact, within this area, it may be difficult to find the name for a stream that is neither a British name nor a 'bourne' name, with only the proposed medieval Denewater (Alre) coming to mind as an exception. Nearly all the major streams names here are of Celtic origin, while the secondary streams are the ones that have been changed to 'bourne' names, but here rarely to any other term used by the Anglo-Saxons for smaller streams.[22] There are no place-names in *broc* ('brook') in middle Hampshire, and *fleot* (stream, flood) occurs only in the *Anglo-Saxon Chronicle* reference to Privet.[23] A superficial examination of southern Hampshire and the Isle of Wight shows that 'bournes' were rare there, with only three examples. In this southern area, there are also few British river names, with none at all for the Isle of Wight and the New Forest.[24] It would be interesting to discover what chronological—or ethnic—factors played a role in the use of *burna*, and in its perhaps selective replacement of British names.[25]

Biological Elements

General Vegetation: *leah* 'wood or clearing' (6); *feld* 'open land or woods' (2); *weald* 'wood' (2); *holt* 'wood' (1); *wudu* 'wood' (1); *mede* 'pasture, meadow' (1); *bere* 'barley, grain' (1); *styfic* 'stump' (1); *stocc* 'stump, log' (1).

Wood-related elements dominate the major place-names, with twelve examples, but only two cases of pasture or arable land away from a woodland setting. This is due to the presence of particular 'forest' parishes, lands which may have been totally wooded in the early Saxon period, and the names of which reflect the land-use before extensive medieval assarting. In middle Hampshire, these are not necessarily the areas of greatest woodland today, but they are universally on high ground between the watersheds. They are areas of poorly drained soil, often of clay or clay-with-flints, and exposed to wind and weather. As such, they would be among the least likely for early agricultural use.

---

[22]   Ibid., p. 923; and noted in Ekwall, *River Names*, p. lxxxvii.

[23]   As *Privotesflod*, *ASC* 757 (*s.a.* 755).

[24]   K. Jackson, *Language and History in Early Britain* (Edinburgh, 1953) map of British river names, reproduced in Gelling, *Signposts*, p. 89, figure 3.

[25]   Gelling believes that the *burna* compound appears very early and that racial affinities of the English settlers was a determinant for its distribution, *Place-Names*, pp. 16-20.

While *styfic* may describe land in the process of clearance (Steventon), the one instance of *stocc* appears to refer to a single burnt stump at Stoke Charity, and had been no doubt a well-known local landmark in the earliest days of the English occupation, but does not necessarily indicate woodland.

Specific Vegetation: *Elles* 'elders' (1); *aesc* 'ash' (3); *Alor* 'alder' (1); *brom* 'broom' (1); *fearn* 'fern' (1); *poppe* 'poppy' (1); privet (1).

This type of name is not very extensive, and with the exception of Privet and Ashe, all are first, or adjectival, elements for site descriptions: *feld, leah, ford,* etc. Specific vegetation names are much more common in local field names.

Animal Names: *Beo* 'bee' (1); *bull* (1); *hund* 'dog' (1); *cran* 'heron' (1); *craw* 'crow' (1); *lavroch* 'lark (1); swine (1); *ticce* 'kid' (1).

Like the specific vegetation names, all the animal names appear as the adjectival first element. It refers to a place frequented or inhabited by the animal, though there is often the possibility that a personal name, or a nickname, was based on an animal name. As with the specific vegetation names, the animal names are more common among field names.

Habitative Elements

Tun 'farmstead' (27); *-ingtun* (8); *hamtun* (4); *ham* (2); *burg* (2); *bur* (1); *cot* (1); *stoc* (3); *worth(ig)* (2); *stede* (2).

As elsewhere in England, *tun* is by far the most common place-name element,[26] perhaps because it had a very long period of use, from at least the seventh century into the late medieval period. There is a notable grouping of *ingtuns* on the south side of the upper Itchen valley, and a group of several *hamtuns* around Overton on the Upper Test. These groups probably represent the fragmentation of two larger estates. The difference between the names of the two groups could stem from their creation at different times, or less likely, a different character of the settlement or tenure at those localities.

Only two villages bear *ham* names, Popham and North Waltham on the north boundary of Micheldever Hundred. This scarcity is apparently general for Wessex, because in Berkshire the *ham* settlements are small and unimportant.[27] These two *hams* are, however, noticeably associated with a Roman road, a correlation that elsewhere has been considered a sign of antiquity.[28]

Burg (meaning fort) appears in the names of two major prehistoric hillforts within the Micheldever valley, and is the common term for such sites, though in some instances in northern Hampshire it has not survived. This term may in fact,

---

[26] Gelling, *Bershire*, pp. 939-942; Smith, *Elements*, pp. 188-198.

[27] Gelling, *Berkshire*, p. 817.

[28] Cox, "Significance of ... *ham*"; Dodgson, "Place-Names from *hamm*"; see note 7.

suggest a re-occupation of the site. *Bur[h]* and *cot* refer to very small places, and appear in the survey at Burcot and Woodmancot.

The three instances of toponyms with the element *stoc* are each appropriate to the meaning of '(dairy) farm dependent upon a larger village of manor.' None of them are major settlements, and Itchen Stoke and Laverstock seem clearly dependent upon neighbouring villages. Ekwall equated Basingstoke in north Hampshire with the *Besinga hearh* 'pagan sanctuary of the people of Baessa,' where Caedwalla reportedly issued a charter dated 688.[29] While Basingstoke is two miles west of Basing, the presumed centre of the 'people of Baessa,' the village of Herriard in the Candover watershed is only four miles south of Basing. Its proximity to Basing may suggest a derivation from *hearh-yeard* 'enclosure of the pagan shrine,' making Herriard an equally likely site of Caedwalla's court, but Gelling considers a more convincing origin in *here-yeard* 'army enclosure.'[30]

Middle Hampshire has two toponyms with *worth(ig)*. Beoworth in the Tichborne Valley is a small place, and its meaning of 'bee enclosure' is no doubt suited to its secluded, woodland setting. This type of *worth* becomes widespread in the eighth century, but there is another use of *worth* that is earlier and is given to more important places. Even though the four villages bearing the name 'Worthy' on the upper Itchen did not receive a secondary appellation until after the Domesday Survey, it is evident that they formed originally a larger, integral estate that was split up in the ninth and tenth centuries. But it is possible that at least a few early *worth* names had an even more specialized use, seemingly that of an area (based on an 'enclosure'?) reserved for a ruler and his immediate followers, as seen in a significant number of *worth* names among the sites associated with royal centres of the early Anglo-Saxon kingdoms.[31]

Social Elements

Folk (1); *preost* 'priest' (1); *abbod* 'abbot (1); *cild* 'youth, prince' (1); *wudu-man* (1); *cyric* 'church' (2); *hearg* 'sanctuary' (1?); *here* 'army' (1?); *speor* 'spear' (1); *Frig* 'goddess' (1).

This group of place-name elements is limited to a few examples. Most are prefixed with *tun*, and are probably a later development, referring to the ownership of the manor (*cild*, *abbod*, etc.). *Wuduman* describes the occupation of the

---

[29]   Ekwall, *Place-Names in -ing*, p. 44; the charter is S25.

[30]   Margaret Gelling, personal communication, 1986.

[31]   A superficial listing of these possible royal *worths* includes: Tamworth (*Tamworthig*), the site of the main Mercian royal palace; Derby (North Worthy); Ixworth, an East Anglian centre of pagan burials; and several important ecclesiastical sites: Polesworth, Brixworth, Worksworth, and Bury St. Edmund's (*Beadricesworth*). King's Worthy on the Itchen is the site of the largest pagan burial group in Hampshire, comprising several hundred burials. A.J. Robertson, *Anglo-Saxon Charters*, p. 20, notes a gate in Canterbury called *vveoweraget* (mid ninth-century) and *Wiwergatan* that apparently lead to the river *Wye*, but which was later called Worthgate, having some association with a *worth* (p. 204).

inhabitants of the 'cots' there. Herriard might have been a pagan sanctuary (*hearg*), perhaps surviving for some time into the Christian period at this isolated spot; alternatively, it could refer to an army (*here*) post or encampment. The *speor-holt* 'wood where warriors regularly got shafts for their spears' might have been set aside for this purpose by a central authority, and there are a number of similar names throughout England.[32] The unusual toponym 'Freefolk' combines two social elements, describing the status of the 'folk' at that place with the first element either 'free' or 'Frig.' As there are no published examples of a named group of freeholders, or a 'folk' that followed an individual, it is more likely that here was a group owing allegiance to the goddess Frig.[33] This folk name probably extended originally over a much larger area, and if similar names were used to identify other pagan Saxon groups, it might help explain why the 'tribal' -*ingas* names have not been recorded for middle Hampshire.

Personal Names

Place-names with personal name elements may be grouped into three categories: simplex, hypocoristic, or diminutive names; dithematic names; and Scandinavian names. They are presented here with their secondary elements and the page reference in Searle's *Onomasticon Anglo-Saxonicum*.[34]

Simplex	Dithematic
Afa-ingtun (62)	Aelfsige-feld (19)
Bicca-ingtun (106)	Ceolbeald-ingtun (129)
Goda-feld (260)	Cynehelm-tun (156)
Eabba-ingtun (175)	Wynsige-tun (524)
Leofa-ingtun (326)	Leofwine-tun (335)
Roppa-leah (404)	
Totta-ford (458)	
Tucca-ingtun (410)	
Tuda-bury (46)	
Ufa-ingtun (465)	

[32]   Smith, *Elements*, 1 (25): 135.
[33]   *OEPN*, 189, has Froyle and Forbury in north-east Hampshire as descended from *Freohyll* 'hill of the goddess Frig', so this attribution to a pagan goddess, while rare here, is not a unique occurrence. For a commentary on this subject, in N. Brooks, M. Gelling and D. Johnson, "A New Charter of King Edgar," *Anglo-Saxon England* 13 (1984), 137-155, esp. pp. 150-151, 154
[34]   William George Searle, *Onomasticon Anglo-Saxonicum: A List of Anglo-Saxon Proper Names from the Time of Beda to that of King John* (Hildersheim, 1959).

Scandinavian	Other Possible Names
Brand-bury (113)	Bulla-dun (120)
Gunhild-tun (271)	Frig-folk (247)
	Papa-holt (papo, 385)
	Styfic-tun (Stuf, stybba, 432)
	Beo-worth (86)

It cannot be assumed that the places given dithematic personal names are necessarily later than those with simplex names, nor are Scandinavian names always the ones associated with the latest sites to be occupied. Some places may have been renamed several times. Sometimes Domesday Book entries incorporated the names of current, or recent owners, making the point that a personal name is more likely to represent a late owner of the land than an original settler.[35]

Interpretation of the Toponymic Analysis

Analysis of the place-names of middle Hampshire permits some general observations. First, there is an over-all even distribution between topographical and biological elements. Habitation elements total about the same number, with *tun* the most common element. This is in no way exceptional to observations made elsewhere in southern England.[36]

The specific distribution of place-name elements reveals a preponderance of wood-related elements along the eastern and northern edges of the area surveyed, with another grouping in the south-west.[37] Continuing into the unsurveyed areas, these name types mark the high ground between watersheds, lands that were least suitable for early woodland clearance and remained heavily wooded into the later medieval period. Similarly, the watersheds between the Micheldever, Candover, and 'Alre' valleys are marked by woodland place-names.

The habitation names *stede* and *cot* appear in woodland areas, and it is possible that these, like *feld*, may be an oblique reference to woodland. *Stede*, however, may be a common name element for the region to the east of middle Hampshire, as several appear in the northeast corner of Hampshire, and there are a large number of *stede* names in Surrey, but none in Berkshire and Oxfordshire.[38] In this area, then, *stede* may be an indicator of settlement by 'Surrey' Saxons up to the watershed of the central Hampshire basin. Furthermore, the many 'shott' (*sceat*) names of north-east Hampshire do not continue into middle Hampshire, with Kempshott parish lying just north of Dummer. These place-names

---

[35]   Gelling, *Signposts*, pp. 162-190; condensed argument on p. 111.
[36]   For comparative distribution patterns, see Gelling, *Berkshire*, pp. 923-944.
[37]   Compare this distribution with that for Wiltshire. Wood names in Eastern Wiltshire are scarce, found only on the watershed south of the Lodden: Gelling, *Place-Names*, p. 204.
[38]   Gelling, *Berkshire*, pp. 938-939.

are also common in Surrey, but appear only once in east Berkshire, and not at all in Oxfordshire.[39]

The *mere* 'pond' names may also suggest a territorial difference. In the upper Candover watershed are three cases of *mere* (Dummer, Broadmere in Farleigh Wallop, and Moundsmere in north-east Preston Candover), which are not found elsewhere in the surveyed region, though the deserted medieval village of Lomer stood on the high ground just beyond the parish of Kilmeston. This pattern may support Gelling's suggestion that the name reflects the importance of water resources in high downland without streams.[40]

Some important place-name elements are *not* recorded for middle Hampshire. Among them are the groups of names with the suffix *ingas* and *ingaham*, which are significant toponyms elsewhere. Ekwall's original monograph on this subject noted that there were two groups of *ingas* names in Hampshire: in the far north (the 'Basing' group), and in the far south (the 'Eling' group).[41] He found an equally strong pattern for *ingaham* names, with only four in Hampshire, all in the south, which he suggested revealed a Jutish influence. Further, the names in *ing* (singular), as opposed to *ingas* (plural) follow this double pattern, with one possible exception at Rypling, a lost tything of Abbotstone. These *ing* names are early, many of them having been taken from minor stream names, and Ekwall proposed that the related *inge* names common in south Hampshire and Kent were another indicator of Jutish settlements.[42]

Other noteworthy absences from the major place-names of middle Hampshire are *ersc* 'ploughed field,' which is common along the Thames valley up to east Berkshire, and *hamm* 'meadowland,' an important toponym in Berkshire, Surrey and Wiltshire. Perhaps the local topography of narrow valleys and high downs mitigates against its use here, though much of Wiltshire and Berkshire has the same terrain.[43] Similarly, *hamstede* does not occur at all here, and this formation is common in Berkshire but rare in Surrey. Another important toponym, *wic*, does not appear in this area, and is also rare in Berkshire, but does have several examples in south Hampshire.[44]

The toponyms of the central Hampshire basin, then, are different in several regards from those of adjacent regions. Certain place-names are not recorded or are found only on the north-eastern edge of the survey area. Elements such as *stede*, *sceat*, and *ersc* were commonly used by the Thames Saxons settling in Surrey and east Berkshire, but apparently did not pass beyond the watershed of the Hampshire Downs into the Hampshire Basin. Furthermore, while the late *ingtun* is common in middle Hampshire, *ingas*, *inga(ham)*, and *inge* are absent, but are important

[39] Ibid., p. 938.

[40] Ibid., p. 936; repeated in *Place-Names*, pp. 26-27.

[41] Ekwall, *Place-Names in* -ing, p. 42; for *ingaham* names, p. 160.

[42] Ibid., p. 217.

[43] Gelling, *Berkshire*, pp. 925-926, 929. For a discussion of *ersc* and *hamm*, see Gelling, *Place-Names*, pp. 234-235, 41-50, respectively.

[44] Gelling, *Berkshire*, p. 942.

elements immediately south and north of the region. The differences in distribution of toponymic elements are clues to the character of the early English occupation of Wessex. The early medieval inhabitants of the central Hampshire basin did not share a dialect of place-name forming characteristics with (and were thus not related to) those people settling the valleys of Surrey and east Berkshire, who were perhaps best described as 'Surrey Saxons' or even 'Middle Saxons.' In Hampshire, these Saxons (and their political allegiance) extended as far as: 1) the *ing* suffix names clustered around Basing, on land drained by the Celtic-named Lodden, which joins the Thames at Reading; 2) in our survey area, the *stede* names of Medstead and Tisted, overlooking valleys draining eastward into the Wey, another Thames tributary. These seem to be clear indicators of a toponymic, and therefore linguistic and ethnic, 'frontier' along the edge of the watershed divide.

No clear definition is yet distinguishable between the place-names of middle Hampshire and those of west Berkshire, an area occupied by West Saxons. Two possibly noteworthy differences are the absence of *throp* (N. Eng. *thorp*) in central Hampshire, and the great rarity of *hamtun* in Berkshire (and again in Surrey), when each is common to the other locale. There is a more telling difference between the survey area and south Hampshire in not only the lack of *ingas* and *ingaham* names in middle Hampshire, but also the near total absence of *ing* names here, understood to be a strong indicator of Jutish settlement. Further, and more detailed, studies of Hampshire toponyms will undoubtedly define more precisely these different place-naming characteristics, as well as pinpointing others, such as that separating the 'Meonware' Jutes from the 'Saxons' of Portchester and Chichester.[45]

In conclusion, the revised chronology of place-name development as presented by Margaret Gelling and J. McN. Dodgson appears to be substantially supported by the patterns of middle Hampshire. First, the earliest stratum of toponyms are those bearing Celtic river names or containing water-related elements. In Berkshire many of these place-names have been attributed to the centres of large early estates or land divisions,[46] and Micheldever may be the principal example of several in Hampshire. The survival of the toponym for a great conglomerate estate could be more often than not a matter of chance, but it was more likely to be preserved if at least the core of the estate passed at an early date into the hands of an ecclesiastical institution.

Secondly, *ham* names, which are typical of early settlement through much of England, here appear at only two small villages, and similar to the pattern observed in Berkshire, they do not play a major role in the formation of

---

[45]   John McN. Dodgson, "Place-Names in Sussex: The Material for a New Look," pp. 54-58, and Martin Welsh, "Early Anglo-Saxon Sussex: From Civitas to Shire," pp. 13-35 in Peter Brandon, ed., *The South Saxons* (Chichester, 1978). See also Barry Cunliffe, *Excavations at Portchester Castle, Vol. II: Saxon* (London, 1976), pp. 301-304. The geographic unity of the broad estuaries east of the Solent suggests an original Saxon 'tribal' unit incorporating the intriguingly axial town locations: Porchester–Cosham–Bosham–Chichester. See D. Hill, *An Atlas of Anglo-Saxon England* (Toronto, 1981), p. 288.

[46]   Gelling, *Berkshire*, pp. 809-812, 823-829; also discussed in *Signposts*, pp. 191-214.

place-names. The absence of *ingas* and *ingaham* names suggests a further ethnic distinction, in this case, from both the Jutes of south Hampshire and the 'Middle Saxon' colonists of north-east Hampshire.

Thirdly, the later pre-Conquest place-names are mainly of the *tun, ingtun, hamtun* variety, all perhaps representing originally dependent, outlying settlements. A group of *ingtun* names on the upper Itchen and a group of *hamtun* names on the upper Test probably result from single large estates that were split up within very short periods, perhaps at single moments. Two instances of more exotic toponyms may be the survival of a pagan tribal unit in Freefolk, and the suggestion of an early royal centre at the Worthies.

Finally, there seem to have been no place-name changes during the early years of the Norman dynasty. Later, the changes that were made, consisted mainly of the addition to the English place-name, of a 'manorial' name, more properly a Norman surname, and later Anglo-Norman. These additions indicate a major change in social customs and self-conception, because the pre-Conquest aristocracy did not bear family names. The effect of this change or rural toponyms, and its far greater influence on estate formation and inheritance, may have been spawned by the Conquest, but only came to maturity after 1100, beyond the period examined in this study.

Appendix C

Advowsons of Middle Hampshire Parishes

The following information on advowsons of the parishes of the Micheldever region is drawn from material collected in *The Victoria History of the Counties of England. A History of Hampshire and the Isle of Wight*, vols. 1-2, ed. Arthur Doubleday (1900-1903); vols. 3-4, ed. William Page (1908, 1911). Abbreviations used here: DB = Domesday Book, Bishop = Bishop of Winchester, N.M. = New Minster (Hyde Abbey).

Bishop's Sutton Hundred (vol. 3):
Bighton (40) DB church, advowson follows manor, N.M.;
Sutton (45) DB church, O.M., Eustace, lord of the manor, gave to Merton Convent;
Bramdean (50) manor held of the king;
Ropley (58) Merton Convent, chapel of Sutton;
West Tisted (62) DB church, not stated if bishop held advowson, but probably did.

Fawley Hundred (vol. 3):
Alresford (306) DB three churches, one probably Medstead. Held by the Bishop;
Avington (308) DB church, possibly Bishop;
Cheriton (313) Bishop;
Beauworth (314) tithing of Cheriton, chapel;
Easton (319) DB two churches, Bishop;
Hinton (322) DB church, Bishop;
Kilmeston (325) DB chapel annexed to rectory of Cheriton;
Martyr Worthy (327) 1251 reference, advowson held by Cathedral;
Medstead (329) probably one of the three DB churches of Alresford, Bishop;
Ovington (331) 1284, king gave Bishop right to advowson;
Owslebury (335) 1351 a vicarage of Marwell Park college of secular priests;
Tichbourne (348) annexed to Cheriton;
Wield (348) 1280 Bishop.

Bermondspitt Hundred (vol. 3):
Preston Candover (377) thirteenth century granted by lord to priory of Southwell;
Dummer(360) DB church probably held with the manor;
Herriard (369) manor;
Nutley (371) Priory of Southwick;
Farleigh Wallop (371) DB held by king, advowson with manor;
Ellisfield (371) DB church, in thirteenth century held by priory of Southwick.

Micheldever Hundred (vol. 3):
Micheldever (393-394) church mentioned in spurious 903 grant.
Not in DB. In 1297 a vicarage with chapels at Northington, Popham, East Stratton and West Stratton.

Buddlesgate Hundred (vol. 3):
Chilbolton (405) Bishop;
Crawley (412) Bishop, had chapel at Hunton;
Houghton (417) DB church, Bishop, a chapel listed probably at North Houghton manor;
Littleton (423) One of nine churches of Chilcomb, Bishop;
Sparsholt (447) one of nine churches of Chilcomb, Bishop;
Stoke Charity (451) DB "Mauger" held church, by fourteenth century was attached to manor;
Wonston (460-461) DB Bishop, with chapel at Sutton Scotney (one of two there in DB?), and chapel at Cranbourne.

Mainsborough Hundred (vol. 4):
Brown Candover (184) church in spurious 903 charter, not in DB, N.M. held advowson;
Chilton Candover (186) 1291 lord of manor presented living;
Woodmancott (187) chapel dependent upon Brown Candover.

Bountisborough Hundred (vol. 4):
Itchen Abbas (192) 1280 Abbey of St. Mary (Nunnaminster), the lord of the manor;
Itchen Stoke (194-195) 1291 a vicarage, lord of manor Romsey Abbey;
Abbotstone (195) manor, Hugh de Port's descendants until 1818;
Swarraton (196) late thirteenth century held by lord of manor, the Knights Hospitalers.

Barton Stacey Hundred (vol. 4):
Barton Stacey (422) DB lord of manor Walter son of Roger de Pistes. Son Miles Earl of Gloucester gave manor and advowson to Llanthony Priory;
Newton Stacey (422) a chapel of Barton Stacey;
Headbourne Worthy (426, 430) DB Cathedral;
Kings Worthy (432) follows the descent of manor of Abbots Worthy, held by N.M.

Evingar Hundred (vol. 4):
Freefolk (284) Chapel dependent on Whitchurch;
Witchurch (303, 304) DB priest, Bishop Henry de Blois gave it to St. Cross Hospital, which still holds advowson.

Chutley Hundred (vol. 4):
Church Oakley (230) manor;
Wooton St. Lawrence (242) 940 charter reference, not in DB, advowson held by cellarer to Bishop.

Overton Hundred (vol. 4):
Overton (217) DB two churches, chapel at Tadley, Bishop held advowson;
Ashe (201) DB follows manor;
Deane (207) manor;
Laverstock (214) DB manor;
North Waltham (222) Bishop Henry de Blois gave to St. Cross Hospital.

Basingstoke Hundred (vol. 4):
Steventon (174) 1238 lord of manor held advowson.

Wherwell Hundred (vol. 4):
Bullington (403) 1228 listed as chapel annexed to Wherwell;
Goodworth Clatford (405) DB prebend of Whewell Abbey;
Middleton (409) prebend of Wherwell Abbey;
Tufton (412) chapelry attached to vicarage of Wherwell;
Wherwell (414) prebend of Whewell Abbey;
Fullerton (413) DB N.M.

Kings Somborne Hundred (vol. 4):
Ashley (442) 1204 confirmation to convent of Mottisfont, from Wiliam Briwere, ca. 1200;
Leckford (449) prebend of St. Mary (Nunnaminster);
Longstock (451) ca. 1200 Briwere gift to Mottisfont;
Farley Chamberlayne (445) manor;
Kings Somborne (480) DB two churches, perhaps a chapel at Upper Somborne, but ca. 1200 Briwere gift to Mottisfont of Kings Somborne and Upper Eldon;
Little Somborne (482) 2104 confirmation of Briwere gift to Mottisfont, later chapelry of Kings Somborne.

Appendix D

Other Hampshire Valley Units (Archaic Hundreds)
(See Figure 5.2)

To the eight valley units detailed in Appendix A, others from Hampshire north of the New Forest coastal lands can be added. Where appropriate, these possible archaic hundreds will be compared to the Anglo-Saxon minster districts proposed by Patrick Hase.[1]

In north-west Hampshire, the Hurstbourne valley was a discrete territorial unit. It comprised the vills of Hurstbourne Priors, St. Mary Bourne, Stoke-at-Bourne, and Hurstbourne Tarant, with smaller manors on the northeastern flank—Woodcott, Crux Easton, Ashmansworth, and Faccombe. The Hurstbourne valley reaches into the Hampshire Downs, which form part of the watershed between the Channel and the Thames catchment basin, and like the similarly situated Candover and upper Test valleys, it had a noticeable upland zone. The Hurstbourne upland comprised the manors of Upton, Vernham Dean, Linkenholt, Combe in Berkshire, and Fossbury and Hippescombe in Wiltshire. The Hurstbourne valley with its upland was a little larger than the territory of the upper Test valley with its upland, though the higher elevation of the former made it less productive.

South of the Hurstbourne valley is the valley of the 'Andover,' a stream name of Celtic origin, which in the medieval period was given to the town, whilst the stream came to be called Ann, and more recently Anton. The villages of Abbots Ann and Little Ann reflect the earlier usage. The Andover territorial unit is large, but compact, and has near its centre the intersection of two important Roman roads, that passing from Silchester to Sarum, and that going from Winchester to Bath. Close to the junction an excavated early pagan Germanic cemetery suggests the strategic placement of such troops in late and sub-Roman Britain.[2] The edges of the Andover catchment area touch some major landmarks: the 'Hampshire Gate' on the north (a pass through the hills there), and the prehistoric hillfort of Danebury on the south. As with the Hurstbourne valley, the Andover valley extended into Wiltshire, with the lands of the Upper and Lower Chute villages draining down to the Test. Patrick Hase suspected that Andover was a possible mother church, though there was no concrete proof.[3]

---

[1]   P.H. Hase, "The development of the Parish Church in Hampshire, particularly in the eleventh and twelfth century" (Ph.D. thesis, Cambridge University, 1975).

[2]   See Martin Biddle, "Hampshire and the origins of Wessex," in *Problems in Economic and Social Archaeology*, ed. G. Sieveking et al. (London, 1976), pp. 323-341.

[3]   Hase, "Parish in Hampshire," p. 311.

On the west side of the Test south of Andover lies the Wallop valley, drained by the Wallop brook, a name that is Celtic or perhaps even earlier. It encompasses the manors of Broughton and Nether, Middle, and Upper Wallop. The valley group is small but clearly defined, similar to that at Tichbourne. Hase did not suggest a location for the mother church here.[4]

South of the Wallop is a valley with a group of manors—East and West Titherley, East and West Dean, East and West Grimstead, and Lockerly—probably associated with Mottisfont on the Test. The western part of this 'Dean' valley extends beyond the border into Wiltshire. Hase considered Mottisfont a mother church.[5] South of the Dean valley is the Wellow/Blackwater valley, which runs into Wiltshire and borders upon the marshlands of Netley separating the New Forest area from central Hampshire.

Other identifiable topographical units are comparable to medieval manorial groupings. On the east bank of the Test, south of Somborne, is a wide catchment basin extending from Michelmersh to Romsey. South of the Middle Itchen (Winchester) unit, was an equally large group of manors with lands draining into the lower Itchen. Hase found these properties to have been associated with the medieval Stoneham manor and probably tributary to this pre-Conquest royal vill. Named from the Roman ruins of Clausentum and controlling the commercial settlement of *Hamwic*, Stoneham's ancient mother church was probably St. Mary's, outside Southampton.[6]

East of this group in low-lying south Hampshire was the small valley of the Hamble, the *Omblea* of Bede.[7] With Hamble at its mouth, but the more important (Bishops) Waltham in its upper reaches, it is not clear which was the original administrative centre. East of the Hamble is the Meon River, the third important river of the Hampshire Basin. The Meon valley is long and fairly narrow, and was probably divided into units based upon the important vills of Tichfield, Droxford, and East Meon, the last of which Hase claimed as a mother church.[8] South of the Meon, the Wallington river drains into the west end of Portsmouth Harbour at Fareham. The east end of the harbour, at Havant, had as upland the area of Chalton, which was a "capital manor."[9]

The watershed marking the north end of the Chalton area is the long high ridge running across Hampshire from Salisbury to Winchester, and extending into Sussex to become the South Downs by the coast. This ridge is cut by the Test, Itchen, and Meon rivers, and elsewhere forms side valleys emptying into these streams. The eastern edge of Hampshire, however, is drained by the Rother into the Sussex Weald and by tributaries of the Wey through the Surrey Weald to the Thames. Selbourne, Alton, Crondall, and Odiham were important centres in the

---

4   Ibid., p. 232.
5   Ibid., pp. 224-228.
6   Ibid., p. 247.
7   *HE* 4.17.
8   Hase, "Parish in Hampshire," p. 303.
9   Ibid., p. 308.

early medieval period; Hase considered them likely to have been mother churches.[10]

Beyond the Hampshire Downs two great territories comprised the group of villages bearing the name Clere, and those surrounding the ancient manor of Basing. A third group may have existed around the deserted Roman city of Silchester, which does not readily fit into either catchment group. The shire boundary cuts across it, bisecting a territory perhaps equal in size to that around Winchester. The border represents the furthest expansion of Mercia during the eighth century, and as a result, the manorial and parish boundaries and even village sites cannot be assumed to be original. Nevertheless, from its water-related place-name, the Clere group probably represents an ancient settlement unit, like Hurstbourne or Meon, where river-named villages show common origins in a valley-wide territory. Basing was a royal manor, the head of a hundred in its transferred identity as Basingstoke, and perhaps the site of a pagan religious centre. Hase believed that both King's Clere and Basing had been mother churches, though there was little supporting evidence.[11]

---

[10]   Ibid., pp. 289, 297.
[11]   Ibid., pp. 314, 320.

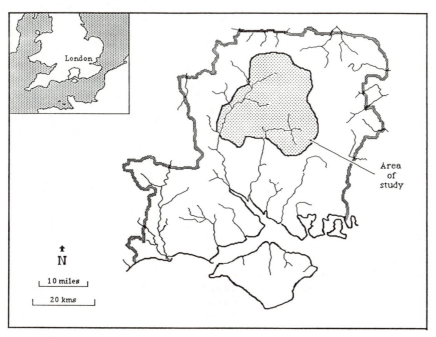

Figure 2.1   Location of Area of Study in Hampshire

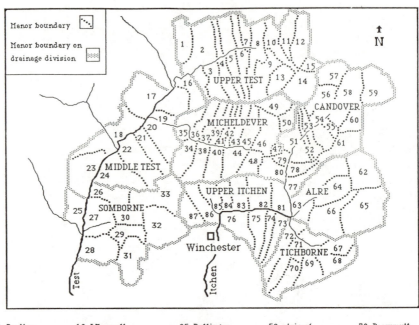

1. Bradley	18. Wherwell	35. Bullingon	52. strip of
2. Whitchurch	19. Bransbury/	36. Norton	Northington
3. Freefolk	Drayton	37. Cranbourne	53. Chilton Candover
4. Laverstock	20. Barton Stacey	38. Wonston	54. Preston Candover
5. Southington	21. Newton Stacey	39. Hunton	55. tract in P. C.
6. Overton	22. Chilbolton	40. Stoke Charity	56. Nutley
7. Polhampton /	23. Longstock	41. Weston Colley	57. Farleigh Wallop
Quidhampton	24. Leckford	42. Godwinsdown	58. Ellisfield
8. Ashley	25. Houghton	43. Northbrook /	59. Herriard
9. Steventon	26. Stockbridge	Micheldever	60. Bradley
10. Deane	27. Kings Somborne	44. Southbrook /	61. Wield
11. Oakley	28. Compton / Brook	Micheldever	62. Medstead
12. East Oakley /	29. Asley	45. West Stratton	63. Alresford
Wooten St. L	30. Little / Upper	46. East Stratton	64. Bighton
13. North Walton	Somborne	47. Burcot	65. Ropley
14. Dummer	31. Farley Chamberlain	48. Papenholt	66. Bishops Sutton
15. Kempshot	32. Sparsholt	49. Popham	67. Bramdean
16. Tufton	33. Crawley	50. Woodmancott	68. Hinton Ampner
17. Middleton	34. Sutton Scotney	51. Brown Candover	69. Kilmeston

70. Beauworth
71. Cheriton
72. Tichborne
73. Ovington
74. Yavington
75. Avington
76. Easton
77. Abbotstone
78. Swarraton
79. Totford
80. Northington
81. Itchen Stoke
82. Itchen Abbas
83. Martyr Worthy
84. Abbots Worthy
85. Kings Worthy
86. Headbourne
Worthy
87. Littleton

Figure 3.1 Early Medieval Manors of Middle Hampshire

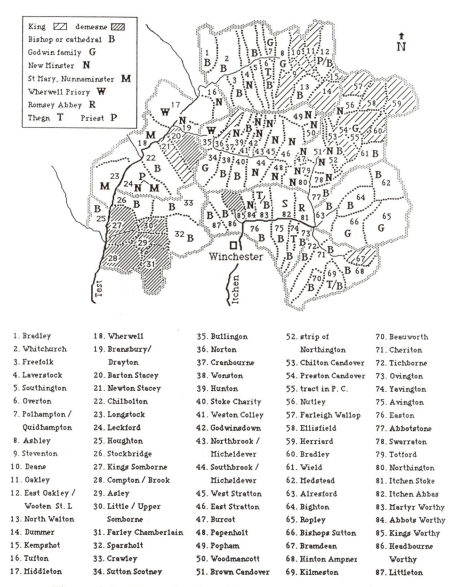

Figure 3.2 Domesday Royal Demesne Land and Folkland

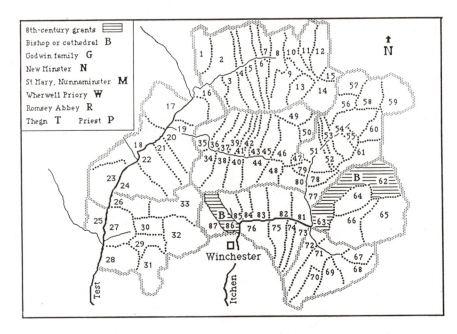

8th-century grants ▭
Bishop or cathedral **B**
Godwin family **G**
New Minster **N**
St Mary, Nunnaminster **M**
Wherwell Priory **W**
Romsey Abbey **R**
Thegn **T**   Priest **P**

1. Bradley	18. Wherwell	35. Bullingon	52. strip of	70. Beauworth
2. Whitchurch	19. Bransbury/	36. Norton	Northington	71. Cheriton
3. Freefolk	Drayton	37. Cranbourne	53. Chilton Candover	72. Tichborne
4. Laverstock	20. Barton Stacey	38. Wonston	54. Preston Candover	73. Ovington
5. Southington	21. Newton Stacey	39. Hunton	55. tract in P. C.	74. Yavington
6. Overton	22. Chilbolton	40. Stoke Charity	56. Nutley	75. Avington
7. Polhampton /	23. Longstock	41. Weston Colley	57. Farleigh Wallop	76. Easton
Quidhampton	24. Leckford	42. Godwinsdown	58. Ellisfield	77. Abbotstone
8. Ashley	25. Houghton	43. Northbrook /	59. Herriard	78. Swarraton
9. Steventon	26. Stockbridge	Micheldever	60. Bradley	79. Totford
10. Deane	27. Kings Somborne	44. Southbrook /	61. Wield	80. Northington
11. Oakley	28. Compton / Brook	Micheldever	62. Medstead	81. Itchen Stoke
12. East Oakley /	29. Asley	45. West Stratton	63. Alresford	82. Itchen Abbas
Wooten St. L.	30. Little / Upper	46. East Stratton	64. Bighton	83. Martyr Worthy
13. North Walton	Somborne	47. Burcot	65. Ropley	84. Abbots Worthy
14. Dummer	31. Farley Chamberlain	48. Papenholt	66. Bishops Sutton	85. Kings Worthy
15. Kempshot	32. Sparsholt	49. Popham	67. Bramdean	86. Headbourne
16. Tufton	33. Crawley	50. Woodmancott	68. Hinton Ampner	Worthy
17. Middleton	34. Sutton Scotney	51. Brown Candover	69. Kilmeston	87. Littleton

Figure 3.3   Eighth-Century Estate Formation

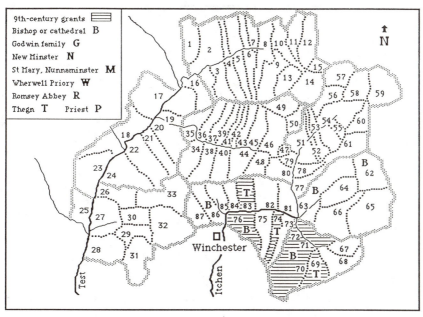

1. Bradley
2. Whitchurch
3. Freefolk
4. Laverstock
5. Southington
6. Overton
7. Polhampton / Quidhampton
8. Ashley
9. Steventon
10. Deane
11. Oakley
12. East Oakley / Wooten St. L
13. North Walton
14. Dummer
15. Kempshot
16. Tufton
17. Middleton
18. Wherwell
19. Bransbury / Drayton
20. Barton Stacey
21. Newton Stacey
22. Chilbolton
23. Longstock
24. Leckford
25. Houghton
26. Stockbridge
27. Kings Somborne
28. Compton / Brook
29. Asley
30. Little / Upper Somborne
31. Farley Chamberlain
32. Sparsholt
33. Crawley
34. Sutton Scotney
35. Bullingon
36. Norton
37. Cranbourne
38. Wonston
39. Hunton
40. Stoke Charity
41. Weston Colley
42. Godwinsdown
43. Northbrook / Micheldever
44. Southbrook / Micheldever
45. West Stratton
46. East Stratton
47. Burcot
48. Papenholt
49. Popham
50. Woodmancott
51. Brown Candover
52. strip of Northington
53. Chilton Candover
54. Preston Candover
55. tract in P. C.
56. Nutley
57. Farleigh Wallop
58. Ellisfield
59. Herriard
60. Bradley
61. Wield
62. Medstead
63. Alresford
64. Bighton
65. Ropley
66. Bishops Sutton
67. Bramdean
68. Hinton Ampner
69. Kilmeston
70. Beauworth
71. Cheriton
72. Tichborne
73. Ovington
74. Yavington
75. Avington
76. Easton
77. Abbotstone
78. Swarraton
79. Totford
80. Northington
81. Itchen Stoke
82. Itchen Abbas
83. Martyr Worthy
84. Abbots Worthy
85. Kings Worthy
86. Headbourne Worthy
87. Littleton

Figure 3.4   Ninth-Century Estate Formation

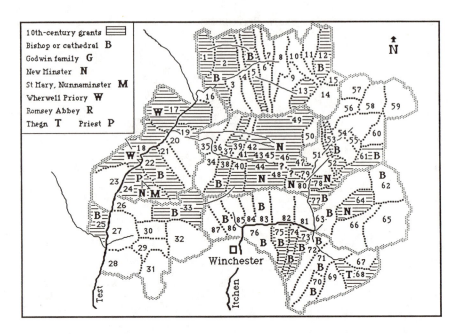

1. Bradley	18. Wherwell	35. Bullingon	52. strip of
2. Whitchurch	19. Bransbury/	36. Norton	Northington
3. Freefolk	Drayton	37. Cranbourne	53. Chilton Candover
4. Laverstock	20. Barton Stacey	38. Wonston	54. Preston Candover
5. Southington	21. Newton Stacey	39. Hunton	55. tract in P. C.
6. Overton	22. Chilbolton	40. Stoke Charity	56. Nutley
7. Polhampton /	23. Longstock	41. Weston Colley	57. Farleigh Wallop
Quidhampton	24. Leckford	42. Godwinsdown	58. Ellisfield
8. Ashley	25. Houghton	43. Northbrook /	59. Herriard
9. Steventon	26. Stockbridge	Micheldever	60. Bradley
10. Deane	27. Kings Somborne	44. Southbrook /	61. Wield
11. Oakley	28. Compton / Brook	Micheldever	62. Medstead
12. East Oakley /	29. Asley	45. West Stratton	63. Alresford
Wooten St. L	30. Little / Upper	46. East Stratton	64. Bighton
13. North Walton	Somborne	47. Burcot	65. Ropley
14. Dummer	31. Farley Chamberlain	48. Papenholt	66. Bishops Sutton
15. Kempshot	32. Sparsholt	49. Popham	67. Bramdean
16. Tufton	33. Crawley	50. Woodmancott	68. Hinton Ampner
17. Middleton	34. Sutton Scotney	51. Brown Candover	69. Kilmeston

70. Beauworth	
71. Cheriton	
72. Tichborne	
73. Ovington	
74. Yavington	
75. Avington	
76. Easton	
77. Abbotstone	
78. Swarraton	
79. Totford	
80. Northington	
81. Itchen Stoke	
82. Itchen Abbas	
83. Martyr Worthy	
84. Abbots Worthy	
85. Kings Worthy	
86. Headbourne	
Worthy	
87. Littleton	

Figure 3.5   Tenth-Century Estate Formation

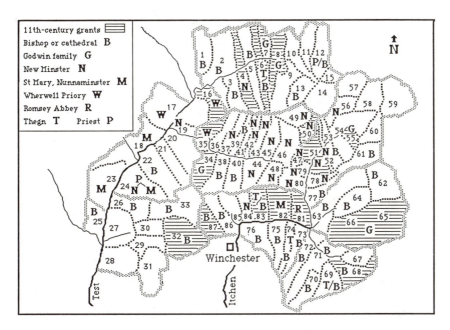

1. Bradley	18. Wherwell	35. Bullingon	52. strip of
2. Whitchurch	19. Bransbury /	36. Norton	Northington
3. Freefolk	Drayton	37. Cranbourne	53. Chilton Candover
4. Laverstock	20. Barton Stacey	38. Wonston	54. Preston Candover
5. Southington	21. Newton Stacey	39. Hunton	55. tract in P. C.
6. Overton	22. Chilbolton	40. Stoke Charity	56. Nutley
7. Polhampton /	23. Longstock	41. Weston Colley	57. Farleigh Wallop
Quidhampton	24. Leckford	42. Godwinsdown	58. Ellisfield
8. Ashley	25. Houghton	43. Northbrook /	59. Herriard
9. Steventon	26. Stockbridge	Micheldever	60. Bradley
10. Deane	27. Kings Somborne	44. Southbrook /	61. Wield
11. Oakley	28. Compton / Brook	Micheldever	62. Medstead
12. East Oakley /	29. Asley	45. West Stratton	63. Alresford
Wooten St. L	30. Little / Upper	46. East Stratton	64. Bighton
13. North Walton	Somborne	47. Burcot	65. Ropley
14. Dummer	31. Farley Chamberlain	48. Papenholt	66. Bishops Sutton
15. Kempshot	32. Sparsholt	49. Popham	67. Bramdean
16. Tufton	33. Crawley	50. Woodmancott	68. Hinton Ampner
17. Middleton	34. Sutton Scotney	51. Brown Candover	69. Kilmeston

70. Beauworth
71. Cheriton
72. Tichborne
73. Ovington
74. Yavington
75. Avington
76. Easton
77. Abbotstone
78. Swarraton
79. Totford
80. Northington
81. Itchen Stoke
82. Itchen Abbas
83. Martyr Worthy
84. Abbots Worthy
85. Kings Worthy
86. Headbourne
Worthy
87. Littleton

Figure 3.6 Eleventh-Century Estate Formation

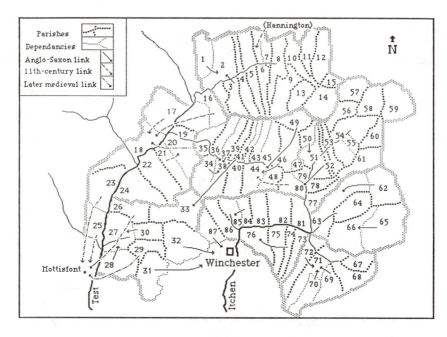

1. Bradley	18. Wherwell	35. Bullingon	52. strip of	70. Beauworth
2. Whitchurch	19. Bransbury/	36. Norton	Northington	71. Cheriton
3. Freefolk	Drayton	37. Cranbourne	53. Chilton Candover	72. Tichborne
4. Laverstock	20. Barton Stacey	38. Wonston	54. Preston Candover	73. Ovington
5. Southington	21. Newton Stacey	39. Hunton	55. tract in P. C.	74. Yavington
6. Overton	22. Chilbolton	40. Stoke Charity	56. Nutley	75. Avington
7. Polhampton /	23. Longstock	41. Weston Colley	57. Farleigh Wallop	76. Easton
Quidhampton	24. Leckford	42. Godwinsdown	58. Ellisfield	77. Abbotstone
8. Ashley	25. Houghton	43. Northbrook /	59. Herriard	78. Swarraton
9. Steventon	26. Stockbridge	Micheldever	60. Bradley	79. Totford
10. Deane	27. Kings Somborne	44. Southbrook /	61. Wield	80. Northington
11. Oakley	28. Compton / Brook	Micheldever	62. Medstead	81. Itchen Stoke
12. East Oakley /	29. Asley	45. West Stratton	63. Alresford	82. Itchen Abbas
Wooten St. L	30. Little / Upper	46. East Stratton	64. Bighton	83. Martyr Worthy
13. North Walton	Somborne	47. Burcot	65. Ropley	84. Abbots Worthy
14. Dummer	31. Farley Chamberlain	48. Papenholt	66. Bishops Sutton	85. Kings Worthy
15. Kempshot	32. Sparsholt	49. Popham	67. Bramdean	86. Headbourne
16. Tufton	33. Crawley	50. Woodmancott	68. Hinton Ampner	Worthy
17. Middleton	34. Sutton Scotney	51. Brown Candover	69. Kilmeston	87. Littleton

Figure 4.1 Early Medieval Ecclesiastical Links

Figure 4.2   Domesday Hundreds of Hampshire

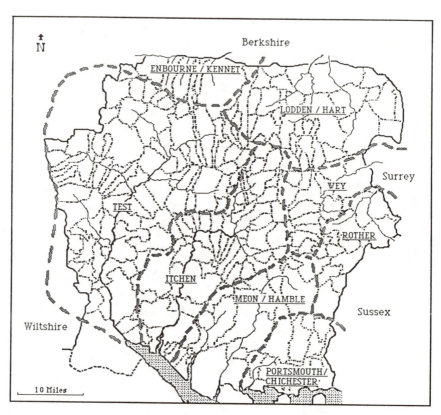

Figure 5.1   Hampshire Catchment Areas

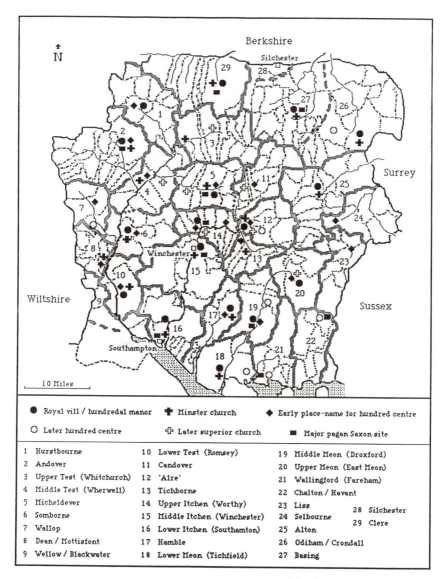

Figure 5.2 Archaic Hundreds of Hampshire

Legend:

● Royal vill / hundredal manor   ✚ Minster church   ◆ Early place-name for hundred centre

○ Later hundred centre   ✙ Later superior church   ■ Major pagan Saxon site

1 Hurstbourne	10 Lower Test (Romsey)	19 Middle Meon (Droxford)
2 Andover	11 Candover	20 Upper Meon (East Meon)
3 Upper Test (Whitchurch)	12 'Aire'	21 Wallingford (Fareham)
4 Middle Test (Wherwell)	13 Tichborne	22 Chalton / Havant
5 Micheldever	14 Upper Itchen (Worthy)	23 Liss
6 Somborne	15 Middle Itchen (Winchester)	24 Selbourne
7 Wallop	16 Lower Itchen (Southamton)	25 Alton
8 Dean / Mottisfont	17 Hamble	26 Odiham / Crondall
9 Wellow / Blackwater	18 Lower Meon (Tichfield)	27 Basing

28 Silchester
29 Clere

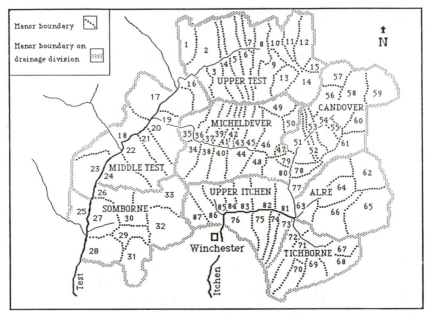

1. Bradley	18. Wherwell	35. Bullingon	52. strip of	70. Beauworth
2. Whitchurch	19. Bransbury/	36. Norton	Northington	71. Cheriton
3. Freefolk	Drayton	37. Cranbourne	53. Chilton Candover	72. Tichborne
4. Laverstock	20. Barton Stacey	38. Wonston	54. Preston Candover	73. Ovington
5. Southington	21. Newton Stacey	39. Hunton	55. tract in P. C.	74. Yavington
6. Overton	22. Chilbolton	40. Stoke Charity	56. Nutley	75. Avington
7. Polhampton /	23. Longstock	41. Weston Colley	57. Farleigh Wallop	76. Easton
Quidhampton	24. Leckford	42. Godwinsdown	58. Ellisfield	77. Abbotstone
8. Ashley	25. Houghton	43. Northbrook /	59. Herriard	78. Swarraton
9. Steventon	26. Stockbridge	Micheldever	60. Bradley	79. Totford
10. Deane	27. Kings Somborne	44. Southbrook /	61. Wield	80. Northington
11. Oakley	28. Compton / Brook	Micheldever	62. Medstead	81. Itchen Stoke
12. East Oakley /	29. Asley	45. West Stratton	63. Alresford	82. Itchen Abbas
Wooten St. L	30. Little / Upper	46. East Stratton	64. Bighton	83. Martyr Worthy
13. North Walton	Somborne	47. Burcot	65. Ropley	84. Abbots Worthy
14. Dummer	31. Farley Chamberlain	48. Papenholt	66. Bishops Sutton	85. Kings Worthy
15. Kempshot	32. Sparsholt	49. Popham	67. Bramdean	86. Headbourne
16. Tufton	33. Crawley	50. Woodmancott	68. Hinton Ampner	Worthy
17. Middleton	34. Sutton Scotney	51. Brown Candover	69. Kilmeston	87. Littleton

Figure A.1 Topographic Units of Middle Hampshire

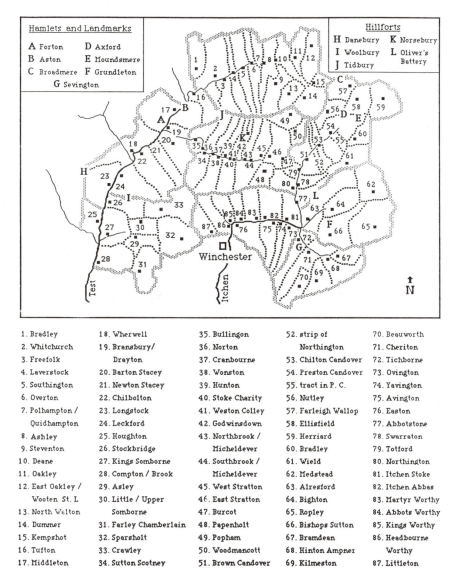

1. Bradley	18. Wherwell	35. Bullingon	52. strip of	70. Beauworth
2. Whitchurch	19. Bransbury/	36. Norton	Northington	71. Cheriton
3. Freefolk	Drayton	37. Cranbourne	53. Chilton Candover	72. Tichborne
4. Laverstock	20. Barton Stacey	38. Wonston	54. Preston Candover	73. Ovington
5. Southington	21. Newton Stacey	39. Hunton	55. tract in P. C.	74. Yavington
6. Overton	22. Chilbolton	40. Stoke Charity	56. Nutley	75. Avington
7. Polhampton /	23. Longstock	41. Weston Colley	57. Farleigh Wallop	76. Easton
Quidhampton	24. Leckford	42. Godwinsdown	58. Ellisfield	77. Abbotstone
8. Ashley	25. Houghton	43. Northbrook /	59. Herriard	78. Swarraton
9. Steventon	26. Stockbridge	Micheldever	60. Bradley	79. Totford
10. Deane	27. Kings Somborne	44. Southbrook /	61. Wield	80. Northington
11. Oakley	28. Compton / Brook	Micheldever	62. Medstead	81. Itchen Stoke
12. East Oakley /	29. Asley	45. West Stratton	63. Alresford	82. Itchen Abbas
Wooten St. L	30. Little / Upper	46. East Stratton	64. Bighton	83. Martyr Worthy
13. North Walton	Somborne	47. Burcot	65. Ropley	84. Abbots Worthy
14. Dummer	31. Farley Chamberlain	48. Papenholt	66. Bishops Sutton	85. Kings Worthy
15. Kempshot	32. Sparsholt	49. Popham	67. Bramdean	86. Headbourne
16. Tufton	33. Crawley	50. Woodmancott	68. Hinton Ampner	Worthy
17. Middleton	34. Sutton Scotney	51. Brown Candover	69. Kilmeston	87. Littleton

Figure B.1   Place-Names of Middle Hampshire

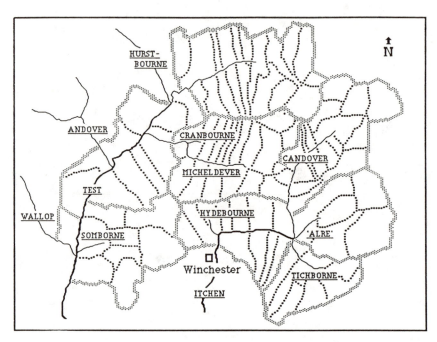

Figure B.2 River-Names of Middle Hampshire

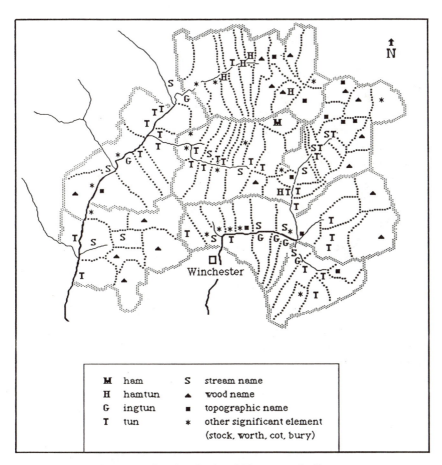

Figure B.3   Analysis of Toponymic Survey

General Index